COVERING POLITICS

POLITICS

A Handbook for Journalists

COVERING POLITICS

A Handbook for Journalists

by Rob Armstrong

Blackwell
Publishing

Rob Armstrong covered politics and government for 32 years, most of them for CBS News. From 1989 to 1998, he was senior radio correspondent for CBS News, covering Congress and national politics. Since 1998, he has been the retired professional in residence at Flagler College, St. Augustine, Florida. He is a graduate of the University of Denver, where he majored in history, and also attended the University of Denver College of Law. He is the author of five other books (including *Covering Government: A Civics Handbook for Journalists,* published by Iowa State Press [now Blackwell Publishing], 2002) and writes a newspaper column.

©2004 Blackwell Publishing
All rights reserved

Blackwell Publishing Professional
2121 State Avenue, Ames, Iowa 50014, USA

Orders:	1-800-862-6657	Fax:	1-515-292-3348
Office:	1-515-292-0140	Web site:	www.blackwellprofessional.com

Blackwell Publishing Ltd.
9600 Garsington Road, Oxford OX4 2DQ, UK
Tel.: +44 (0)1865 776868

Blackwell Publishing Asia
550 Swanston Street, Carlton, Victoria 3053, Australia
Tel.: +61 (0)3 8359 1011

Authorization to photocopy items for internal or personal use, or the internal or personal use of specific clients, is granted by Blackwell Publishing, provided that the base fee of $.10 per copy is paid directly to the Copyright Clearance Center, 222 Rosewood Drive, Danvers, MA 01923. For those organizations that have been granted a photocopy license by CCC, a separate system of payments has been arranged. The fee code for users of the Transactional Reporting Service is 0-8138-0918-5/2004 $.10.

Printed on acid-free paper in the United States of America

First edition, 2004

Photos published by permission: Back cover: Rob Armstrong–courtesy of Betsy Lee Photography, 544 Wood Chase Drive, St. Augustine, FL; Conversations: Candy Crowley–courtesy of CNN; Bob Schieffer–courtesy of Karen Cooper/CBS News; Marvin Kalb–courtesy of Martha Stewart; Brit Hume–Fox News Network, LLC; David Broder–courtesy of *The Washington Post* Writers Group; Brian Lamb–courtesy of C-SPAN; Elaine Povich; Jamie Dupree

Library of Congress Cataloging-in-Publication Data
Armstrong, Rob, 1949–
   Covering politics : a handbook for journalists / Rob Armstrong.—1st ed.
     p. cm.
   Includes index.
   ISBN 0-8138-0918-5 (alk. paper)
   1. Press and politics—United States. 2. United States—Politics and government. I. Title.

PN4888.P6A74 2004
070.4'49324'0973—dc22

2004003942

The last digit is the print number: 9 8 7 6 5 4 3 2 1

Dedication

For Mother, Dad and Barbara, with love and thanks

Contents

Acknowledgments

Once again, my wife Barbara Stafford has allowed her life to be disrupted, her intellect to be tapped, her patience to be tried, her legal expertise to be exploited and her editorial skills to be tested so that I could write another book. That she did it all with grace, wit and good cheer is a testimony to her strength of character. I could not have written it without her.

A. Dawn Rogers agreed to work with me again as my research assistant, and again her help was invaluable, her enthusiasm for the project was infectious and her ability to find odd and arcane bits of information was uncanny.

The people at Blackwell Publishing (formerly Iowa State Press) continue to awe me with their skill, dedication and professionalism. Publisher Mark Barrett approached this book with enthusiasm and constructive suggestions from our first discussion about it. It was a delight to work with project manager Lynne Bishop and veteran editor Arnold Friedman again.

I am deeply indebted to all of the busy academic, political and journalistic professionals, most of whom are quoted by name in the text, who allowed me to tap their vast store of knowledge and generously gave their time for lengthy interviews and follow-up phone calls. I am especially grateful to my former boss Larry McCoy, who is now with Dow Jones Newswires, and CBS News correspondent Howard Arenstein, who took the time to go through the manuscript with critical eyes and help improve it.

My students and former students were, as usual, test subjects for much of this material, and my faculty colleagues at Flagler College generously offered suggestions and encouragement. Flagler College President Dr. William T. Abare Jr. has been consistently enthusiastic and supportive. So have Academic Dean Paula Miller, Communication Department Chair Dr. Tracy Halcomb and Dr. Caroline Dow.

Larry Janazich of the Senate Radio and TV Gallery and Tina Tate and Gail Davis of the House Radio and TV Gallery went out of their way to help facilitate my access to Capitol Hill in this age of heightened security.

My deep appreciation to my dear friend Tom Taylor, just for being there. And to my mother and father, Murray and Freda Armstrong—how do I say thank you for all the caring, nurturing, help, wisdom and love they've given me through the years?

Section I
Basic Background

1

Overview

Those of us who were cutting our journalistic teeth during the 1960s and '70—the Johnson Administration and Vietnam, the Nixon Administration and Watergate, and the heyday of the Beatles—believed that was the Golden Age of political reporting. To young reporters like me, Timothy Crouse's best seller *The Boys on the Bus* (Ballantine Books, 1974) was more than an interesting chronicle of Democrat George McGovern's unsuccessful 1972 run for the White House; it was Talmudic. The reporters were bigger than life. They were the Titans of covering politics. We wanted to be like them. We wanted to be a part of it. We wanted to know all the players. We wanted to plumb the deepest depths of candidates and campaigns.

We wanted to be able to drink (not to mention write) like Hunter Thompson of *Rolling Stone*, analyze like Johnny Apple of *The New York Times*, ask questions like Walter Mears of the Associated Press, and perform on camera and microphone like Roger Mudd of CBS News. We wanted to be in on all the behind-the-scenes stuff that makes a political campaign such an adventure.

Crouse's book was in part responsible for the development of a politico-journalistic subculture that still exists, a subculture of ultimate insiders. He painted a picture of a political reporting process that verged on inside baseball—sometimes too inside. These ultimate insiders often wrote as much for each other and for the political establishment as for the reading, viewing and listening public.

David Broder of *The Washington Post*, one of Crouse's *Boys on the Bus* and one of the most respected political journalists in the country, says there's a place for political reporting aimed at insiders as well as that aimed at a broader audience. "If you're lucky enough to work at a paper like this you can write some pieces that really are for the insiders," he said. "I wrote a column about the South Carolina Democratic debate [Sunday, May 4, 2003] that probably 90 percent of the readers weren't very interested in, but I wrote it because I knew there would be a lot of conversation about it in the political world."

Most journalists and most news organizations do not have the political clout of Broder or the *Post*. Reporters, editors and producers need occasionally to take a step back and consider whether the stories that are being published or aired are designed to impress other insiders and one's competitive peers or whether they are designed to inform, enlighten and educate the news organization's consumers.

Broder underscored the fundamental reason for covering politics and politicians: "These people are going to make decisions that are going to affect your life as a citizen. They're going to raise or cut your taxes. They're going to go to war or keep you out of a war. These are consequential things. And that's where we need to keep our focus."

Even veteran journalists must be reminded every now and then that the job is about reporting, writing and presenting stories that are new, accurate, factual, fair, interesting and have impact on the audience they serve. "I believe that journalism and journalists have an almost sacred responsibility to provide valuable information to the consumer, to the citizen, to keep the level of citizenship high, to keep the vitality of democracy high," said Marvin Kalb, former CBS and NBC News correspondent and senior fellow at Harvard's Shorenstein Center for the Press, Politics and Public Policy in Washington.

Covering politics, like covering the functions of government and the impact those functions have on citizens, requires journalists to understand and synthesize a vast array of material. Myopia can be an occupational hazard. There is always a risk of getting too close to the people and to the stories being covered. Failure to deliver useful and pertinent information to one's audience can contribute, over time, to public distrust, mistrust, cynicism and skepticism about politics and politicians. In some cases the media have been part of the problem because of the way political stories have been focused and framed.

"To get to the heart of a story you sometimes have to tell the story that touches the heart," said Tom Mattesky, deputy bureau chief for CBS News in Washington. "You do that by relating large and complex issues to real people and everyday life. And that's the cornerstone of reporting that goes beyond statistics and political rhetoric. It is important to point out that there often are life and death issues that affect our pocketbooks. And we must constantly be aware that the policies our politicians are debating might actually determine whether people can put food on their tables, can put gas in their cars, can afford to pay for health care in their retirement."

For most political journalists and people who like politics, the word "politics" conjures up exciting images of public policy debate, candidates, races, speech making and handshaking in the quest for votes. But that is just the tip of the iceberg. Politics is a process that begins long before a candidate is selected or chooses to pursue an elective office, and continues long after the votes are cast, finally devolving into the process of governance. Journalists who cover politics must have a thorough understanding of the whole time-line—potential candidates testing the waters, what motivates people to seek elective office, the ceaseless task of raising money, campaign organizations, the influence of political parties on candidate selection, the issues that shape candidates and campaigns, and the role of the various cast members in the drama that is politics, including consultants, pollsters, spinmeisters, opposition researchers, interest groups, fund-raisers and, ultimately, the voters.

In the post-Watergate years, politics has generated a substantial level of public cynicism and doubt. "Politician," to some people, is a dirty word. Politics itself is seen as fraught with intrigue, scandal, character assassination, corruption and even dishonesty. The political history of the last half of the twentieth century is littered with examples: Richard Nixon, Gary Hart, Wayne Hays, Jim Wright, Dan Rostenkowski, James Traficant and Bill Clinton were all ethically and/or legally challenged. But that is not the entire story and it is up to political journalists to add perspective, context and texture.

People who strive for a career in political journalism or those already on that track should know that politics is too important to the fabric of our national culture to cynically dismiss and trivialize the whole process as an exercise in sleaze. On those occasions when scandal is the story, cover it.

The purist, some would say elitist, approach to political journalism is to focus exclusively on the weighty issues and policies that affect people's lives. That is to ignore the realities of the marketplace, and political reporters often find themselves caught between those weighty issues and those occasionally sordid elements that capture the public's attention.

There is an undeniable public appetite for stories of scandal and corruption. During the Clinton-Lewinsky scandal people told pollsters that they thought there was too much coverage and the media were going too far. At the same time TV ratings went up when programs about the scandal aired. Some news executives demand reporting that panders to the basest tastes of their audience in order to boost ratings and readership, and attract advertisers and maximize advertising revenues. Some consultants actively promote sensational coverage over the public policy debate of a campaign. A Louisiana politician was once quoted as boasting, "The only way these people won't vote for me is if they catch me in bed with a live boy or a dead girl." Some news organizations immediately set out to uncover that scenario.

"We have in some cases been too quick to ascribe ulterior political motivation to what politicians are doing," noted Candy Crowley, CNN's senior political correspondent. "Not all votes, not all policy positions are determined by personal political motivation. They all have political impact. But we, too often, have a tendency to confuse the two. In fact it's very hard to know what somebody else's motivation is, and sometimes we're not as careful as we need to be about our judgment of why someone does something. We need to be a little more attentive to what the political effect is going to be."

Serious political reporters walk a fine line. The successful ones manage to strike a balance and cover all manner of stories within the political realm, including scandal, corruption, governance, public policy debate and the machinations of the electoral process. James Toedtman, associate editor of *Newsday*, refers to it as "keeping your gyroscope running." It is the job of those covering politics to report as much of the whole picture as possible, to analyze and explore the various facets of the candidates, the campaigns and the issues that shape them, and to avoid the pitfalls of presenting the races as one-dimensional or just reporting the horse-race aspect of the contest. These days, that's a difficult and full-time job.

The political process in America has become an almost non-stop cycle. The late Rep. Morris Udall (D-Ariz.) once confessed some disillusionment with it. He lamented, "You have to start raising money for your next campaign the day after Election Day." Money plays such an overarching role in politics that reporters must be keenly aware of how it is raised, how it is used, the role of contributors and campaign finance reform. (See chapter 10.1, 10.2 and 10.3.)

Reporters also must have a working knowledge of the rules and regulations that govern the political process in their particular areas of coverage. State and local rules regarding everything from application and filing deadlines to limits on campaign contributions vary widely. (See chapter 4.)

Certainly, there are those who argue that covering politics is just like any other kind of journalism. Sociologist Herbert Gans of Columbia University hypothesizes in his book *Democracy and the News* (Oxford, 2003) that the news media overblow their own importance in the political scheme of things. Gans suggests that the media have greater visibility than actual influence, that the *Boys on the Bus* are just passengers, not drivers.

Gans's hypothesis presupposes that the object of political journalism is influence. That supposition is flawed. Political journalism is the straightforward business of covering the candidates, campaigns and issues for one's readers, viewers or listeners, without the imposition of the journalist's biases, prejudices or opinions. It's the same basic stuff that applies to any journalistic endeavor. Informing the public— delivering the news—may result in a type of influence that manifests itself in the form of reexamined, reinforced or changed views, but that's not the objective of the reporting itself.

There is a link between the public's lack of interest in politics, politicians and the political process, and the type of political news coverage to which people are exposed. It is often a vicious cycle: people say "I have no interest in politics," thus they don't consume political news, thus they say they don't like political news coverage, thus they don't know about the candidates or the issues, thus they have no motivation to vote, thus when the people elected don't address their concerns their views of the process and news coverage of it are reinforced. That may be oversimplified, but there's more than a grain of truth in it.

Political scholars have long used voter turnout as a bellwether of public interest and involvement, and they point to non-presidential primary elections to illustrate the degree to which voters are disengaged. Non-presidential primaries often attract fewer than 10 percent of the eligible voters. Non-presidential primaries also generate far fewer news stories, on average, than general elections or presidential primaries. Many political journalists and scholars suggest that more news coverage would generate greater public awareness and interest.

Political reporters are critical of the entire process of electoral government. When they do their jobs as they should, they are the synthesizers of information for their audiences. They square contradictions and make complicated information understandable. It is the job of political journalists to be able to say to an elected official: "How come you said one thing to one group on Monday and something else to another group on Tuesday?" The general public does not follow the statements of those running for office, or those already elected, as carefully as journalists must.

Reporters can probe for answers that politicians may skirt or circumvent in such public forums as town hall meetings. How is the plan going to work? How much will it cost? Who's going to pay for it? Why is your plan better than what is in place now? Who will benefit? Who will not? Candidates love to paint with broad brushstrokes. Good political journalists examine the details and explain to the voting public what it all means.

Good political journalism looks beyond the name-calling and smokescreens. It tells voters, "Plan A will do this, cost this and have this direct impact on you. Plan B will do that, cost that and have that direct impact on you." Political stories that follow the candidates' broad generalizations generate less interest than stories that tell readers, viewers and listeners what something means specifically for my community, my neighborhood, my family and me.

Some news media critics suggest that it is better if a voter listens to what a candidate or official says and draws his or her own conclusion. In theory, that's exactly as it ought to be. But with the avalanche of information generated by candidates and their supporters, the vast majority of readers, viewers and listeners are not going to take the time to filter through it all and cull out the facts. In addition, when there are questions to be asked, politicians have not proved themselves very eager to let the public or the news media have at them one-on-one. At public question-and-answer sessions voters generally get only one question, which the politician will answer (or spin) as he or she wants. When politicians submit to questioning from journalists, there are follow-up questions and attempts to cut through the spin. Where the spin prevails, reporters must expose that to the voters and point out that the politician did not answer the question.

David Broder observed that in the 2000 presidential race, Democrat "Al Gore did not have a single news conference" after he got his party's nomination. "That's ridiculous," he said.

The premise of what follows in these pages is that there is much that is good in political journalism but there is much that could be better. This volume seeks to highlight what works, and explore techniques and strategies for making political journalism better. Political journalism is scrutinized through the eyes of some of the country's top political journalists, scholars and political professionals.

Covering politics is fundamental to the American system of government. Those who do it have an obligation to the people they serve to make their coverage as good as it possibly can be. Beyond that, for reporters it is a wonderful way to make a living. In conversation after conversation with some of the best political reporters in the country, the word "fun" came up over and over again.

Broder still loves the job after more than 40 years. "The people who go into politics tend to be more energetic, more imaginative, more ambitious and often more idealistic than the people you meet in other areas of work. The payoff for me is having an excuse to hang around with people like that. . . . It's fun to be dealing with people who are, in a lot of cases, the children of people that I started out covering. There are a lot of second generation politicians, including the current president, whose fathers and mothers I knew in public life. . . . The other part that's fun is you never know where the story's going to end up."

"It's great fun," said *Newsday's* political reporter Elaine Povich. "Political reporting is the most fun you can have with your clothes on. . . . It's more fun than covering sports because the winner is only determined at the very end and there's an awful lot of chess maneuvering. To watch these people strategize and try to work around each other is some of the most fun you can have."

2

The American Tradition

The political process in the United States, including the way the news media cover politics, politicians and public policy, has evolved throughout the nation's history. What exists today bears little resemblance to what men like James Madison and Alexander Hamilton envisioned in 1787. The architects of the Constitution did not devise an electoral system that provided for political parties or even direct representation beyond the House of Representatives at the federal level. Nonetheless, the stampede toward a two-party government, with direct electoral representation at virtually all levels, started during George Washington's administration.

The adversarial, yet symbiotic, relationship between the news media and politicians predates Washington's inauguration, going back to colonial times. Modern political journalism in America has its roots in the 18th century. Standards, ethics, technology, public appetites, business demands and methods of delivery have all changed, but the role of the news media as a conduit of information about what politicians are doing and how it affects citizens remains fundamental.

2.1 All Politics Is Local

Democrat Thomas P. "Tip" O'Neill, a gregarious Irishman from Massachusetts, was Speaker of the House for 10 years in the 1970s and '80s. He was a big, shambling man with shrewd political instincts. It is said that there wasn't a hand in Boston that he didn't shake at least once. He is credited with first uttering the political mantra "all politics is local."

O'Neill and those who practice his brand of retail politics— pressing the flesh, going door to door, making personal contact with as many constituents as possible—believe that the way to get elected and keep getting elected is for politicians to keep their fingers on the pulse of those who vote for them. They are keenly aware that public concerns change, that issues of import shift and vary.

Virtually every politician represents a finite geographic area, and it is incumbent on those journalists who cover politics to be intimately familiar with the areas and the people who live there. The only office in American politics that is truly national in scope is the presidency. Senators and governors represent states; members of the U.S. House of Representatives, state senators, and members of the lower chambers of state legislatures are elected from individual districts of varying sizes; mayors and city council members represent cities and districts or wards within cities. O'Neill would have told you that every politician is influenced by the values, morals, concerns and passions of the people who elect them; and any politician who ignores the folks back home does so at his or her political peril.

Democrat Ann Richards, the former governor of Texas, told a group of CBS News correspondents in a background session right after the Republicans took control of both the House and Senate in the 1994 mid-term congressional elections, that American politics is a two-part process, "getting elected and governance." She observed that a politician can't do anything unless he or she wins and whether he or she gets elected again is determined to a great degree by what they do when they're in office.

Journalists need to be keenly aware that covering elections is only a part of covering politics. Much post-electoral news coverage falls down because of several key flaws in the way reporters do their jobs. First, journalists who cover only the horse race (the who's ahead, who's coming from behind, what are the crises, gaffes and scandals of the campaign?) have not laid the groundwork for covering the success or failure of a politician's governance. Second, journalists do not look back enough at what was said during the campaign when the campaign is over. Third, journalists on daily deadlines (in the case of newspaper reporters) or hourly deadlines (in the case of many broadcasters) become so enmeshed in the story of the moment that they neglect to explore the larger picture of how the events of the present relate to what the candidate said during the campaign, and how they square with the values, morals, concerns and passions of the folks back home. Journalists, too, need to consider Tip O'Neill's mantra—all politics is local. (See chapter 7.4.)

Part of the tapestry of covering politics, however, is examining and exposing the limitations on what a single politician can do. "Legislating is the art of the possible," said Sen. Conrad Burns (R-Mont.) during the final negotiations that led to enactment of the Telecommunications Act of 1996. If one legislator cannot persuade enough other legislators to go along with his or her amendment, language, concept, issue or codicil, it will not become part of the final product.

Throughout the history of politics and government in America, the development of coalitions, alliances and partnerships has been a pivotal part of the process. The political development of the United States Congress grew out of the philosophical differences between key members of the Washington Administration. Issues such as taxation, development of a national bank, interstate commerce, westward expansion and slavery were all pivotal issues on which early coalitions and alliances played an important role in the evolution of political parties.

Today, journalists should be aware of the issues around which political coalitions are built and alliances are developed. Geography remains a good place for reporters to start their analysis. Urbanites often have different priorities than people who live in suburbs; rural residents have different priorities than people who live in cities. Racial, ethnic, religious, socio-economic and educational differences all provide grist for the journalist's mill. Political party affiliation in certain areas is always critical.

Issues, compromises and coalitions sometimes do not go along party lines. Recent federal examples of legislative cooperation across party lines include Republican Sen. John McCain of Arizona and Democratic Sen. Russ Feingold of Wisconsin working together on campaign finance reform, and Democratic Sen. Edward Kennedy of Massachusetts and former Republican Sen. Nancy Kassebaum of Kansas working together on the portability of health insurance.

Locally and in state legislatures, the practice is similar. Party lines have been crossed and bipartisan coalitions have been built in various parts of the country over such issues as public school funding, real estate development, and medical malpractice insurance. Reporters need to understand why the coalitions and compromises have worked or not.

The best journalists covering politics are like jugglers, keeping lots of balls in the air at once. They naturally report on the horse races (which candidates are winning and losing). But beyond the horse race stories there are stories about the personalities of those running and those elected, the issues of concern to the politicians, the issues of concern to the voters, the deal making and coalition building that go into the politics of governance, and trends that will shape campaigns and races down the road. (See Chapter 5.)

2.2 Politics and the Press—Strange Bedfellows

Throughout the history of the United States, the relationship between the news media and politicians has been stormy, contentious, even hostile, while at the same time it is symbiotic, a marriage born of necessity and held together by mutual interests. It is often compared to a couple waltzing with both trying to lead. Dick Lamm, the former governor of Colorado, once caustically likened it to the great apes picking fleas off each other. Others have described it in even more-graphic and less-flattering terms.

Politicians have long railed against the news coverage they received. In his 1828 campaign against John Quincy Adams, Andrew Jackson became furious when a newspaper described his mother as a prostitute and him as her illegitimate child. Boss Tweed, the overlord of New York's political machine Tammany Hall, loathed the political cartoonist Thomas Nast, who regularly skewered him. "Give 'em hell" Harry Truman did just that to Henry Luce, the Time-Life mogul, and David Sarnoff, president of RCA, owner of NBC, for what he described as "not telling the truth" about him. Richard Nixon, after his unsuccessful bid to be governor of California in 1962, told reporters that they won't have "Dick Nixon to kick around any more." Vice-President Spiro T. Agnew called the news media "nattering nabobs of negativism."

In many cases modern politics has escalated that kind of name calling into full-blown hostility. Michael Freedman, vice president of communications and a professorial lecturer in journalism at The George Washington University, related an incident that underscores the depth of the adversarial relationship between politicians and the news media. Freedman served as press secretary to Democratic Rep. David Bonior of Michigan in the early 1990s.

The attitude of the senior staff was that "the news media is the enemy," he said, describing his first day on the job. "The first thing I was told—not by the congressman, but by a senior staff member—when I joined Bonior's office was 'We hate the press!' I was stunned. My jaw dropped. I thought to myself what am I doing here then?"

In fact, the attitude is common on Capitol Hill and Bonior's office was far less hostile than many. For a lot of congressional press secretaries, the job is to keep reporters as far from the senator or House member as possible unless there is a specific message to deliver. "The mind-set within the congressional offices is extraordinarily different than what a lot of journalists think it is," said Freedman. "It is entirely subjective to the point of view that the member might be advocating or opposing about an issue. Why would [a senior staffer] say 'we hate the press'? The answer largely lies in [the fact that] the members of Congress cannot control the press and . . . they are somewhere between skeptical and cynical about that which they cannot control."

Attempts to control the news media and what is covered are commonplace throughout the political process. "Campaigns are filled with tension," said CBS News radio correspondent Bob Fuss, who covered the 1992 campaign of Bill Clinton. "There's a constant battle between reporters and the handlers who are trying to manipulate us in such a way that the story is always positive."

He cited a specific example: "The Clinton campaign had particularly obnoxious young people who were helping to handle the press. For a while they used ropes whenever they wanted to keep us away from him—and that was fairly frequently because there were a lot of embarrassing stories during the campaign that we wanted to ask him about. They would come out and corral us with these ropes. And after a while the TV crews would simply carry scissors and knives, and whenever a rope appeared it got cut."

As a practical matter, politicians cherish and covet uncritical media coverage and, as often as not, the media oblige. Still pictures and TV video of politicians cutting ribbons, kissing babies, receiving awards and giving their standard campaign speeches are the delight of politicians. (See chapter 10.5.) A congressional press secretary once said to me that he loved a certain small town newspaper in the district because the paper ran the congressman's press releases word for word, without editing them.

All politicians pay lip service to a free, unbridled press and reporters who dig below the surface, but in reality, most would be delighted if reporters did their digging and investigation only into the activities and positions of their opponents. As a practical matter, a lot of political reporting involves finding out what's going on out of public view. The late CBS News correspondent Lem Tucker once described the art of covering politics as "watching a wrestling match under a rug." He said, "You know there's a whole lot going on but you don't know who's doing what to whom. Our job is to find out who's doing what to whom and to report it." Stage-managed events—speeches, award ceremonies, ribbon cuttings and the like—are designed to thwart reportorial investigation and provide a platform for uncritical, unfiltered, unsynthesized news coverage of the politician.

Modern White House press offices have become adept at keeping the news media so busy covering carefully-staged events that reporters have precious little time for real reporting. Political campaigns at many levels—U.S. Senate, U.S. House of Representatives, governor, and even mayor in such big cities as New York, Philadelphia, or Chicago—have adopted the same strategy of overwhelming the media with staged events.

Ronald Reagan and his media guru, Michael Deaver, were masterful at manipulating the media. Reagan, a former actor, delivered speeches brilliantly and Deaver seldom presented the media with a backdrop that didn't flatter his star. As a result, the public rarely saw a bad picture or heard a bad sound bite of Reagan. The politicians stage an event; the news media dutifully cover the event. The politicians get ink and air time; the newspapers and electronic news organizations get stories, pictures and sound. Everybody wins, except the voting public, who get precious little real information about the office-holder, candidate or the issues involved.

While covering stage-managed events is a part of covering politics, journalists—reporters, editors, producers, still photographers and videographers—need to keep in mind that it should not be the primary responsibility of covering politics. The definition of "news" implies that what you are presenting to your readers, viewers and listeners is new and important, something relevant with a direct or indirect impact on them. Ribbon cuttings, award ceremonies and baby kissings are seldom new, important, relevant or significant to anybody except to the politician who is getting his or her face in the news. (See chapter 10.4.)

Some news organizations are satisfied simply to cover an event with a candidate or officeholder and call it political reporting. This kind of coverage is cheap and easy; it requires very little investment of time or journalistic effort on the part of a reporter or on the part of the organization. News executives and editors often need a peg—in the jargon of the business—in order to consider a political story. For example, a candidate visiting a nursing home can be the peg for a story on that candidate's position on Medicare or Social Security. A politician cutting a ribbon to open a new fire station can provide a peg for an analysis of whether that politician kept his or her campaign promises about spending priorities on public safety.

Good political reporters often use events as news pegs, in order to sell stories to their bosses, even when those bosses are not predisposed to airing or printing serious political stories. "It helps if you're doing something on the anniversary of an event, for example," said Helen Dewar, veteran *Washington Post* reporter. "It makes sure your story doesn't sit around gathering dust, that it gets in by that deadline. The imminence of some kind of action can help give a story some kind of relevance."

Some events are simply so big that they become the news on their face. When the president of the United States visits your town to appear with a local candidate, the event, itself, is newsworthy and merits coverage. Purists will argue that political journalists have an obligation to look beyond the event to the political motivation for holding it and to expose the expected impact on the local electorate; the fact is that a presidential visit to a local community overshadows virtually all types of analytical coverage.

President George W. Bush's campaign appearances during the 2002 election campaigns in key senatorial and gubernatorial contests were considered a daring new political gambit for a sitting president. Tom Mattesky, deputy Washington bureau chief for CBS News said it followed on media expert Michael Deaver's stage-managing techniques during the Reagan Administration and used new technology in a calculated strategy to maximize favorable coverage for the president and his candidate while pushing the opposition into the background.

"Everything now is done deliberately, whether it's the location of a speech . . . or even the decision of where to go and when," said Mattesky. "What you're seeing is an unfettered continuous presentation of one side. . . . Let's take Jacksonville, Florida. It would be very unusual to see the Democratic candidate getting anywhere near the amount of face-time on Jacksonville television that [Republican Gov.] Jeb Bush got with his brother. They set up these events with the president and the candidate he's promoting so that it's impossible to crop him out. The candidate's literally as close to the president as his Secret Service agents are. It's highly orchestrated. The backdrops are carefully selected. And the whole intent is to not just get total coverage on the 6 o'clock news but to get coverage on the noon news and, for that matter, to break into programming while the president is in that city to maximize the candidate's face time with the president on local TV."

It is nearly impossible for a reporter, especially a local reporter, to do anything but cover the event the way the White House and the local candidate want. As Mattesky noted, "There is no better backdrop, no better campaign prop, than Air Force One." If one definition of news is something unusual or out of the ordinary, for most cities a visit by the president qualifies, and achieving any measure of balance in coverage is difficult.

The journalistic concepts of objectivity, fairness, accuracy, balance and reporting the truth are relatively modern. American newspapers grew out of the pre-Revolutionary tradition of information dissemination by pamphlet and broadsheet. Point of view and opinion were an accepted part of news coverage. Those people who held a particular point of view or political opinion largely bought and read the newspaper that embraced their viewpoint.

Early newspapers routinely smeared politicians with whom they disagreed in the vilest and often the most inaccurate and even fabricated terms. John Adams was called a monarchist, pro-British royalist and servant of the merchant class. Thomas Jefferson was excoriated by newspapers that supported Adams in the election of 1800. On October 6, the *Connecticut Courant*, for example, wrote that "Mr. Jefferson is an enemy to the Constitution . . . and wishes its destruction." The article went on to suggest Jefferson was a "spendthrift . . . libertine . . . [and] atheist" and asking is this man "qualified to make your laws, and to govern you, and your posterity . . . ?" This was presented as a news article, not an editorial.

Other highly partisan newspapers of that era thought nothing of labeling political candidates as murderers, drunkards, thieves, bastards and otherwise morally unfit to hold public office. Truth, fairness and factual accuracy were not early journalistic values and the unrestricted injection of opinion into news stories was the norm. *The New York Times*, for example, reported the 1860 election of Abraham Lincoln as an "[a]stounding triumph of Republicanism" and declared the election as representative of Northern "indignation" over "the menaces of the South."

Many newspapers still have editorial policies that reflect political points of view, though virtually none stoop to the level of invective that was common, if not dominant, from 1787 to the Civil War era. Most modern newspapers restrict their opinions to their editorial or op-ed pages and take pains not to let opinion seep into hard news coverage.

Significant numbers of people believe that the news media, in general, are politically biased and infuse news coverage with opinion and biased decision making. Conservatives often point to CBS News and *The Washington Post* as examples of liberal bias; liberals accuse Fox (network) News and *The Washington Times* as examples of conservative bias.

"There's a complicated dynamic," said Dotty Lynch, CBS News's senior political editor. "I think it's fair to say that the press corps is more liberal in the aggregate than the general public." The perception of a political preference, she said, has had an impact on political coverage, not because of bias in stories, but because of the relationships between reporters and those they cover. "Republican operatives often have a chip on their shoulder about the media. They think we're not going to give them an even break. They think we're out to get them. They don't feel as comfortable with reporters as Democratic press secretaries. Democratic candidates tend to be more accessible than Republicans. The big exception to that, of course, was [2000 presidential candidate and senator] John McCain [R-Ariz.] who liked reporters, had a staff that liked reporters. And he wound up getting extremely favorable coverage."

"Some people on the right think that reporters are political activists who are out to advance an agenda. That's not true," said Brit Hume, Fox News's chief Washington correspondent, who calls bias, especially liberal bias, a "very serious problem."

He suggested that in order to combat bias a reporter must guard against allowing his or her own personal views to creep into the way the story is told. The key is language and an awareness of the impact of words. "You can find neutral language. But there's a problem with neutral language. It tends to be dull. So therein lies the difficulty and the dual challenge of political journalism. How to be interesting and be fair."

Jamie Dupree, news director for the Washington Bureau of Cox Radio, said the reality and the perception may be quite different. "As we get a new crop of reporters every year who have grown up with Fox News, with [conservative talk show host Rush] Limbaugh on in the car that maybe their parents were listening to, I tend to think the question soon may be whether the news media have gotten too conservative. People will laugh when they read that. But there's a pendulum with everything and now it's swinging the other way."

Broadcasters have long been keenly aware of the notion of political bias, a legacy of the Federal Communication Commission's "fairness doctrine," that dates to 1949. With the popularity of radio news during World War II and the looming development of television, the FCC sought a method by which to preserve the air waves as a public trust. In 1941, during the Franklin D. Roosevelt Administration, the commission suggested that radio stations not editorialize at all. Under President Harry Truman, the commission moved to require radio and TV stations to air all sides of controversial issues and opposing political points of view.

My first media job was as a news reporter and occasional talk show host on radio station KTLN in Denver in 1967. We were called "moderators" and were instructed in emphatic terms not to inject our personal opinion into our programs. We were to encourage as many different points of view as possible. The news policy was equally firm: in covering politics or public controversies, get as many opposing points of view as possible and keep your own opinions to yourself. Two years later, in 1969, the U.S. Supreme Court upheld the constitutionality of the fairness doctrine in *Red Lion vs. FCC*, only to have the FCC repeal the doctrine in 1987.

Despite the ongoing debate, even among respected professionals, in my experience political journalists take pains to examine their own personal biases and to make certain that they do not color, cloud or obfuscate their reporting. While not every journalist adheres consciously to the Code of Ethics of the Society of Professional Journalists, most—virtually all of the really good political reporters—follow the code's most important tenets either consciously or unconsciously.

Among the most important elements of the SPJ Code are to "seek truth and report it. Journalists should be honest, fair and courageous in gathering, reporting and interpreting information. Journalists should: Test the accuracy of information from all sources and exercise care to avoid inadvertent error. Deliberate distortion is never permissible." The code goes on to suggest journalists should "[e]xamine their own cultural values and avoid imposing those values on others." Critical to political news gathering and reporting, the SPJ Code of Ethics warns journalists to "[d]istinguish between advocacy and news reporting. Analysis and commentary should be labeled and not misrepresent fact or context." (The entire SPJ Code as well as the organization and other useful information for journalists can be accessed at www.spj.org.)

In addition, most political journalists believe that it is never proper for the journalist to inject his or her own opinion into coverage of candidates, campaigns, races or public policy debates. Most political journalists adhere to a high standard of fairness and go to great lengths to ensure the accuracy of their stories. Most political journalists understand that neither the reportorial process nor product are ever perfect, but their professional integrity mandates that they strive constantly to make it better and get the facts right.

2.3 The Two-Party System

The Founding Fathers didn't pay a great deal of attention to the likelihood that political parties would develop in the new nation they sired. Of course, political parties had been common in Europe, especially in Britain. But the idea of political parties is not mentioned in the Constitution itself, nor in most of the writings tangential to it. Some of the men who had input into the development of the Constitution believed a system of political parties in the new country would, in fact, be harmful.

James Madison, the primary architect of the U.S. Constitution, dealt with the mechanics of creating a government for the fledgling country. He devised the three branches of government, separation of powers, and checks and balances. He outlined the concept of a president as head of the executive branch and the Electoral College as the mechanism by which presidents would be elected.

The electoral process devised by Madison does not specifically envision political parties. The Constitution is vague with regard to the methods and manners of elections, leaving it to the states to select the dates and times of elections and determine who is qualified to vote. Article I, Section 2, says representatives "shall be . . . chosen every second year by the people of the several states." Article I, Section 3, says senators shall be elected by the state legislatures (which was changed to direct, popular election by the Seventeenth Amendment in 1913). And Article II, Section 1, says that the president shall be picked by the Electoral College. The electors are appointed "in such manner as the legislature . . . [of each state] may direct."

As a result there was no uniformity in early elections. It wasn't until 1848 when Zachary Taylor was elected president that the voting occurred on the same day across the country.

Madison's writings indicate he understood instinctively that the popularly elected House of Representatives would be the most political of the legislative branches, because of the diversity of the people electing representatives. However, there is little in *The Federalist Papers* to indicate Madison foresaw the political nature of the body manifesting itself in the development of formal political parties. There was little political intrigue or posturing in getting the new legislative branch off the ground in 1789. A few congressional races were contested, but for the most part, the men who played pivotal roles in state government during and immediately after the American Revolution were elected to the first national government.

The first presidential election was void of politics. In fact, accounts of that election make it appear more like a coronation than the result of a political process. Everybody assumed that George Washington, the man who had led the military struggle against the British monarchy, would be the first president. Washington's first election was all but by acclamation. He had no formal opponent nor was there any kind of campaign. The assumption was that Washington stood for what Americans stood for, and that was that.

Washington himself was opposed to the kind of philosophical battles that accompanied political parties in Britain, and urged a unified, somewhat monolithic, political structure. Thomas Jefferson believed that the United States would have only one political party—his. Neither vision lasted long.

The surprise was the speed, after the 1789 election, with which the lines between two distinct political philosophies and ideologies surfaced. The underpinnings of the first American political parties have roots that go back to Revolutionary times and involve geography, economics and widely-disparate views on the role of government. The parties themselves began to take shape during Washington's first administration and grew rapidly during his second. The divisions created the framework of what has come to be known as the American two-party system.

A philosophical rift among some of the men in key government positions gave rise to two distinct political camps, a situation that erupted into full-blown name-calling and mudslinging during the election campaign of 1796. That race pitted two heroes of U.S. independence—John Adams and Thomas Jefferson—against each other. The divisions were also becoming evident in Congress, with the distinctions playing out both in campaigns for election to the House of Representatives and in the development of coalitions and alliances for the passage of legislation. The importance of one side or the other having a majority in Congress soon became evident. The majority would control the agenda, key congressional offices and the committees that oversaw legislation.

The first political parties were the Federalists and the Democratic-Republicans. The Federalists—such men as Alexander Hamilton and John Adams—were proponents of an active federal government, a national economic policy that promoted banking and commerce, and development of good relations with Britain. The other camp, the Democratic-Republicans (who often called themselves simply Republicans and who are identified as Jeffersonian Republicans by some historians) were represented by Thomas Jefferson and James Madison. They believed in a small and non-intrusive central government, a narrow interpretation of the U.S. Constitution, *laissez faire* economic policy along the lines of the economic philosopher Adam Smith, states' rights, and a closer U.S. alignment with France than Britain. The Federalists were linked closely with Northern businessmen, bankers and manufacturers; the Democratic-Republicans were closely linked with Southern farmers and landowners. These geographic differences would set the stage for the development and evolution of the two parties over the next half century.

By the end of the first Adams-Jefferson presidential race in 1796, and as the 1800 rematch approached, much of the debate over policy and personality played out in the newspapers. Almost all newspapers of the day supported one side or the other. Those that supported Jefferson were calling Adams a monarchist and King John the First; those that backed Adams labeled Jefferson everything from an anarchist to an extremist and a dangerous Jacobin (after the often brutal post-revolutionary ruling party in France).

During Andrew Jackson's first term (the early 1830s), the Democratic-Republicans were undergoing internal changes, one of which was the transition to calling themselves Democrats. Jackson is the first president to do so. During Jackson's second term he managed to alienate some of his Southern supporters to the point that they bolted the Democratic Party. They banded together with the Federalists, more out of anger at Jackson than because of political ideology. Their muscle in opposing Jackson and his policies resulted in a new coalition and generated a new name for the Federalists. They adopted the name of the old English political party, the Whigs. In 1836, Democrat Martin van Buren easily defeated three Whig challengers and the Democrats dismissed the new coalition as weak and directionless.

Any real weakness proved to be short-lived and the Whigs started gaining strength in Congress in the 1838 mid-term elections. Public sentiment was shifting and two years later Whig William Henry Harrison relegated van Buren to one term as president. That campaign gave rise to one of the most memorable campaign slogans to that point—Tippecanoe and Tyler too. Harrison had led U.S. troops successfully in battle against an Indian confederacy in 1811 and defeated them at Tippecanoe Creek, after which he was nicknamed Old Tippecanoe. John Tyler was the vice presidential nominee.

Harrison died only a month after he was sworn in and Tyler served out the rest of his term. By the end of the Harrison/Tyler Administration, the United States was expanding rapidly westward and the issue of slavery was becoming a dominant factor in American politics. The primary question was whether the new states being admitted to the Union should be slave states or free states. The Democrats, with their predominantly Southern base, saw no problem with extending slavery into the new states. The mostly Northeastern Whigs (and a burgeoning Western-based third political party known as Free Soilers) were, for the most part, politically and morally opposed to slavery and its geographic expansion.

That issue was the subject of a strategy meeting in the depths of winter 1854, in icy Rippon, Wisconsin. By summer of that year the Whigs had decided to change the name of their party to Republican and to oppose the expansion of slavery to the West.

Six years later Abraham Lincoln would become the first Republican president, the issue of slavery would become so volatile that the South would ultimately secede from the Union, and the country would be plunged into a bloody Civil War. At the same time, the development of the two major political parties in the United States was complete and the Republicans and Democrats live today.

The Republican Party is frequently referred to as the GOP, which stands for Grand Old Party. According to the Republican National Committee's web page (www.rnc.org), the phrase dates back to the 1870s and a reference to the "gallant old party" in the Congressional Record. Subsequent newspaper and magazine headlines referred to the GOP and the Grand Old Party. For journalists, both GOP and Republican Party are acceptable references in both print and broadcast.

The Democrats and the GOP have, effectively, been in transition during the 150 years from the Civil War to the dawn of the 21st century. An array of issues has molded the fabric of the two political entities. Industrialization, unions, World War I, the Great Depression, World War II, the emergence of the atomic age, the Cold War, the Civil Rights movement, Vietnam, Watergate, taxation, government spending, military policy and globalization have all played a role in the political evolution of the United States and its two principal political parties. Along with the thumbnail chronology of political development, journalists must understand how the issues and personalities helped shape and continue to shape the political landscape.

2.4 Third Parties and Independents

While the United States is considered to operate with a two-party political system, third parties have enjoyed a rich and often colorful history, and abound today. Depending on which list you look at, there are as many as 50 parties other than the Democrats and Republicans active in the country. Some have had extremely short shelf-lives. One or more parties have probably been hatched and expired as this chapter was being written.

Some of the better known third parties include the Communists, Socialists, the Green Party, Libertarians, the Right to Life Party, the Reform Party, the Natural Law Party, U.S. Taxpayer Party and the American Conservative Party. A few purport to represent various extreme views and the fringes of society, and include the American Nazi Party, the Pansexual Peace Party and the Pot Party.

Third parties go back to the early 1800s. The Anti-Mason Party,

Anti-Jackson Party, Free Soilers and Know Nothings all pre-date the Civil War. The Greenbacks, Prohibition Party, Populists and Socialists roughly coincided with each succeeding decade after the Civil War.

No third party presidential candidate has ever been elected, but several have had significant impact on the overall electoral process and won enough of the popular vote to have garnered votes in the Electoral College.

President Theodore Roosevelt, who had already served two terms as a Republican, garnered 88 electoral votes in 1912 under the standard of the Bull Moose Party. In 1948, South Carolina's Democratic governor, Strom Thurmond, left that party to run on the anti-integration and anti-civil rights Dixiecrat ticket and won 39 electoral votes. (Thurmond, who died in 2003, served in the U.S. House of Representatives and later as a U.S. senator as a Republican.) In 1968, Alabama Gov. George Wallace, elected as a Democrat, led the American Independent Party in the presidential race against Republican Richard Nixon and Democrat Hubert Humphrey. Wallace prevented either of the other candidates from winning a majority of the popular vote, but Nixon handily won the electoral vote, 301 to 191, over Humphrey. Wallace picked up 46 electoral votes.

One-time Republican Rep. John Anderson ran for president as the candidate of the National Unity Party in 1972. More recently H. Ross Perot founded and ran for president on the Reform Party ticket in 1992 and consumer advocate Ralph Nader ran as the Green Party candidate in 2000. Neither won any electoral votes, but some political observers believe that Perot's presence divided the Republicans more than the Democrats and allowed Democrat Bill Clinton to defeat Republican incumbent George H. W. Bush in the 1992 race. They also posit that Nader's candidacy helped Republican George W. Bush win by a whisker over Democrat Al Gore in 2000.

Political pros, especially those connected with the two major parties, often dismiss third parties as trivial. They declare that third-party candidates can't win and anyone who votes for one of them is wasting a vote. That's not entirely true. Minnesotans elected former professional wrestler Jesse Ventura, who ran on the Reform Party ticket, to be their governor in 1998. Maine has frequently elected independents to the governor's mansion; most recently, Angus King served from 1995 to 2003. Oregon, North Dakota, Alaska and Connecticut all elected third-party governors during the 20th century.

Independents and third parties have regularly elected members to the U.S. House and Senate. The dean of Independents in the House is Bernard Sanders of Vermont, once the Socialist mayor of Burlington. He was first elected in 1990.

Republican U.S. Sen. James Jeffords, also of Vermont, stunned his fellow Republicans in 2000 by bolting the party and becoming an Independent. That moved the Senate from GOP control (50 Republicans and 50 Democrats but with a Republican vice president to break ties) to the Democratic column.

While reporters must exercise caution in not overemphasizing the importance of third parties, they often provide colorful candidates and non-traditional views of many issues. Just as too much coverage of them does not serve the public well, neither does ignoring them or marginalizing them. Some of the more intriguing and newsworthy third party candidates during the last three decades included Communist Angela Davis, conservative columnist Pat Buchanan who has run under several standards, and baby doctor Benjamin Spock who ran for the White House as the candidate of the Peace & Freedom Party in 1972, the same party that nominated Black Panther Eldridge Cleaver four years earlier.

Covering third parties requires a little additional digging on the part of reporters. It's always a good idea to do a little homework about the party, what it stands for and the background of the candidate or candidates. It is not unusual for political reporters to view third parties as more of a circus sideshow than a serious part of the political process.

It is hard to overstate the amount of sneering and derision on the part of a significant number of respected national newspeople in 1998 when Jesse Ventura announced his candidacy for governor of Minnesota. All the big name journalistic pundits thought either the state's attorney general, Hubert "Skip" Humphrey III, grandson of the former Democratic vice president and presidential candidate, or St. Paul's popular and well-known Mayor Norm Coleman would win handily. But on Nov. 3, 1998, it was Ventura, the former pro wrestler, former actor, former radio talk show host, who was the last man standing, and the journalistic pundits were wiping the egg from their faces.

A Conversation with Bob Schieffer

News chief, Washington correspondent: CBS
Host: *Face the Nation*
Author: *This Just in—What I Couldn't Tell You on TV* (Putnam, 2003)

A good sense of humor seems to be the hallmark of most newspeople. It's an understatement when it comes to Bob Schieffer. He is witty, droll, often downright funny, not to mention being one of the most well-connected political reporters in the country. Yet there's still a hint of Texas in his voice and, even after more than four decades in Washington, a whole lot of Texas in his heart and soul.

I encountered Schieffer one night in late October 1976 in the second floor men's room of the CBS News Washington bureau. He was toweling down after a shower following grueling days on the campaign trail.

"How are you, Bob?" I asked.

"Hammered," he replied with a touch of Texas twang. "I feel like somebody put me in a sack and just beat me."

Schieffer is a genuine star, but I have never seen that stardom get in the way of his work ethic or drive for journalistic excellence. He always makes that one last phone call, checks that one last fact, buttonholes that one last politician. He is a consummate professional.

I knew a little of his background from many conversations during stake-outs or while listening to endless debates on Capitol Hill, but I took this opportunity to ask about it in detail:

B.S.: "I had always wanted to be a reporter. When I was a kid I was the sports editor of the junior high school paper, sports editor of the high school paper and editor of the annual. Unfortunately, what my mother thought I needed to do was be a doctor, but when I got to college no one else thought that. I enrolled in pre-med. I fooled around with that for two years and realized that creative writing was not going to get you very far in chemistry. So I switched to journalism, which is always what I wanted to do. When people asked me what led me to journalism, the true answer is comparative anatomy.

"I didn't have a very good college career. I did manage to graduate on time. But college is what you put into it. I'm one of those who believe that you can get a very good education at a poor college and you can get a very poor education at a good university. It's up to you. I put nothing into it and as a result I didn't get very much out of it. I like to think that by now I've read all the books I should have read, but when you come right down to it, I'm basically self-educated."

R.A.: *Didn't you start as a print reporter?*
B.S.: "Actually I started as a radio reporter working in the newsroom of a little radio station in Fort Worth. It paid the grand sum of a dollar an hour. I was in college and this was just after I switched to journalism. I was not a disc jockey. I was a reporter. We had these panel trucks and we'd cover what I call the three R's—wrecks, rapes and robberies. When there was a wreck I'd go out there in the panel truck and broadcast a report live from the scene over a two-way radio.

R.A.: *You were way ahead of your time in the trend toward live coverage.*
B.S.: "Oh, yes. We called ourselves the station that pioneered and developed on-the-scene news coverage in the great Southwest. What we didn't tell people was that the entire news department was made up of TCU [Texas Christian University] students. I learned a lot. None of us knew anything about it at the time. But we learned by doing.

"After that I met the night police reporter at the *Fort Worth Star-Telegram*, who was Phil Record. When Phil got promoted to night city editor he recommended me to take his place at the *Star-Telegram* as the night police reporter. It's the first time they ever hired anybody from radio, but that's how I got into the newspaper. Then I stayed there and went to Vietnam in 1965.

"When I came back, one of the local television stations, the NBC affiliate in Dallas, invited me to come out and talk about the war. Afterward they offered me a job, 20 dollars a week more than they paid me at the newspaper. I'm one of the first print guys who got into TV for the money. I really did need the 20 dollars.

"To give you an idea of pay scales in those days, I had been making 135 dollars a week at the paper. They'd given me a 10 dollar raise, combat pay when I went to Vietnam, from 125 to 135 dollars. They offered me the extra 20 dollars at the TV station which took me to 155 dollars and that seemed like all the money in the world. That's how I got into TV. And after a couple years there I came to CBS."

R.A.: *When did you first cover politics? Was it a local campaign?*

B.S.: "Yes. When I was at the radio station, we had a mayor's race. That was my first time to think about politics. I had always been interested in politics. After I went to the paper, when I came back from Vietnam, they were actually going to make me the political reporter when I was offered the job at the television station. So I had been covering politics along the way.

"My first campaign while I was at the television station was in 1968 when [Minnesota Democrat Hubert] Humphrey came through Texas.

"My first national campaign was when I came to CBS and did the McGovern campaign [in 1972]. I was one of the *Boys on the Bus* [Timothy Crouse's book written about that campaign.] And it was a great campaign. Everybody knew that McGovern was going to lose. It was like being in the stands of a football game when the score is 60 to nothing. Everybody knew how it was going to come out. But it was my first campaign, and first campaigns are sort of like first loves—you never forget them.

"As I look back on that campaign it really was the last issue campaign. McGovern was against the war. [Republican incumbent Richard] Nixon was for it. McGovern got drubbed, but it was a campaign in which you knew what McGovern stood for and you knew what Nixon stood for. All too often today we write about staying on-message and we don't really check to see what the message is.

"Since that campaign, most of the campaigns have tended to be about image. And in recent years they are almost exclusively about which candidate raises the most money. In about 95 percent of our campaigns now, the candidate who raises the most money wins.

R.A.: *They raise more money, thus they get their message out more, thus we cover them more, and it becomes a self-fulfilling prophecy?*

B.S.: "Yes. And they get on television. The campaigns are waged almost exclusively on television. In recent years in Fort Worth, where I grew up, I can't remember when a candidate for governor came there and held a public rally. It's just not cost-effective. You can reach so many more people on television. When a candidate comes to town he goes to see the people who contribute to campaigns and he holds a news conference at the airport.

"I'll tell you one story that's in my book about how much politics has changed. The first politician I ever saw was Lyndon Johnson. I was 10 years old and we heard he was coming to the vacant lot where we played baseball on the north side of Fort Worth. Dad took me down to see him and the reason that we went was because we heard he was coming in a helicopter. We'd never seen a helicopter.

"So all of a sudden up in the sky here was this airplane with no wings and this voice comes over an electronic bullhorn. 'This is your candidate for the United States Senate, Lyndon Johnson. I'll be down to see you in a minute.'

"Well we didn't know if it was God, Lyndon Johnson or what. It absolutely terrified us. Here comes the helicopter and it lands. Johnson gets out and gives this rousing speech, and at the end of it he takes his hat off and throws it into the crowd. He waves and moves on.

"I told this story many years later to Jake Pickle, who was the long-time [Democratic] congressman from Austin, Texas. Jake says, 'Oh, yeah. I worked in that campaign. That was my job. I was the hat catcher.'

"I said, 'What?'

"He said, 'Yeah. I would always drive ahead to where the helicopter was going to land and I'd stand on the front row. You know Lyndon was tight. He wasn't going to waste a hat on a political rally. He'd take that hat off and he'd just throw it to me. Then I'd run around to the back of the helicopter, give it to him and he'd fly off to the next stop.'

"I think back on that and I can remember every detail of that day. It was fun. I was with my dad. It was exciting. And by comparison I can't remember a single campaign commercial that I heard or saw in campaign 2000. And the other part is that I'm glad I can't remember because they were so sleazy and so superfluous that I don't want to remember what they said. But in those days [1948] politics was an amateur sport.

"The campaign chairman was somebody who worked in the community, the state chairman was usually a businessman or labor leader. These were people that had other jobs. Now what's different about politics is that it has given over all of these jobs to professionals. Too often now the point of politics seems to be to raise money for these cottage industries that have sprung up around it. We have these consultants now who are experts at raising money. We have pollsters who are experts at demographics.

"When Lyndon Johnson came to our community, he got a chance to see who we were, how we looked, how we dressed. He had a feel for the community and we got a feel for him. It was an interactive process. Now, if a politician wants to know who lives in that part of town he just goes to a pollster who gives him a demographic breakdown. Somehow I don't think he has as good a feel by looking at a set of numbers for that neighborhood as Lyndon Johnson did when he took the trouble to come there.

"That summer of 1948, Lyndon Johnson would make as many as 17 campaign stops a day in that helicopter as he campaigned across Texas. Now the only time that politicians hold public rallies is to use them as a backdrop for making a television commercial. Because the television commercials cost so much, that has driven up the price of campaigns.

"This will never happen. This is truly putting the toothpaste back in the tube, but if I had my way, I'd probably go back to the old smoke-filled room, the old precinct convention, the state convention, the place where the local people selected the candidates. In my view, that was more participatory. The candidates were much closer to the people than they are today."

R.A.: *So the rise of political consultants, handlers, strategists and pollsters is the problem?*

B.S.: "The professional consultant has one objective, and that is to win. Once the election is done, whether he wins or loses, he takes his money and goes to the next town and gets ready for the next election. In the old days, when this was an amateur sport the Democratic chairman of the incumbent's committee in Fort Worth and the Republican chairman of the challenger's committee both lived in the community. And if they won, they got to share in the spoils. But if their guy lost, they had to live with it, because it was their town and their community.

"When you're running a campaign and you know that you're going to have to live with the consequences when it's over, you tend to run a different kind of campaign. That's another reason that these campaigns have become so vicious and so nasty. The political consultant who runs a campaign and gets paid for it doesn't care what the impact is going to be on the people on the other side. He doesn't really care what the impact is going to be on the community. Because once it's over he can move on to the next town. If you're homegrown and have to live in that town and you have to live in that town win or lose, you're going to run a different kind of campaign."

R.A.: *Dirty campaigns are nothing new?*

B.S.: "There has always been a dark side to politics. And there has always been negative campaigning. In the old days it was called street talk or a whisper campaign. What's happened is that what used to be street talk and the whisper campaign is now on television. We have taken these things that used to be whisper campaigns and elevated them to the level that we actually put them in television ads. We can circulate them more widely and in a sense give them more credibility than they deserve."

R.A.: *You've won a lot of praise over the years for your interviewing style on* Face the Nation. *What kind of preparation do you do?*

B.S.: "I always try to have a game plan. I don't write out the questions in advance that I'm going to ask people when they come on *Face the Nation*, but I try to stake out areas that I want to make sure that I cover.

"Another thing that I always do is write the name of the person I'm interviewing at the very top of the page. The reason why is that at the 1976 Democratic convention in New York, at the end of the convention the four floor men were Roger Mudd, Dan Rather, Mort Dean and myself. Walter Cronkite said, [imitates Cronkite] 'Now we want to turn to those stalwart floor men Roger Mudd, Dan Rather, Morton Dean and. ...' And for what seemed like an hour, Walter could not remember my name. Finally Dan said, 'It's Bob Schieffer, Walter.'

"'Oh, yes, of course!' [Laughs.]

"It happens to the best of us. I always thought if Walter Cronkite could forget my name I could probably forget the name of whoever I was interviewing, so I make it a policy to always write down the name, because I just know that some day, some place, my mind is going to go blank.

"Everyone's mind goes blank at one time or other. I'll never forget one time when Jimmy Carter had a news conference at the White House. He called on me and the moment he did my mind just went absolutely blank. Now this is being broadcast on national television. My bosses in New York are watching and I didn't want to say, 'Well, thank you, Mr. President, but I really don't have a question.' Can you imagine the bosses in New York sitting there and saying, 'We're paying Schieffer to cover the White House and he can't even think of a question to ask the president?'

"I couldn't come up with anything else, so just off the top of my head I said, 'What's the deal on the Russians?'

"Well, it turned out he had something he wanted to say about the Russians. And he used my question—which was a non-question—as a platform to put out this statement about the Russians, which made the front page the next day of *The New York Times* and we used that evening on the [CBS] *Evening News*. But the only reason I came up with that was my mind had gone blank."

R.A.: *Any pitfalls or dangers you want to flag for young reporters?*

B.S.: "It's easy to be overcome with your own self-importance. Politicians don't pay attention to you because you have a cute personality or because they're looking for someone to run around with or be friends with. They're paying attention to you because you're a reporter and you represent a news organization and you can influence the public, the people who vote for or against them.

"In Fort Worth, when I went to work at that radio station, the boss said to me one day, call up the mayor and see if you can get him to say something about this story. I thought that the mayor wasn't going to take a call from me. But I did and his wife answered the phone and she yelled, 'Hey, Tom, it's Bob Schieffer from KXOL on the phone.' They knew who I was because I worked at the radio station. I was stunned that I could get through to the mayor. But that was because I worked for a news organization."

3

Legal Benchmarks

The American political landscape is far different today than it was even a half century ago, much less in 1787 when the U.S. Constitution was adopted. Philosophical, social, technological and legal changes have played a significant role in shaping the modern American political system. Congress and the courts have played a pivotal role.

Political reporters not only need a fundamental understanding of the history and function of the political process, they also need some grounding in the legal underpinnings of it. Just consider all the political reporters who went to work on Election Day 2000 and didn't emerge from the legal and constitutional thicket that election engendered until more than a month later. Every reporter who covered that election and its aftermath will tell you that they came out of it with a vastly greater understanding of election law and its constitutional foundation than they ever imagined possible. Most of them will tell you they wish they had known more earlier.

3.1 The Right to Vote

Every school child is told that the right to vote is fundamental to American democracy. The fact is that the right to vote has become a fundamental citizen right only in relatively recent times; historically it was not so. Nor has the development of the right to vote been smooth or rapid.

The framers of the Constitution envisioned only limited direct popular representation in the new nation's government, relying instead on a scheme of indirect representation. The Constitution, as first ratified in 1787, required a direct popular vote only for members of the House of Representatives. The president and vice president were elected by the Electoral College; the U.S. senators were elected by the state legislatures and were not popularly elected until 1913, after ratification of the 17th Amendment.

State legislators and governors were elected by popular vote, although it was by no means representative of the society at large. Legal restrictions on who was allowed to vote severely limited actual participation in the process. In every state, only white male citizens had the right to vote. Twenty-one was the minimum age for voting. Women, slaves, free African Americans, and Native Americans were not enfranchised regardless of age. For the first 78 years of U.S. history nobody saw much problem in that, except those people who were locked out of the system. Once it was identified as an issue to be reckoned with, it was changed only slowly and with political rancor and social discord.

There were discussions about the abolition of slavery going back to pre-Revolutionary times. There was debate in 1775 and '76, in the Continental Congress in Philadelphia, about whether language regarding the institution of slavery should be incorporated into the Declaration of Independence. In those days the phrase "all men are created equal" was narrowly construed. Never did most framers of the new U.S. Constitution envision the right to vote being extended to anyone other than white men.

Only in the aftermath of the Civil War was the white male grip on the right to vote loosened. The 15th Amendment, ratified in 1870, theoretically gave African Americans the right to vote, although that right was limited in many Southern states by poll taxes, literacy tests, *de facto* (if not *de jure*) denial of voter registration for blacks and other legal mechanisms designed to circumvent the amendment. The Civil Rights Act of 1957 (revisited by Congress in 1960) sought to provide legal protection for African American voters. And the 24th Amendment, ratified in 1964, outlawed poll taxes in federal elections.

Nonetheless, black voters experienced extreme difficulty in some places when they attempted to vote in the 1964 presidential election. Dr. Martin Luther King Jr. led a march from Selma to Montgomery, Alabama, where he hoped to present a list of grievances to the governor. Police stopped the marchers in Selma and used clubs and teargas on them. The next year Congress easily enacted (and President Johnson signed) the Voting Rights Act of 1965. A year later the U.S. Supreme Court rejected an appeal that the Voting Right Act was unconstitutional.

The full suffrage of women lagged behind the history of voting rights for African Americans, even though many African Americans were denied their voting rights until well after women as a matter of practice. Even as the largely underground women's suffrage movement gained strength in the early 20th century, the male-dominated power structure was both condescending and patronizing toward women. Suffragette Susan B. Anthony was derided and ridiculed in her time, and women in general were dismissed by arrogant and chauvinistic men as not intelligent enough to participate in politics. Ultimately in 1920, the 19th Amendment gave women the right to vote nationwide.

A footnote in voting rights history from the Republican National Committee notes that a dozen states, all with Republican-controlled legislatures, were ahead of the curve and had given women the right to vote prior to ratification of the 19th Amendment. In 1916, Republican Janette Rankin of Montana became the first woman elected to the House of Representatives, where she served for three decades. A devout pacifist, Rankin was the only person to vote against U.S. entry into both World War I and World War II.

Until 1961, people who lived in the District of Columbia paid federal taxes, were subject to federal laws, were required to serve in the U.S. military, but were not represented when it came to electing D.C.'s most important resident, the president of the United States. The 23rd Amendment provided for the District of Columbia to be represented in the Electoral College. It provides for the number of electors equal to the "number of senators and representatives in Congress to which the district would be entitled if it were a state, but in no event more than the least populous state." In short, that means the district has three electors in the Electoral College. (See chapter 3.2.)

In 1971, the age barrier was lowered. The 26th Amendment extended the right to vote to "citizens of the United States, who are eighteen years of age or older." That amendment was the direct result of the Vietnam War and the draft. It sparked an unprecedented level of grassroots political activity on college campuses. Students in my class at the University of Denver involved in generating support for the amendment reasoned that if young men were old enough to be drafted, to be sent into combat to kill, and be killed, for their country, they were certainly old enough to vote for or against those who sent them to war.

One statutory benchmark in the history of the right to vote was congressional passage of the 1993 National Voter Registration Act, the so-called Motor Voter Act, which sought to strike down the remaining barriers to voter registration by racial minorities and people with physical disabilities. Among the provisions of the bill: people can register to vote when they get or renew their driver's licenses, they can register by mail, or they can register in person at such agencies as social service offices and state offices providing disability benefits.

Congressional backers of the Motor Voter Act argued that it would increase voter registration and thus increase electoral participation. Penny Halyburton, supervisor of elections in Florida's St. Johns County, says it's not as successful as its supporters had predicted. "More people are registering and most of our people are registering with DMV [the Department of Motor Vehicles]. About 60 percent do register with DMV . . . but we're not seeing a higher voter turnout."

While the courts have upheld the constitutionality of the act, critics also claim it has generated fraud and abuse.

Voter turnout—or the lack of it—remains an ongoing issue in modern electoral politics. The United States routinely elects a president with fewer than 60 percent of eligible voters casting ballots. Some midterm congressional elections draw less than 50 percent. And in some state, local and primary elections a 30-35 percent turnout is considered good. In sharp contrast, when Nelson Mandella was first elected president of South Africa—the first election there after the end of apartheid—more than 95 percent of the nation's voters cast ballots, many of them standing in the hot sun for two days for the privilege.

Politicians know that in close races, organizations that get their candidates' supporters to the polls have the edge. In New York's Harlem, for example, churches often organize get-out-the-vote drives in which church members will pick up voters, take them to the polls and drive them home again. The same thing happens in other communities such as Little Havana in Miami and senior citizens' centers in Phoenix.

As political races get down to the wire, reporters should monitor various core constituencies within their coverage areas to see if a candidate has managed to energize his or her core supporters or, on the other hand, whether core constituencies are not particularly enthusiastic about the performance of a given candidate. The pulse of various communities can often provide an alert reporter with an indication of voter turnout and thus how the election might turn out.

In addition, the number and nature of undecided voters can be significant. Reporters ought to keep an eye on the percentage of the electorate that is telling public opinion pollsters that they are undecided. Usually, the percentage of undecided voters shrinks rapidly as Election Day approaches. If a large number of people say they are still undecided within a week of the election, that can signal a story that's worth following. Reporters need to find out why there are so many undecided voters and what candidates do in the last days of a campaign to sway those undecideds.

A follow-up story can be whether the undecided voters cast ballots at all, and if so, what moved them to vote, and if not, why not.

3.2 The Electoral College

For journalists covering presidential politics, the Electoral College usually becomes a tangential element to a news story once every four years when presidential elections are held. In modern times the electoral winner has usually been declared unofficially before returns start coming in from the West Coast. Every so often, however, such as the 2000 race that pitted Republican George W. Bush against Democrat Albert Gore Jr., the Electoral College is the story. (See chapter 3.3.)

Normally, the Electoral College meets several weeks after Election Day. The votes are tallied in each state and, by practice and tradition, the person getting the most popular votes in that state is awarded that state's electoral votes. The first person amassing 270 electoral votes is then determined to be the next president of the United States. Some of my students have difficulty with the concept that the national popular vote is not a factor in determining who is elected; the key is the vote in each state. Thus is it possible to have one person win the national popular vote and not be elected president.

That, of course, has happened several times in U.S. history. In 1824, John Quincy Adams was clobbered in the popular vote. (He also lost in the Electoral College. But no candidate won a majority in the Electoral College and as a result it fell to the House of Representatives, under the provisions of the 12th Amendment, to select the president. Adams won.) In 2000, Gore beat Bush by a little more than half a million popular votes but lost in the Electoral College. (Bush ended up with five electoral votes more than the 270 needed to give him a clear majority and preclude action by the House of Representatives.)

A common question is why the president of the United States is not elected by popular vote. The answer goes back to the development of the Constitution. The intent of the framers of the Constitution in establishing an Electoral College was to balance two concerns: minimizing the likelihood that the most important official in the country would be elected by popular political whim, while providing some measure of accountability to the voters of each state. James Madison, in *Federalist Number 39,* defended indirect election of the president, noting that electors serve for a specific and limited period of time and that there is popular consent to their service at least at some level. He wrote, "The president is indirectly derived from the choice of the people."

Alexander Hamilton expanded on the reasoning behind indirect election of the president in *Federalist Number 68,* saying that the Electoral College system works to afford "as little opportunity as possible to tumult and disorder." He also commented on the underpinnings of keeping the Electoral College within individual states: "[A]s the electors, chosen in each state, are to assemble and vote in the state in which they are chosen, this detached and divided situation will expose them much less to heats and ferment . . . than if they were all to be convened at one time, in one place."

Periodically, amendments to the Constitution have been proposed to abandon the Electoral College in favor of direct, popular election of the president, but to date none has obtained the requisite two-thirds of both the U.S. House of Representatives and the Senate to be sent to the states for ratification.

The role and function of the Electoral College is delineated in the Constitution. Political reporters as well as government reporters (often the same people) must have a basic understanding of how it works. This is part of how I described it in *COVERING GOVERNMENT: A Civics Handbook for Journalists* (Iowa State Press, 2002):

"Electors are picked by the states to vote for president and vice president. The number of electors is the same as the number of members each state is entitled to in Congress, a minimum of two senators and one representative. As an example, Connecticut has two senators and six representatives for a total of eight electoral votes. Today, there are 538 electors—435 members of the House, plus 100 senators, plus 3 electors from the District of Columbia. (The 23rd Amendment added in 1961 gives D.C. representation in the Electoral College.) It takes a majority or 270 electoral votes for a candidate to be elected president.

"The electors vote in their respective state capitols and send their sealed ballots to the president of the U.S. Senate, who opens them, tallies the votes, and certifies the results in front of the entire Congress. The person receiving the most votes for president is elected. . . .

"The Constitution specifically gives the right to establish and administer election rules to the state legislatures. That includes setting up the practices and policies for picking members of the Electoral College. . . .

"The language of the Constitution is not specific with regard to either choosing electors or binding their votes. As a result there is no uniformity. Some states have laws requiring electors to vote for the person receiving the majority of popular votes in the state. Others select a slate of electors pledged to each candidate on the ballot and, based on the popular vote within the state, empower the electors pledged to the person receiving the highest number of votes. Still other states put slates of electors on the presidential election ballot, either grouped with the candidates they support or labeled as supporters of a given candidate. Finally, there are states that do not put legal bounds on electors, and simply rely on the tradition that electors vote for the person receiving the most popular votes in a state. Fewer than a handful of electors in U.S. history have not voted as the voters of their state did.

"Nonetheless, during the post-election turmoil in 2000, when there was a mathematical possibility of a tie vote in the Electoral College, there was some quiet exploration by Democratic candidate Albert Gore's camp regarding electors who might vote other than for the winner of the popular majority in states that do not legally bind electors. The Gore campaign was concerned about the election being decided by the House of Representatives, which had a Republican majority. . . .

"After electors meet in their various state capitols to cast their votes, the tally sheets are sent to the president of the Senate, the sitting vice president. . . . If the Electoral College vote is a tie or if no candidate wins a majority, then the election of the President falls to the House of Representatives. The result is not determined by a majority vote of the 435 members of the House. Each state delegation meets to vote separately and each state then receives one vote for president, which does not eliminate the possibility of a 25–25 tie vote in the House."

The Senate votes on a vice president in any event. If the House of Representatives fails to elect a president, then the vice president serves as president under the rules of presidential succession.

3.3 Bush versus Gore 2000

The millennium presidential race turned out to be the most controversial in more than a century. After an election night that saw the major television networks embarrass themselves by first calling Florida for Gore, then retracting it, then calling it for Bush and again retracting it, the morning after the election dawned with the electoral storm still raging over the Sunshine State and the outcome of the presidential race still uncertain.

During that night and in the following days there was much to criticize in the news coverage. Many reporters and news organizations seemed to have been caught off guard and were unprepared for events as they unfolded. It went well beyond the mistakes in calling and un-calling Florida. It revealed some fundamental flaws in the preparation of many journalists. Even some respected veteran reporters delivered incomplete, misleading and inaccurate information about what was going on and why. Many had problems reporting about the function of the Electoral College and what would happen in the event of a tie. Some were unable to explain to their viewers or readers why there is no uniform national electoral process and why the state of Florida operated the way it did. Many reported that what was happening was "unprecedented." It wasn't.

Florida had been involved in the bizarre 1876 presidential race in which Republican Rutherford B. Hayes was ultimately elected over Democrat Samuel Tilden. That contest went to the U.S. Congress because of widespread vote fraud in Florida and two other states, South Carolina and Louisiana. Florida sent the president of the Senate three different sets of Electoral College ballots. Hayes became president as the result of an electoral commission established by Congress. The establishment of the commission was outside the Constitutional provisions for deciding unresolved Electoral College votes. And the ultimate political nature of the commission prompted some newspapers that backed the Democrats to dub the president "Ruther-fraud" B. Hayes.

The 2000 Florida controversy did not involve vote fraud, but it certainly did involve ineptitude at many levels. Among other things, it introduced a whole new vocabulary to our electoral lexicon. The "chad" became a household word. Chads are the little squares or circles that get punched out of punch-card ballots, such as those used in 2000 in Palm Beach County. If the chad is not punched all the way out, it can be a hanging chad, dimpled chad, or pregnant chad. The nation was treated to television news pictures of election workers using magnifying glasses to check the chads of hundreds of ballots by hand.

All the recounting took time. Under Florida law, the secretary of state in Tallahassee was to certify the election results on November 14, just a week after the election. The recounts in four counties were not finished. A series of legal battles ensued and the November 14 deadline passed. Ultimately the Florida Supreme Court ruled that the recounts could continue beyond the deadline and declared that the results of the recounts must be included when the secretary of state certified the results. The Republicans appealed and the United States Supreme Court heard the arguments on Friday, Dec. 1, more than three weeks after Election Day.

GOP attorneys told the justices that Article II, Section 1, of the Constitution clearly vests the state legislatures with the power and responsibility of enacting election laws and that the action of the Florida Supreme Court amounted to an unconstitutional infringement on the authority of the state legislature, in effect, rewriting the state's election law by judicial fiat.

On December 8, the Florida Supreme Court, all seven justices named to the high bench by Democratic governors, ruled that not only should the recount continue, but that a mandatory hand recount should take place in all of the state's counties. Republicans in the Florida House of Representatives defied the state's Supreme Court and met on Tuesday, Dec. 12, to vote for an Electoral College slate that would cast Florida's electoral votes for George W. Bush.

Late that same night, the U.S. Supreme Court rejected the position of the Florida Supreme Court and allowed the election results to be certified for Bush. Among other things, the majority of the nation's high court held that the variations in recount methodology endorsed by the Florida Supreme Court amounted to an unconstitutional violation of the "equal protection" clause. The majority opinion stated, "The Supreme court of Florida has said that the legislature intended the state's electors to 'participat[e] fully in the federal electoral process.' . . . That statute, in turn, requires that any controversy or contest that is designed to lead to a conclusive selection of electors be complete by December 12. That date is upon us, and there is no recount procedure in place under the state Supreme Court's order that comports with minimal constitutional standards. . . . [W]e reverse the judgment of the Supreme Court of Florida ordering a recount to proceed."

The majority opinion drew a scathing dissent authored by Justice John Paul Stevens, in which Justices Ruth Bader Ginsburg and Steven Breyer joined. Stevens wrote, "In the interest of finality . . . the majority effectively orders the disenfranchisement of an unknown number of voters whose ballots reveal their intent—and are therefore legal votes under state law—but were for some reason rejected by ballot-counting machines." He concluded, "Although we may never know with complete certainty the identity of the winner of this year's presidential election, the identity of the loser is perfectly clear. It is the nation's confidence in the judge as an impartial guardian of the rule of law."

That night was not a triumph for radio or television journalism and speaks volumes about the pitfalls of being on-the-air live as a complicated event unfolds. The net result may have captured the drama of the moment but it did not provide as much useful information as the implications of live news coverage would suggest. When the decision was released by the Supreme Court press office, it was breathlessly delivered to freezing correspondents outside the courthouse. They found themselves confronted with a lengthy and complicated document.

"We watched wonderfully seasoned correspondents standing on the Supreme Court steps reading the decision on the air, trying to make sense out of a huge volume of information as they were reading through it," said Michael Freedman, professorial lecturer in journalism at The George Washington University. Put bluntly, they fumbled around trying to find the bottom line and in the process reported a hodgepodge of confusing and occasionally misleading information. The initial assessments included a declaration that it appeared to be a victory for Gore and another stated that the Florida Supreme Court had been upheld. They finally sorted it out.

In retrospect, viewers and listeners would have been better informed if the broadcast networks had waited to go on the air until somebody had actually read the decision and was able to report what was in it. The reality of the journalism business for electronic reporters was that competitive pressures and public interest compelled live coverage. There was no other option. Newspapers had the luxury of being able to digest the data before racing to report it.

The next day, Albert Gore conceded. "Now the U.S. Supreme Court has spoken. Let there be no doubt, while I strongly disagree with the court's decision, I accept it. I accept the finality of this outcome." Throughout all the legal wrangling George W. Bush enjoyed the thinnest of leads in the Florida vote count—fewer than a thousand votes most of the time, fewer than four hundred once. On Monday, Dec. 18, 2000, the vote of the Electoral College was received and certified by the president of the Senate, the sitting vice president, who ironically was Albert Gore. It was 271 to 266 with one elector abstaining.

3.4 The Federal Election Commission

Money and politics are inextricably linked. (See chapter 10.1.) And while the politicians have always had a vested interest in obtaining as much money as possible to finance their political campaigns, there has long been an undercurrent of discontent with regard to the influence and power of money in the political process. Historically, efforts to limit, control and/or regulate the flow of money into the political system have met only limited success. The reason for this is that the people charged with enacting campaign reform laws owe their power and positions to the *status quo* and have little practical motivation to make wholesale changes to it.

In 1905, Republican President Theodore Roosevelt threw his support behind a bill to limit the level of campaign contributions. Roosevelt believed that wealthy individuals and corporate interests had a disproportionate level of influence because of the money they contributed. Forty-two years later, in 1947, a bill sponsored by Republican Sen. Robert Taft of Ohio attempted to further limit the influence of corporate money on the political process and to regulate spending in federal elections. Congress attempted to strengthen the law again in 1966. But the bills were fraught with loopholes and had little real impact on campaign funding and the role of money in the political process.

By 1971, Congress was persuaded that updating and consolidating the measures passed between 1907 and 1966 would help to rein in the flow of unrestricted campaign contributions and curb abuses. The House and Senate enacted the Federal Election Campaign Act to regulate the financing of federal elections. Among other things, that act imposed strict financial disclosure requirements for candidates running for federal elective offices—president, Senate and House of Representatives—along with political parties and political action committees, known as PACs.

In the aftermath of the Watergate scandal in 1974 Congress adopted a series of amendments to the 1971 act in the name of campaign finance reform, including the income tax check-off for public funding of presidential campaigns. The next year, 1975, Congress established the Federal Election Commission (FEC) to administer and enforce the provisions of the Federal Election Campaign Act.

Congress revisited campaign finance reform again in 1976 and 1979 in an effort to address objections to the act contained in the 1976 Supreme Court decision in *Buckley vs. Valeo*. In that case the high court struck down most of the expenditure limits in the Federal Election Campaign Act, saying, in effect, that campaign contributions are a form of political expression that is protected by the First Amendment. "The act's expenditure ceilings impose direct and substantial restraints on the quantity of political speech. . . . [L]egislative restrictions on advocacy of the election or defeat of political candidates is wholly at odds with the guarantees of the First Amendment." (See chapter 3.5.)

The FEC defines its own role as an independent regulatory agency with a specific mandate to administer the public funding program, facilitate public disclosure of campaign finance documents, clarify the law through regulation and advisory opinions prepared for candidates and organizations, help candidates understand and comply with the law, and enforcement.

There are six commissioners appointed by the president with the advice and consent of the Senate. They serve staggered six-year terms with two seats subject to replacement every two years. No more than three commissioners may be members of the same political party.

Critics of the FEC, such as The Cato Institute, a conservative think-tank, note that the commission is controlled by people with a vested interest in the political process, and that the people making the rules are the same people who are being regulated. Incumbent Democratic and Republican officeholders are in charge and, as a result, third parties, challengers and independent candidates have little clout with the agency.

Political journalists should be aware that the FEC maintains a database of various federal campaign finance activities, including identifying large contributions and their contributors and the activities of PACs. In addition reporters can obtain such useful documents as summaries of campaign activities, presidential candidates' personal financial disclosure statements, audit reports, files on completed enforcement actions and copies of advisory opinions. The public records office is the place to start and much of the information is available online.

The FEC press office is also accessible online. (The agency's web site can be accessed at www.fec.gov and has been redesigned in recent years to be more reporter-friendly.)

The FEC deals only with races for federal offices, but every state has some version of an election commission or agency to oversee all other elections. Many states place elections under the office of the secretary of state. Most have a subset of municipal and/or county election officials as well to oversee elections at the local level.

3.5 The McCain-Feingold Bill

On March 27, 2002, President George W. Bush signed the McCain-Feingold Campaign Finance Reform Bill, also known as the Bipartisan Campaign Reform Act of 2002 or BCRA. Republican Sen. John McCain of Arizona and Democratic Sen. Russ Feingold of Wisconsin had been talking about reforming the way political campaigns were financed for the better part of a decade. Several versions of their bill had been the object of heated congressional debate for years.

Two of the main, and most controversial, features of the bill prohibited unlimited so-called "soft money" contributions and imposed restrictions on issue advocacy ads, such as television commercials, on behalf of or in opposition to a candidate run by an interest group immediately prior to an election. Until enactment of the BCRA, soft money was unregulated money contributed to political parties by corporations, advocacy groups, labor organizations, PACs and, occasionally, individuals. That money could then be spent on behalf of a candidate. Reporters should understand that "hard money" is contributed directly to candidates and has long been subject to state and federal regulation.

The McCain-Feingold Act limited issue advertising by corporations, non-profit organizations and labor unions. Those groups were prohibited from airing messages that included the picture or name of a federal candidate within 30 days of a primary election or within 60 days of a general election.

In addition, the limits on individual contributions to candidates in federal elections (presidential and congressional) were increased from $1,000 to $2,000 per election, and financial disclosure requirements on the part of campaigns were strengthened.

Passage of the act and the fact that the president signed it were hailed by supporters of campaign finance reform as a major step toward cleaning up and reforming the financing of federal election campaigns. They declared that it would end nasty attack ads and make candidates less beholden to the corporations, advocacy groups, and labor organizations that contributed vast sums of unregulated money.

"It will prevent unions and corporations from making unregulated soft-money contributions—a legislative step for which I repeatedly have called," said President Bush in the statement he made at the signing ceremony. "Often these groups take political action without the consent of their members or shareholders, so that the influence of these groups on elections does not necessarily comport with the actual views of the individuals who comprise these organizations. This prohibition helps to right that imbalance."

Nonetheless, the president cited "flaws" in the bill that "present serious constitutional concerns." Bush's concern echoed that of major critics of the measure, notably that limiting how people spend their money is tantamount to limiting speech.

Lawsuits challenging the BCRA were filed almost before the ink on President Bush's signature was dry. Republican Sen. Mitch McConnell of Kentucky was the leading opponent of the bill. A special judicial panel made up of three federal judges—two from U.S. District Courts and one from a U.S. Circuit Court of Appeals—was appointed to hear the initial challenges to the campaign finance reform law. On May 2, 2003, the panel delivered a highly contentious, complicated opinion that ran more than 1,600 pages.

Among other things, the panel said political parties have a right to raise and spend soft money that is protected by the free speech provisions of the First Amendment. However, they said that protection does not extend to money raised or spent for speech in support of or in opposition to candidates for federal office. In addition, the regulations regarding the 30- and 60-day ban on issue ads were struck down and replaced with another rule conjured up by the court.

Appeals were filed by everybody involved in the original court action almost immediately. "People on both sides have interpreted it whatever way is most favorable to them," said *Newsday* political reporter Elaine Povich. The stage was set for a showdown before the nation's highest court, which agreed to consider the case in an expedited fashion and deliver its ruling before the 2004 presidential primaries began.

Experts and political scholars tried to anticipate what the court might do. Larry Sabato, professor of political science and director of the Center for Politics at the University of Virginia, was one of many who looked to an earlier campaign finance decision as a guide: "[T]he Supreme Court did say in Buckley v[ersus] Valejo that, whether we like it or not, in our system, in a capitalist representative democracy, money is speech."

On Wednesday, Dec. 11, 2003, the Supreme Court handed down a 300-page 5–4 decision that upheld the law's most controversial and far-reaching restrictions on political money. The court specifically upheld the ban on soft-money contributions and the limitations on issue-advocacy ads by special interest groups.

In a blistering dissent, Justice Antonin Scalia pointed to other recent free speech decisions that included upholding the rights of cable TV operators to air sexually explicit shows. He wrote: "Who could have imagined that this court would smile with favor upon a law that cuts to the heart of what the First Amendment is meant to protect: the right to criticize the government."

The court's majority noted that "we are under no illusion" that Congress will not return to the issue of money and politics.

The political pros started preparing for the possibility the Supreme Court would uphold the law long before the decision was rendered. In May, days after the appellate panel's decision, congressional Democrats kicked off an effort to raise soft money by circumventing the McCain-Feingold restrictions. They created two groups not connected to the Democratic Party, but clearly embraced by the Democratic leaders in Congress, to solicit soft money. GOP groups were also formed.

Sabato said this was not an unexpected development. "I have always felt that if you try to dam the flow of political money in one place, the money—the water—which is very powerful in a democracy will simply cut a path around the dam and it will show up someplace else."

"The problem is there are so many channels in a country like ours in which money can move from the private sector into the political sector that regulatory schemes almost always break down very quickly," said *The Washington Post's* political columnist David Broder. "I'm skeptical that any group of lawyers can write regulations that other lawyers won't quickly find ways to evade."

Broder added that there might be a solution. "I would like to see public funding tried on a larger scale. It may not be a panacea either but I think it would create the potential for people who might otherwise not be in a position to mount an effective campaign to do so. And as far as I'm concerned, if you can't insulate politicians from contributors—which I think is impossible—what I'd really like to see the campaign finance system do is try to close the gap between challengers and incumbents."

As this book goes to press, there is no serious move afoot to expand public funding of political campaigns.

For political reporters it is an absolute certainty that, regardless of the Supreme Court decision about the McCain-Feingold Act, you will never be at a loss for a story if you follow the money. Who's donating it? Who's raising it? How is it being spent? As CNN's senior political correspondent Candy Crowley noted, "Money is the mother's milk of politics." (See chapter 10.1, 10.2, and 10.3.)

4

The Process

The architects of the Constitution envisioned seeking and holding elective office as a necessary public service. They saw participation in representative government as both a noble and a temporary calling based on accountability of those elected to those who elected them. In *Federalist Number 57*, Alexander Hamilton or James Madison (it is not clear which man wrote it in 1788) said that "the elective mode of obtaining rulers" allows the citizens to select "men who possess most wisdom to discern, and most virtue to pursue, the common good of the society." Politics as a career was not part of the original scheme.

The founders thought they had created a civilized and well-orchestrated system that would produce a government of gentlemen. They did not contemplate today's level of partisan combat and rancor, and one can only imagine that Hamilton or Madison would find the political process of today nothing short of blood-sport awash in money and undermined by the vast array of interests other than the "common good of the society."

Modern political journalists must understand the basics of the process in order to put what happens in the electoral arena into perspective for their readers, viewers and listeners.

4.1 Stand or Run

Political candidates in many parts of the world, including Britain, Ireland and Canada, stand for election. In modern American politics, they run for office. That was not always the case. Immediately after the American Revolution and well into the 19th century, presidential candidates stood for election, fearing that actively running or campaigning for the position would make them appear overly hungry for the mantle of power, a vestige of the tyranny against which the Revolutionary War was fought.

The Whig Party nominee for president in 1852, Mexican-American War hero and former Army Gen. Winfield Scott, is often credited with being the first presidential candidate to actively campaign for office. He was handily defeated by his lesser-known Democratic opponent Franklin Pierce, who followed the tradition of his predecessor, President James Polk, in sending letters to key supporters on campaign issues. He did not engage in personal appearances or speech-making.

For a half century thereafter, a tradition developed that trailing presidential candidates would campaign and leading candidates would stay home. Some political historians have dubbed the latter "front porch campaigns." Republican Theodore Roosevelt thought it undignified for an incumbent president to go out campaigning and asking people for their votes. In 1904, he won a landslide without ever leaving his estate, Sagamore Hill, in Oyster Bay, New York.

William Howard Taft was the first sitting president to take to the campaign trail. He undertook a railroad campaign, an 18,000-mile political odyssey all around the country in 1912. That was the birth of the modern tradition of incumbent presidents, as well as their opponents, hitting the road in the quest for votes. Only four years later, presidential candidates would discover the power of campaigning through the mass media. Democrat Woodrow Wilson used newspapers and billboards in his 1916 reelection bid. Eight years after that, Republican Calvin Coolidge campaigned via radio. Republican Dwight Eisenhower was the first presidential candidate to use television for campaign advertising, in 1952. (See chapter 10.3.)

Campaigns for the U.S. House of Representatives have always been livelier and more political. That is due, in part, to the fact that congressional districts were relatively small compared to the size of the entire country and, in part, because Madison and the other architects of the U.S. Constitution created a perpetual motion system with every representative up for election every two years. (U.S. senators were not popularly elected until 1913 when the 17th Amendment became part of the Constitution. By then modern campaigning for office was the norm.)

The "stump" speech became a part of the American political process in early House campaigns and in races for local and state offices. Candidates would simply climb up on any tree stump to give them a little elevation and deliver their speech to whomever was in earshot. Personal contact was the principal way politicians communicated at the local level, and congressional districts were of a size that a candidate could easily make personal appearances all over.

Appearances by candidates were also a source of public entertainment, a tradition that continued until the dawn of the age of television. Stephen Hess, senior fellow at the Brookings Institution and one-time speechwriter for President Dwight Eisenhower noted that even as late as 1958 people would crowd into places like the Baltimore Armory to listen to a political speech. "It was still entertainment," said Hess.

Television dramatically changed the nature of political campaigns. A presidential candidate can reach more people with one televised airport campaign rally than Taft did during his entire railroad campaign in 1912.

4.2 Candidates

The scope of offices for which candidates run covers a wide spectrum. The top elective office in the country is president of the United States, even though the president is not elected by popular vote. (See chapter 3.2.) Other federal offices include United States senator and United States representative.

The governor is the top elected official in all 50 states. The lieutenant governor occupies the number two spot in 44 states; six states—Arizona, Maine, New Hampshire, Oregon, West Virginia and Wyoming—have no office of lieutenant governor. In some states the governor and lieutenant governor are elected separately; in others they run as a ticket, like the candidates for president and vice president.

There is no uniformity in the names and duties of other state elective offices. Among the most common ones: state senator, state representative (in every state but unicameral Nebraska), attorney general, secretary of state, insurance commissioner, agriculture commissioner, education commissioner, treasurer, comptroller and highway or transportation commissioner. The exact titles vary. Some states elect Supreme Court and other lower court judges.

Mayor is often, but by no means always, the top elected official in a city or other municipality. Other common elective offices in cities, towns, and counties include: city council member, county council or commission member, sheriff, judge, clerk of the court, supervisor of elections, tax collector, school board member, and various members of boards and/or commissions responsible for transportation, airports, environment, planning and zoning, building and construction supervision, public health and public utilities.

A person can often become a candidate simply by declaring an intention to run. Some state political party rules require candidates to register with their various parties in the case of partisan elections. Many states require a filing of candidacy with the local supervisor of elections or election commission in the case of local offices, or with the office of the secretary of state in the case of state offices. Some states and/or parties require potential candidates to collect signatures on petitions in order to secure a place on the ballot. In the case of states and localities, the signatures must be those of registered voters; in the case of parties, the signatures usually must be of voters registered to that particular party.

In the case of federal offices, the Federal Election Commission says a candidate is any "individual who seeks nomination for election, or election to federal office." In addition a person is defined as a candidate by the FEC if he or she has raised or spent more than $5,000 or authorized another person or committee to raise and/or spend more than $5,000.

Federal law recognizes exploratory committees as legitimate campaign entities, usually involving presidential hopefuls, designed to research the feasibility and prospects of a person running for office. There is no federal filing requirement for exploratory committees, although if the person subsequently becomes a declared candidate then all contributions up to the time of the declaration must be reported to the FEC.

State and political party rules regarding filing, disclosure and contribution limits vary. Reporters must make themselves familiar with the specific rules in their particular coverage areas. Florida's St. Johns County is typical. Penny Halyburton, the county supervisor of elections, said the process is not complicated. "Once a person decides to run for public office and files the appointment of a campaign treasurer with the appropriate filing officer, the person is then considered a candidate and may begin receiving contributions and making expenditures to further their candidacy. They don't want to begin raising money before they file that statement . . . because it's against the law." In addition candidates must have a separate campaign bank account.

In some states a filing fee is required. In California, for example, there's a $3,500 filing fee for anyone wishing to run for governor, and the candidate must present petitions with the signatures of 65 registered voters. In Florida, candidates can use one of two methods. The candidate must either pay a filing fee, which is a percentage of the annual salary of the office sought as established by statute, or collect signatures on petitions. "Most people choose to run by petition," said Halyburton, citing several practical advantages. "They can start off their campaign several thousand dollars ahead of the game and they also meet the people by going door to door" to gather signatures.

As a general rule, where candidates' names can be placed on the ballot by the petition method, the local and/or state election supervisor or commission must check and verify the signatures to ensure that the people signing are registered voters, residents of the state or district, that the signatures are authentic, and that the addresses are correct.

Some states and local jurisdictions have limitations on how early candidates may declare their intentions to run. North Dakota, for example, prohibits congressional candidates from filing their nominating petitions more than 150 days prior to the primary election. Others, like Florida, have no limits. "They can start any time," said Halyburton. "They could actually come in today [April 28, 2003] for 2010."

For the most part, incumbents tend to announce their intentions to seek reelection later than the declaration of candidacy by their challengers. Given the political safety of incumbents at every level, the reelection announcement of somebody who already holds the office is seldom a journalistically big deal. (See chapter 6.3.) Even when a sitting president announces he'll seek a second term, it's rarely an earthshaking news event. But when an incumbent decides not to seek reelection, that is often big news.

Reporters should always keep an eye on the playing field as this process unfolds. When incumbents decide not to run again or to seek other offices—a state representative, for example, decides to run for governor—the ripple effects can create multiple story opportunities.

4.3 Elections

Elections fall into several categories. Primary elections begin the electoral cycle and are held to select the candidates who will bear the standard of a political party. In most states, there's no primary election for an office in which only one candidate has declared. State law governs the electoral process and the laws vary widely. Usually primaries take place several months before the general election (which is always in November, with the exception of states, such as Virginia, that have separate dates for municipal balloting.) In the presidential election cycle, the primaries start in New Hampshire in January. For state and local offices the primaries in most states are usually, but not always, in September.

Generally, there are three types of primary elections: closed primaries, open primaries, and crossover primaries. The terminology is not consistent from state to state, and reporters covering politics need to find out exactly what the law is in the area where they work. Generally closed primaries are those in which only registered Democrats may vote for Democratic candidates and only registered Republicans may vote for Republican candidates. (This effectively locks out independent voters, non-affiliated voters, and/or voters registered with third parties.)

Open primaries usually allow voters who are registered independents or those who are unaffiliated to select which party's candidates they wish to vote for. (Virtually every state with this option requires the independent to pick one party or the other for the entire ballot, not for individual offices.) In many open primary states, voters registered with a particular political party may vote only for that party's candidates and only independents have the option.

Crossover primaries allow voters from any party, as well as independents, to select which party's candidates they want to vote for. For example, Democrats may opt to vote in the Republican primary and vice versa. Voters may make a new party selection in each primary election. When inquiring about what kind of primaries exist in the various states, reporters should check the specifics of the terminology. There are locations where "open" and "crossover" are used interchangeably and allow everybody to select which party's slate they will vote for in every primary.

General elections are usually held on the Tuesday after the first Monday in November in even numbered years. For federal elections this is a matter of law, established by Congress. It was established as the Election Day for United States representatives in 1875 and for senators in 1914 after the previous year's ratification of the 17th Amendment allowing for popular election of senators. The Federal

Election Commission notes that Congress did not want elections to fall on November 1 because it is All Saints Day, with special religious significance to Roman Catholics, and because many businesses did their books on the first of the month and they didn't want business finances to impact the electoral process.

Periodically, there is debate in Congress or within the political parties over whether to change the date of federal elections. The debate is usually associated with a discussion of low voter turnout. Proposals range from moving Election Day to Saturday or Sunday, to making it two days over a weekend, to establishing it as a national holiday, to voting by mail or Internet. So far there has been no serious move in either the House or the Senate to change the date.

States, on the other hand, have wide latitude as to when elections are held. Most hold their state elections, votes on ballot initiatives and ratification of constitutional amendments on the Tuesday after the first Monday in November. But some set aside other dates for local and/or municipal elections. Virginia's constitution, for example, requires that municipal elections be held in June. Some states allow for certain offices, such as mayors, to be elected in odd numbered years.

Louisiana has an unusual system in which general election day for the rest of the country in November is effectively an open primary election, with every candidate from all parties appearing on the ballot. In races where no candidate wins a majority (50 percent plus one vote), there is a runoff election pitting the top two vote-getters against each other. It is not unusual to have two candidates from the same political party on the runoff ballot.

Races with more than two candidates on the ballot for one office are common. State laws vary with regard to whether a candidate may be elected with a plurality (getting the most votes without obtaining a majority) or whether a majority is required for election, with provisions for runoff elections for the highest vote getters.

4.4 Nominating Conventions

Many state political parties have long used a process for nominating candidates for office that begins in the smallest of political jurisdictions, individual precincts, and ends at a district or state convention. The precinct caucus is the most basic of grassroots politics. Party members meet on a specific day within a precinct—often at a private home, church basement or other community meeting room—to pick delegates. Supporters of the various candidates try to get as many of their fellow supporters as possible to attend the caucus. The candidate who has the most supporters gets the most delegates to take to the next step in the process, the district or county convention. Each precinct is allowed a specific number of delegates.

Those precinct delegates then go to the district or county convention where a similar process takes place, and again the delegates are apportioned based on which candidate had the most support. The next step is usually the state party convention. (In the case of a district or local office, the winner of the vote at the district or county convention would be the party's nominee.)

The idea of national nominating conventions for the office of president, and along with them adoption of the national party platforms, didn't emerge until the 1832 election. Republicans nominated Henry Clay; Democrats tapped incumbent Andrew Jackson, who won easy reelection. The national convention process was a natural extension of the local and state process. Delegates elected at the state party level went on to the national convention.

From the 1970s on, many states moved away from the caucus and convention process in selecting party candidates. They have adopted a process that centers on primary elections. Some state parties have abandoned the convention process altogether, although the parties have preserved a vestige of the national convention process in the nomination of a presidential candidate.

The state of Iowa clings to the caucus system for picking delegates to the presidential nominating conventions. It is one of the dwindling number of caucus states and is traditionally the first stop along the presidential campaign trail. In 2004, Iowa's caucuses were held Monday, Jan. 19, the earliest date ever.

In most recent presidential elections, there has been little drama in the national political conventions. It has been clear who the victors would be as a result of primary elections, and the nominating conventions have deteriorated into little more than political formalities with little news value. Usually the parties' nominees are established within a few months of the first presidential primary election in New Hampshire in January.

At all national conventions since 1956 the candidates—in the rare cases when there was more than one candidate still in the race by convention time—have been nominated and the first convention ballot has decided the winner. In most cases the spectacle has been carefully orchestrated for prime time network television. The last time a nomination battle went to more than one ballot on a national convention floor was at the 1952 Democratic convention in Chicago. Adlai Stevenson won the nomination on the third ballot.

Supporters of the transition to the primary system at all levels of candidate selection argue that it allows more people to participate directly in the process. They say that the old caucus and convention system favored party regulars and activists who got involved early and made the decision for the rest of the citizenry long before most people even knew who was running. The view is not universal.

"Things were better before the primary system," said Bob Schieffer, chief Washington correspondent for CBS News. "Under the old system people actually watched the national conventions because that's how you found out who the candidate was going to be. Now they're just a long infomercial. People say that we're losing interest in politics because the ratings for these conventions are so low. That's absolutely wrong. The reason people don't watch the conventions any more is because they're boring. Who wants to watch an infomercial? No one."

The primaries are starting earlier and earlier in presidential politics. In 1996, the season began in late February, with most primaries in March. In 2004, the season started in January, right after the Iowa caucuses, and by February the frontrunners were clearly established. The Democrats held their first nine-candidate debate in May 2003. CNN's senior political correspondent Candy Crowley said, "The 2004 campaign began before the 2000 race was decided, before the Supreme Court handed down its decision" in *Bush vs. Gore.* (See chapter 3.3.)

"I've been thinking about it since I left the 2000 conventions," said Cox Radio's Jamie Dupree. "I'm already planning where I'll go and what primaries I'll cover." That was eight months before the 2004 New Hampshire primary.

There are no signs of the expansion of the political season being reversed.

"I think a great deal of the reason people have lost interest in politics is because of the primary system we've developed," said CBS's Schieffer. "I know you can never go back to the way it was. I know that there were faults and things that were not good about it. But I don't think the system we've developed now is very good."

A Conversation with David Broder

National political correspondent and columnist: *Washington Post*
Author or coauthor: seven books, including *Democracy Derailed: Initiative Campaigns and the Power of Money* (Harcourt, 2000)

Ask any political reporter in the country for a list of the best in the business and David Broder's name will be near the top of them all. He is the Tiger Woods, the Wayne Gretzky and the Michael Jordan of political journalists. Publications have been stumbling all over themselves for years trying to come up with new and appropriate accolades with which to describe Broder. He's been called "the dean" of American political reporters so often it's almost become a cliché. He's been given enough awards, recognitions, and plaudits (among them the Pulitzer Prize and the 4th Estate Award from the National Press Club) to fill a small warehouse.

In Washington, a city filled with big names and often even bigger egos, David Broder is a reporter's reporter. There's nothing flashy about him, no superstar aura, no flash and glitz. He is soft-spoken. He is a courteous gentleman of the old school. He still answers his own phone and returns his own calls. For more than 40 years his work ethic has been among the most rigorous and exacting in the newspaper business.

He spends his Mondays at the University of Maryland's Philip Merrill College of Journalism. His students are blessed. I hope they know that study-

ing reporting with David Broder is like studying the Ten Commandments with Moses. Yes, he's that good.

Yet he is something of an anomaly in a highly competitive business where nice guys often finish last. He is a genuinely nice person.

His first campaign was the Kennedy-Nixon contest in 1960. He says a great deal has changed since then, much of it for the better.

D.B.: "This has gone from being a boy's game to being a men's and women's game—covering politics. And that's had an enormous impact, and a very positive impact.

"When I think about somebody like [the late Ann] Devroy [former *Washington Post* reporter] who absolutely set the standard for coverage of the White House. . . . She had an absolutely perfect bullshit detector. And people like Jim Baker [former secretary of state] and Marlin Fitzwater [President George H. W. Bush's press secretary] knew that they couldn't get away with anything with her and so they leveled with her. I used to listen to her end of the conversations in the newsroom. It struck me so often that I couldn't be as tough as a guy in dealing with them, as she could as a woman. People see things differently. And having women in the political press corps has really changed things.

"A dramatic example of that—I went up to Buffalo [N.Y.] to cover the first debate between Rick Lazio and Hillary Clinton. I thought Lazio had done pretty well. He'd been on stage with a world celebrity and he hadn't drooled. Every woman reporter there picked up instantly on the fact that Lazio had walked over to her and crowded her, moved from his podium to her podium, invaded her space. And that was the thing that the public picked up on. That was not a gentlemanly thing to do. It's not just gender, it's race too. You've got a much more diverse press corps now and that's a great advantage."

R.A.: *Who did you like covering the most?*

D.B.: "There are a lot of them that I like. The first is special. The first time you do anything it's very special. The 1960 campaign was a great campaign. You had two young men—everybody thinks of Kennedy being young, but Nixon was a young man in 1960—and they both knew that it was going to be a very close election. They both ran flat out from day one. And the other thing that made it special—we didn't realize how special at the time—[was] obviously television. After all we had the first television debates.

"Politics wasn't entirely a spectator sport at that time. People wanted to feel that they were part of it. So the crowds were huge, not just at downtown rallies, but along the roads from the airport into town. People would bring their kids to see somebody who might be president going by. And we didn't have all the security that developed subsequently. So the people were really in that campaign."

R.A.: *Anybody you particularly disliked covering, or would care to say in print?*

D.B.: "I wrote very critically in columns about the Nixon campaign in 1972. Basically what I said was he was going through the pretense of a campaign, but was actually stiffing people, not dealing with the questions that either the reporters or that the public were asking. He took a campaign—a time when voters should be able to get their questions answered—and turned it into an artificial, empty exercise. I think I said in one of those pieces that if the publishers of the country had any backbone they'd tell Nixon that unless and until he'd start making himself available for at least some questions, they weren't going to spend the money to send people around the country for this parody of a campaign."

R.A.: *Actually, I've got a quote from one of your columns in the 1972 campaign. You wrote that "the Nixon entourage seems to be stifling dialogue."*

D.B.: "That was the point I was trying to make. . . . Maybe that was naive on my part but because we've certainly seen news management by presidents and presidential candidates become more and more routine. But it was new enough at that point, and it really offended me.

"The view I developed was that campaigns really, properly, belong to the voters. And what behooves us as political reporters is to spend enough time ourselves with the voters that we get a pretty clear idea about what their concerns are, what questions they've got. And then we need to try to nudge the candidates into addressing those concerns, instead of just saying that it's up to the candidate what they talk about, or accepting it when their consultants and managers say that this isn't a good issue for us or it's a good wedge issue for us to turn on some fraction of the electorate."

R.A.: *How careful do young reporters have to be to avoid being seduced by campaigns and reporting just what the campaigns want?*

D.B.: "Part of our job is basically to describe what's happening out there. So some of our coverage is driven and should be driven by what the candidates choose to talk about. But we can't be deaf and blind to other things that are going on. And that's why I think it's useful to get away from the bus or the plane from time to time and bounce what's happening in the campaign off the voters and see what they're making of it. And finding out what questions they have that are not being answered."

R.A.: *What's your technique for taking the pulse of the public?*

D.B.: "I certainly didn't invent it. It's a very old-fashioned kind of reporting. It's not that complicated. You pick precincts that have interesting voting histories. Most of the time these turn out to be ticket-splitting precincts where people can go one way or the other. You tend not to go to the 90 percent Republican or 90 percent Democratic districts. . . . Voting statistics are very available in this country. You can get them in the courthouse. You can get them from campaigns. It's not that hard to do.

"The first requirement for anybody covering politics is know where the damned votes come from in your community, because there are places in every community that are the swing areas. They tend to decide elections. And if you're covering the campaign you need to know where those areas are, because I guarantee you the candidates know where those areas are. That's where they're going to concentrate and that's where you ought to be doing your reporting. Then you basically knock on doors.

"The best times to do it are starting around 3 or 3:30 in the afternoon. Before that you get only retirees. And retirees are important but you want a mix. And depending on the part of the country you're in you can work until 7:30 or 8, some places 8:30, without interrupting people too much.

"Then you have conversations. It's not like polling. It's very different from polling. It's asking them what's on their minds. You're not coming with a fixed set of questions and asking them to respond."

R.A.: *How do you get folks to open up and tell you what their hopes and worries are?*

D.B.: "Once people are persuaded that you really are interested in what they think, they open up. There is an initial skepticism you've got to overcome at every door. I mean, you're sitting having supper or watching TV and you don't expect some damned reporter from *The Washington Post* to come knocking on your door. So you've got to get past that initial skepticism. But once you've persuaded them that you really are interested in what they're thinking then people open up and often in a very eloquent way.

"Typically I start with a very open-ended kind of question: 'I'm not from around here, tell me how things are here?' And they'll talk about anything that's on their mind. Sometimes people will tell you that we just had the worst incident at the school. Or the factory where my brother-in-law works has gone from two shifts to one shift. They'll tell you what's on their mind and then you're in a conversation. And it's a conversation that they've established, not one that you've established."

R.A.: *Does that set up a template for your story?*

D.B.: "Yes. Exactly. And what we try to do—because we have the luxury of having a really good polling unit at the *Post*—is go out and do a lot of door-knocking and relay our impressions to our pollster and then he can use those to frame questions and ask those questions to enough people that you get some statistical backup or refutation of the impressions you're getting in the living rooms. It's hard work, but it's the most important work we do in understanding campaigns."

R.A.: *Manipulation? Has it become more pervasive?*

D.B.: "No question they've gotten bolder about it. In the last campaign Al Gore did not have a single news conference from the day of the convention to the day of the election. That's ridiculous. But our only power is in telling people what's going on. We can't order them [candidates] to do something. But we certainly ought to tell people when we see that kind of a pattern developing and then let the public make a judgment whether it's important to them or not. It's gotten much more manipulative."

R.A: *Back in 1991, E. J. Dionne wrote an interesting book called* Why Americans Hate Politics. . . .

D.B.: "Terrific book."

R.A.: *Do Americans hate politics any more or any less than they did back in '91?*

D.B.: "People are very cynical about politics. Perhaps more than they are entitled to be. My friend Jack Germond is working on a book that basically makes the argument that politicians are better than you think they are. People are persuaded that they're all a bunch of crooks, that all they want to do is line their pockets, take care of their friends, sell out the public. He thinks that's wrong and I think that's wrong, too. There is a huge level of public cynicism about politics and that's reflected in the press. You've got people who do not want to cover politics, because they think it's sleazy."

R.A.: *Doesn't the news media feed this cynicism with gotcha journalism?*
D.B.: "Yes. We are not innocent in this process. Reporters are fight promoters. If there's not a good fight going, we'll try to get one going. We love conflict. And the public despises conflict in government.

"They don't believe or understand that the Founding Fathers thought that it was important to build in conflict between the branches and between state and federal governments. Checks and balances are a part of the Constitution. People will say to you, 'Why don't they just do what's right, instead of going at each other all the time?' As if everybody agrees on what is right.

"It's also the case that the partisanship has been particularly intense in recent years, in part because the parties are so evenly balanced that almost any issue which comes up causes either side to ask, is it going to help us or is it going to help them? And often they never get beyond that."

R.A.: *With profound public cynicism about the media and profound public cynicism about the politicians, is the democracy in danger?*
D.B.: "I think the greater risk is the loss of confidence in representative government. People don't think that the people they send to city hall or the state legislature or to Washington really represent them. I think that's a more serious problem. Two things that measure the extent of that are the decline in voting and . . . the rise of direct democracy, the initiative process as a way of bypassing representative government. Citizens are writing laws in a way that the founders never imagined being done in this country."

R.A.: *You wrote a book about that. You are not a big fan of the initiative and referendum process?*

D.B.: "No, because it's being used by people who are very clever and who have the resources, who can raise the money to put issues on the ballot. And they promote them with advertising campaigns. It has none of the checks and balances that are part of our constitutional system. You never have to deal with the opposition. Basically if you can get 50 percent plus one, you can write the law or the damned [state] constitution to suit yourself. And that's happening all over the country."

R.A.: *So ballot initiatives have been effectively taken over by special interests?*

D.B.: "It was conceived as a noble idea and there are circumstances where there's a justification for it as a safety valve. But the way it's been used in the last 25 years—to set budgets and to make social policy and particularly to rewrite state constitutions—is fundamentally at odds with the way in which our system of government was designed to work."

R.A.: *Have you ever had a reportorial disaster, had a story blow up in your face?*

D.B.: "The worst experience I had on a campaign was in 1976 in the Wisconsin [Democratic] primary. I was working out of NBC that night in Milwaukee. And a man named Dick Scammon, who was a great statistics person, was calling the election for NBC. And at some point—8:30 or 9:30—he called the election for [Arizona Rep. Morris] Udall and I believed him and wrote a lead based on that. As it turned out [Jimmy] Carter won by doing better than anybody expected in the rural areas. That was the hardest phone call I ever had to make. I had to phone the national news desk and I said, 'I think we've got a problem. This lead of Udall's is melting pretty fast.'"

R.A.: *What was their reaction?*

D.B.: [Laughs.] "They said, 'Yeah, we got a problem!'

"I don't know how many papers had gone out, but thank goodness nobody has ever waved one in front of me. But I'm sure there were several thousand copies that night that had Udall winning the Wisconsin primary. I was lucky because the Milwaukee paper—the *Sentinel*—had done the same thing and on television the next day Carter held up the *Milwaukee Sentinel* on his television interviews not *The Washington-damned-Post*."

5

Roadmap for Reporters: Getting Started

Today's campaign trail is a remarkable thoroughfare. It is a multi-lane freeway with no speed limit, a clogged and congested one-way urban street, a quiet country lane, and even a wilderness track that you need a guide like Sacagawea to locate. Journalists who travel the campaign trail have a vast array of high-tech toys and tools at their disposal to make the job of political news gathering and reporting easier—e-mail, cellular phones, text messages, faxes, scanners, beepers, BlackBerries, laptops, Palm Pilots and the Internet.

All the gadgetry can help, but it won't substitute for the fundamentals of basic journalism in preparing. The good news for young reporters is that once you have started the process of preparation, you don't have to go back and do it all over again every election cycle. After you've done it once it becomes a matter of building on and editing what you have already established.

5.1 Packing for Your Trip on the Campaign Trail

Even before any candidates have announced their intentions to run, political reporters need to make themselves aware of who's who in politics in their area. Answering some preliminary questions will provide the roots of both a phone file and personal database. Start with a simple list of names. For each person on the list, collect phone numbers, office addresses, home addresses (if possible), e-mail addresses, and the names of any key aides or assistants who might be helpful along the way. Then start building on the basic data (see chapter 5.4):

- Who are the current elective office holders and what offices do they hold? (Get as many names and positions as possible and remember that often people holding one office are using it as a stepping stone from which to run for another office.)

- Who are the key political party officials in your city, county and state?
- Who ran for office and lost in the last election? What are they doing now? (Frequently people who ran once will run again. Democrat Mark Warner ran unsuccessfully for the U.S. Senate before he staged a successful campaign for governor of Virginia. Republican Karen Stern ran unsuccessfully for the Florida state legislature before staging a successful campaign for a seat on the St. Johns County Commission.)
- Who are the behind-the-scenes players? (What interest groups in your area are politically active—corporations, unions, action groups, PACs, business or professional associations and citizen-based organizations—and who heads these groups? Who are big campaign contributors?)

Once you've answered these questions, start gathering information about issues. What's on voters' minds in your area? What issues were significant in the last campaign cycle, and are the same issues important now? What new issues face the candidates this cycle?

Be aware that information coming from candidates and campaigns may not be reliable or completely accurate. Many incumbents, for example, have a tendency to augment the history of the last campaign and their accomplishments in office as they get closer to the next election. Old newspaper clips and Internet stories can form the foundation of research into what issue positions they really took in their last campaign and what they've really done in office. Reporters should be armed with some basic political information in addition to the issues. What kind of campaign was it? Was there negative advertising? By which side? How much money did the incumbent raise and spend? How much did his or her opponent raise and spend? Is last cycle's loser likely to challenge the incumbent again? Or seek a different office?

Talk to the local political parties and their officials. What are the parties looking for in candidates? What's on the radar screens of the behind-the-scenes players and the political pros? What do they expect to be the big issues? You are looking for differences and similarities. Defining an issue or problem will lead the reporter to the solutions proposed by the various candidates; that can form the foundation of interesting and informative stories.

By the time you compile this information and put it into a personal database, your initial list of names will start to have some depth and texture. There's no substitute for doing your homework and laying the groundwork well before the campaign ever gets started. The more you do in advance, the better your coverage will be along the campaign trail.

There also is no substitute for personal contact, what a lot of reporters call "face time." Telephone calls are great and save a lot of time, but once you've compiled your list of important pols and operatives, make it your business to meet with as many as possible. It is especially important to meet with incumbents or current officeholders. With the exception of those prohibited from running again by state term limit laws, it is always a good bet that the incumbent will run for office again.

Look into your reportorial crystal ball and try to figure out who is a likely challenger. Try to determine if any challenger has the potential to make the race competitive. Does the challenger have personal wealth or has the challenger raised large amounts of money? Has the incumbent done anything while in office to anger the voters and make him- or herself vulnerable to a challenge? Does the district have a history of electoral volatility?

The better the incumbent and the potential challengers know you, the more likely you are to be able to get an interview at the height of the campaign, when they're swamped and you're on deadline. The better they know you, the easier it is to get and confirm information in the heat of the political battle. Knowing the key people is critical at all stages of political coverage and it cannot be overemphasized.

When House Speaker Jim Wright (D-Texas) resigned in 1989, Deborah Potter, now executive director of NewsLab and then a tenacious CBS News correspondent, was among the first to break the story. Wright had been charged by Rep. Newt Gingrich (R-Ga.) of violating House ethics rules involving speaking fees and a book that Wright had written.

"Basically what you have to do is to find out who really knows something, somebody who can sort the wheat from the chaff," she said. "When you have a really big story, everybody purports to know something but very few people really do. So knowing who's really close to an individual, who really has their ear and vice versa allows you to put weight on different things that you're hearing. The closer you get to the actual individual, the better off you are."

A reporter, like Potter, who has taken the time to get beyond the politician's press secretary and chief of staff will be rewarded. In covering any kind of political story, the ability to get in touch with your sources quickly can make the difference between breaking the story and being one of the also-rans. "Some of the people who are close to the individual are not public personalities," added Potter. "Some of them are his friends who have nothing to do with politics."

She suggested a technique. "Doing profiles is a great way to find those people early in a campaign. When you find the people who are the kitchen cabinet, if you will, make those connections when you're covering a campaign and stash them away, and go back to those people during the governance phase after an election and you've got a relationship that you've built over time. And you can go to them and say how's he thinking about that or how might he be thinking about that."

The closer you get to Election Day, the harder it is to get one-on-one face time with the candidate. Access dissipates in direct relation to how well a candidate is doing and how high the office is that's being sought. It's always easier to get an interview with a candidate for the county commission than it is with a candidate for governor. A personal relationship, albeit a thoroughly professional relationship, often pays dividends, but it's no guarantee.

"The candidate who has the longest shot is the one you're going to be able to get closest to," said CBS Radio News correspondent Bob Fuss.

Your own past coverage can play a role in the level of access you're granted. If you've recently written or aired a story or stories the candidate or campaign thinks were too critical, you may find yourself relegated to the pack of other journalists covering the race, shouting questions as the candidate gets into his or her car for the next event. Obviously that will not prevent you from running a critical story.

What news organization you work for will also play a role in the level of access you get. Many candidates and campaigns court local news outlets and would rather grant an interview to one of them than to a national organization. Even presidential candidates will devote significant portions of their daily schedule to interviews with local reporters from swing states or areas where a few votes may make the difference between winning and losing.

President George H. W. Bush used that strategy frequently during his 1992 campaign against Bill Clinton. The Bush campaign would park the national reporters who were traveling with him in some press room or holding area while Bush would do local TV interviews. We were not permitted to see or hear what was said until the interviews aired, and in many cases we were, conveniently for the campaign, back on the campaign plane winging our way to the next stop, unable to do anything about it even if news was made in one of the interviews. Clinton did the same thing. Expect more of it.

5.2 Archiving Sound Bites and Quotes

On Sunday evening, March 31, 1968, I watched, with the rest of the country, as President Lyndon B. Johnson announced, "I will not seek and I will not accept the nomination of my party for another term as your President." My phone rang shortly thereafter and it was the news director at the radio station, KTLN, where I worked. "We need reaction," he said. "Can you come in." It was not a question.

I did and spent the next several hours making and recording phone calls and preparing them as sound bites—in those days we called them "actualities"—for the Monday morning newscasts. (I put the sound bites on audiotape cartridges and wrote lead-ins for the anchor to read.) It was my first major political story. I was a novice. I remember floundering around trying to figure out whom to call and what to ask. The news director gave me some names and home phone numbers and I dutifully made the calls and produced the requisite tape. In retrospect, I was woefully ill-prepared for that first foray into political journalism. I didn't know the players. I didn't understand their relationships to each other. I didn't have the savvy to ask more than the most rudimentary questions.

On Wednesday, June 5, 1968, I was working for another radio station in Denver. I awoke to the news that Robert F. Kennedy had been shot in Los Angeles. I went to work that morning at KDEN radio knowing what to expect: Get local reaction! Before I left home I dug out my notes from what I had done just over two months earlier and was, at least, a little better prepared. I still had some names and phone numbers. I also was better equipped to ask questions. Since the LBJ announcement I had made it a point to keep an eye on what the people I had interviewed were saying about such things as the presidential campaign.

It was the Saturday following Robert Kennedy's assassination that I learned another valuable lesson about how to cover politics.

"Let's catalogue and save some of this [taped sound bites]," said the boss, legendary Denver journalist and broadcaster Gene Amole. "We may need some of it later on." The tiny area that served as the station's newsroom was cluttered with reels of tape and scripts from the previous week.

I spent much of the weekend making index cards and tape labels noting who spoke, the date, in-cues, out-cues and a few words about what was said. In those days, our high-tech operation involved a manual typewriter, some shelf space and a little metal file box for index cards. The audio retrieval system was crude. I put the reel-to-reel tapes of each sound bite in chronological order. Starting with the first, I spun it onto a large, empty reel in order to create a master reel. I spliced some leader-tape to the first and spliced in the next sound bite, noting the number and order on each index card and on the tape box. When the reel was full I rewound it onto another empty reel and that was tape #1. And so it went.

To find the sound bite you wanted, you'd physically count as the brown audio tape and white intervals of leader tape passed when you hit "fast forward" on the playback deck. It was unsophisticated, but effective. I don't recall if Gene Amole used the word "archive," but what I had done was to create a rudimentary archive of our Robert Kennedy material.

Today, most radio stations are digital and the sound can be retrieved simply by calling up the right track on a CD or mini-disc. Many television stations and networks are in the process of making the transition from analog to digital as we go to press. Video retrieval using a file server and an interactive database allows producers to find the shots they want almost instantaneously from a huge volume of material. PGA Tour Productions has one of the most advanced systems of this type at its World Golf Village headquarters in St. Augustine, Florida. If you want a shot of Tiger Woods, for example, hitting a four-iron from a fairway bunker it can be in your hands in seconds. Similar systems for video retrieval are on the market now for TV newsroom use.

Even as unsophisticatedly as we did it at KDEN radio in 1968, for political journalists it is never too early to start archiving and cataloguing sound bites (for radio and TV folk) and quotes (for print people). The computer is a wonderful tool for such tasks. It allows journalists to create databases of their own that will form the foundation of future coverage. Today most news organizations, large and small, have some sort of database that reporters can tap into for this type of work. The best political reporters all have some kind of personal archive and database in addition to their news organization's systems.

The payoff is in fast, reliable access to quotes and sound bites that will enable you to add depth and dimension to your stories and coverage. Ways in which you will use your archived material include stories comparing current and past positions, stories that seek to hold politicians accountable for what they said in the past, stories that compare one candidate's position with another candidate's position, stories that reflect the evolution of a policy or issue, stories that illustrate campaign promises, and even obituaries. There is really no limit to when and how you'll use your archive.

5.3 Establishing Coverage Priorities

In addition to contact lists and archiving quotes and sound bites, there are several other preliminary steps necessary before launching a journey on the campaign trail.

First, reporters need to find out exactly what offices are going to be up for election in the next cycle—including local and state offices. Which of those offices are partisan and which are nonpartisan? (In a lot of areas, judges are elected; however the electoral methods vary from partisan to nonpartisan to a simple vote of yes or no on whether to retain the judge. School boards and county commissions are also frequently nonpartisan offices. Nonetheless, reporters should be aware that there is a lot of politics in nonpartisan races. Just because the candidates don't have party labels doesn't mean they're not political animals.)

Second, reporters need to track the races, incumbents, potential challengers and likely issues in order to prioritize coverage. Competitive races—those in which no candidate is a shoo-in—are always interesting. An open seat, one in which an incumbent is not seeking reelection, is generally more interesting than one in which there is little doubt that the incumbent will be reelected.

Third, see if any of the challengers are independently wealthy. Money is a great equalizer. Political science professor Larry Sabato, director of the University of Virginia's Center for Politics, said a candidate who is willing to spend his or her personal wealth on a race can "convert a non-competitive race into a competitive race."

Sabato used the example of the 1996 U.S. Senate race in Virginia. Democrat Mark Warner challenged incumbent Republican John Warner. "John Warner, who won the first time in a very competitive race, has always won since with 70 or 80 percent of the vote. The reason why that one became competitive is because Mark Warner spent about eleven million dollars from his own pocket and another couple of million he was given extra from other people. The incumbent only spent five or six million. He didn't think he'd have a race. He was wrong. Turned out to be 53/47 [percent]. And so you always look for a candidate who can spend 10 or 20 million out of his own pocket. The odds are that's going to become a competitive race."

Mark Warner lost that Senate race but subsequently was elected governor of Virginia.

Many of the biggest newspapers, broadcast and cable networks, and major local television stations have full-time political units or individuals who deal constantly with the news organization's political coverage. Other, mostly smaller, news organizations slip into "campaign mode" when it becomes necessary. Busy news executives often delay making coverage decisions until the campaign is looming. A good political reporter who has tracked races, candidates and issues can play a key role in determining the amount and type of coverage the organization will mount.

Preliminary organizational decisions need to be made on allocation of human resources, or deploying your troops as the military would say. Management should be encouraged to become engaged earlier rather than later in the campaign cycle in order to provide enough time for political reporters to prepare adequately. Readers, listeners and viewers are shortchanged when reporters are not prepared. (Most serious political reporters don't necessarily wait for their marching orders from the brass before they start getting ready for the campaign trail.)

There are several ways to cover key races and the coverage decisions have a great deal to do with the size of the organization making those decisions. For example, *The New York Times* can devote scores of reporters to coverage of various races and campaigns; *The St. Augustine (Fla.) Record* may be able to assign only one or two reporters to cover them all.

One way for news managers to approach political deployment is to assign one reporter to follow one or more races. This is the standard procedure at many small and medium-sized news organizations. Another, the approach used by the broadcast networks and major national newspapers in presidential races, is to assign a reporter or team (reporter and producer) to cover each candidate, with reportorial balance achieved by giving equal time, weight and play to all of the reporters. (This is, of course, more feasible after the nominating conventions than during the primaries when the field is often very crowded.)

5.4 Free-Form Databases

My students look at me as if I am the world's oldest living human when I talk about the way we covered the news back in the 1960s and '70s. In those days, a free-form database was a filing cabinet. Today's political journalist has an arsenal of weapons to choose from, most importantly the computer.

Long before the candidates have announced or filed to run, reporters should be gathering information about the candidates and the issues. (See chapter 5.1.) One of the best ways of storing that information is in a free-form database. These databases are also frequently called "personal" databases or "flat" databases, to distinguish them from "relational" databases, which require the purchase and installation of a database manager. Most news organizations have some kind of database manager and a relational database to assist reporters in their work. (One common use for a relational database and database manager is in tracking political money. See chapter 13.1.)

For reporters, the downside to storing information or keeping sensitive files in the news organization's data management and retrieval system is that other people within the organization may have access to it. Every reporter I know has files and information they want to keep strictly private. A personal free-form database accomplishes this.

Basically, a free-form database is a group of documents or files compiled by the reporter. Virtually every reporter has his or her own system of filing and saving the data. Most use diskettes or rewritable CDs for storage, especially for sensitive information that they may not want accessible to other people in their news organization. Diskettes and CDs can be easily carried around with the reporter if he or she is working in the field, an impossibility with the old-fashioned file cabinet. The data itself can be entered manually, scanned or even downloaded from the Internet.

What reporters include varies widely, but most reporters want a way of identifying issues and statements with candidates, usually over a period of time. Many reporters create a file labeled with the name of the person being chronicled. In the file go individual documents, usually statements slugged with a subject and date. Thus, when the reporter wants to find out what John Doe was saying about real estate development during his run for the state House of Representatives in 1998, to compare it with his stand now in his bid for the state Senate, the reporter simply clicks on the John Doe file and looks for documents titled "real estate development" and dated 1998.

Free-form databases generally do not allow you to search by keywords or phrases, so it is a good idea to limit the content of documents to one or a few subjects. When you're on deadline it can be agony to have to plow through a whole speech or the transcript of an entire news conference to find the particular quote that's germane to what you're writing.

While print journalists can carry a small library of notes and data with them on a few CDs or diskettes, radio and TV journalists rely heavily on sound bites and video clips usually archived at the station or news organization's headquarters. Nonetheless, many reporters and producers carry notes of what's available in audio and video in their free-form databases. The old index cards I prepared when Robert Kennedy was shot have given way to this new technology. In fact, many big news organizations index their archives on a file server that's accessible by logging on to the organization's own computer network.

Reporters who cover politics usually avail themselves of as many tools as they can. That means not only being familiar and dexterous with using the data and systems of their news organizations, but it also means keeping a personal free-form data base.

5.5 Taking Notes, Keeping Notes

Reporters are assiduous and often compulsive note takers. Today, in order to keep track of all those notes, it is important to enter them into your free-form database with some kind of file or document name that will allow access to them when it is needed. Remember that in your free-form database, a keyword search is outside the realm of most laptops or PCs, unless you have purchased and installed a database manager. Scanners allow you to file your notes without manually entering them into the database.

The CIA and other intelligence organizations live in fear of exposing what they simply call "methods and sources." In the spy business, exposing the ways intelligence is gathered and the people who are providing information can be a matter of life and death. In political news coverage, the methods are pretty well known, and exposing the identity of a confidential source seldom results in consequences as dire as a threat of physical harm. Nonetheless, every reporter has information that he or she would just as soon not have become public knowledge. Who within the campaign is providing you with inside information? What are your sources for information about private polling or focus group information? Do you have the candidate's unlisted home phone number or private cellular phone number? Who in the opposition camp is providing you with information?

To protect your sources, be extremely careful when you scan your notes into your computer and confine them to a database. If you file them onto a CD or diskette, assume that it can be accessed by someone other than you if you should lose it or leave it lying around. The same is true if you scan your notes onto your hard drive. Even if you have purchased encryption software and/or lock the file with password access, do not assume it is 100 percent safe. Multi-user file servers, such as those at many major news organizations, are especially vulnerable to snooping and hacking.

Even if someone is authorized by virtue of the conditions of your employment to look into your files—someone such as your boss, your editor or your producer—there are things you will want to keep private. The best way to do this is simply not to file the information at all, but few of us have the capacity to memorize all of our phone lists or address books.

Some reporters go so far as to code the most sensitive information in their own notes. Methods of individual coding include giving extremely sensitive sources fictitious names, inverting phone numbers, and transposing the digits in phone numbers. One reporter I knew in Denver would invert the first three digits, invert the next four digits, and then write them in Chinese characters.

Remember, computers are vulnerable. If hackers can get into the NASA computer that docked the space shuttle or snarl up the network of Bank of America, somebody can probably get to your information.

5.6 Developing Outside Sources

For reporters committed to serious political coverage, an ongoing part of the job is to have access to outside sources and experts, those who are not currently part of the active political process but who have institutional and/or personal knowledge of the players and the program. Naturally geography limits access to a great degree. Reporters in Washington have a smorgasbord of political experts from whom to pick and choose. On the other hand political reporters in Cheyenne, Wyoming, or Lewiston, Maine, will have a much more limited universe of outside sources and experts.

The political pros who run campaigns, devise strategies, take the public pulse, conduct the polls, focus groups and the like are valuable, but reporters must compartmentalize them. Very few are neutral; very few will provide unvarnished information or analysis. Use them. Cultivate them. But always be wary. Always seek a second view, opinion or analysis, preferably from somebody on the opposite side of the political spectrum.

Academics can be extremely useful to journalists. A lot of cities and towns have a college or university; some have more than one. It is worth spending a few hours meeting the people in the various political science or government departments. Some respected political journalists have joined the academic ranks. Find out about them. What's their point of view? What are their credentials? How good are they at providing analysis? And for broadcasters, are they good talkers? A quote in a newspaper can be constructed from a sentence full of hemming and hawing; broadcasters need to have people who can spit out what they have to say in fairly concise form. College professors tend to be good at this because they are used to getting up before groups of people and speaking coherently.

Elder statesmen—former office holders—also can be useful, although they, too, have a political point of view. Nonetheless, they often can provide colorful and insightful analysis of the issues, process and campaigns. (In 1989, during a bruising political tug-of-war between Republican President George H. W. Bush and Democrats on Capitol Hill over U.S. trade policy with China, it added texture and color to a series of stories I did when I obtained an interview with former GOP President Richard Nixon, the first U.S. president to meet with Mao Tze-Dong, the chairman of the Chinese Communist Party. His insight was fascinating.)

Section II
The Campaign Trail

6

Candidates and Campaigns

For reporters covering politics, the question of who is running is often paramount in determining whether a race will be interesting and/or competitive. Who is running will impact on how much news coverage a race will generate. The bigger the names, the more interest there will be; the higher the office, the more interest there will be.

The 2004 presidential race began before the ink was dry on the Supreme Court decision that made George W. Bush the winner of the 2000 contest. (See chapter 3.3.) Stories appeared in all the news media about who would challenge Bush. Would defeated Democrat Albert Gore run again? If not who would? When Gore decided not to run, nine other Democrats quickly jumped in. The first political stories in every election cycle generally revolve around who's going to challenge the incumbent.

Sometimes political stories are simply so obvious they can't be ignored.

The year 2003 saw a highly unusual situation in California. There was a special recall election to determine whether Democratic Gov. Gray Davis, elected less than one year earlier, should be removed from office. The vote would be two-pronged: should Davis be recalled and, if so, who should replace him. The whole process produced a two-month cornucopia of political stories. For political reporters it was the best of all possible worlds, featuring political intrigue, movie stars, allegations of sexual harassment, an array of interesting candidates and negative advertising.

An early question was whether movie star Arnold Schwartzenegger, a Republican, would enter the race. He ultimately did. But there were other serious candidates, including Democratic Lt. Gov. Cruz Bustamante. In all there were more than a hundred candidates. The supporting cast included a woman who appeared in billboard ads in various scanty outfits, a homeless man who lived beneath a freeway underpass, *Hustler* magazine publisher Larry Flint, former TV star Gary Coleman and a street artist who declared the race "performance art."

Within the last two weeks of the campaign more than a dozen women came forward to accuse Schwartzenegger—who was then the clear frontrunner—of sexual misconduct, including fondling their breasts and other inappropriate touching on various movie sets. The Davis campaign was quick to suggest the possibility of criminal conduct on the actor's part. On Tuesday, October 7, California voters gave Davis the boot and elected Schwartzenegger to be the Golden State's next chief executive.

6.1 Testing the Waters and Taking the Plunge

Whether a person is considering a run for president or county commissioner, the process begins months, if not years, before there is any kind of official announcement. The process is similar for all elective offices, but on a scale of newsworthiness, the higher the office being sought the earlier in the process it is likely to produce news. In addition, the higher the office being sought, the more likely it will be that the players are well-known personalities. A person considering a run for the White House has probably been elected to several subordinate offices—senator, representative, governor. On the other hand, somebody running for city council or county commission may be running for the first time.

Most candidacies begin with a simple discussion, or several discussions, among close friends, family and associates. It is at this stage that the candidates start asking serious questions. What will a campaign mean to me and my family? What will it mean to my job? Am I up to the challenge of running for office? Can I raise enough money to run? What do I stand for? What are my values? Who will I be running against? Will I have a primary opponent or opponents in my own party? Do I have a chance of winning?

If a reporter has done advance work, identifying the potential candidates and those people close to them, it is likely that at this stage somebody will acknowledge that the person is considering a run. Depending on the person considering a candidacy, this may be worth a story of some kind. Is he/she well known? Does this person already hold an office and is the run for a different position? Is it an open seat? Does this person address issues that are of concern to your readers, viewers or listeners? Is there likely to be an issue or issues of major controversy in the election? Is the person controversial?

Often the next step is for the potential candidate to test what he or she stands for by meeting with voters. This can be done by the potential candidate appearing at one or several of the local service clubs, churches, synagogues, social organizations or even small gatherings in people's homes. The purpose is threefold: to see how the prospective candidate presents him- or herself, to take the pulse of the voters and hear their concerns, and to see if the candidate resonates with the voters. Do people like what this person has to say about what's on their minds? At this stage it's all highly unscientific. While these types of events help the potential candidate decide whether to take the plunge, they also present excellent opportunities for reporters to examine the person and what he or she stands for.

Presidential hopefuls usually start in Iowa, the first caucus state, and New Hampshire, the first primary state. They will start testing the waters as early as two or two-and-a-half years in advance of the election. Even before they make their first test run into one of those key states, prospective presidential candidates, their aides and consultants draw up plans. "Every candidate has a plan for everything—a plan for health care, a plan for Social Security," said deputy CBS News Washington bureau chief, Tom Mattesky. Those plans provide a blueprint for the potential candidate's policy agenda.

As they are devising their policy plans, people considering a run for the White House often form exploratory committees both nationally and in key states long before they make a formal declaration of candidacy. Presidential hopefuls often have local supporters, friends and/or advisors who appear as surrogates for the candidate. These surrogates test the person's plans and positions on various issues and in turn deliver feedback to the candidate and/or the organization on what's selling and what's not. Once the committees and/or local surrogates have been identified, it is important for political journalists to make contact with them and add them to their databases and Rolodexes.

The same type of process prior to a formal declaration of candidacy often takes place with people considering a run for other major offices—governor, U.S. senator, representative. Naturally, there are variations attendant to the circumstances of the race, the geographic location, the personality of the potential candidate and the amount of money the potential candidate has. The process is significantly scaled back as the level of the office sought diminishes. Advance preparation and testing for a school board race will be less than the advance preparation and testing for a state senate race.

If the office being sought is president, senator, representative, or governor, the potential candidate and his or her closest advisors will usually meet with a pollster somewhere during the decision process. Potential candidates (or sources close to those people) seldom tell reporters about such meetings, unless the results turn out to be incredibly or unexpectedly favorable to the person. Polls are expensive and most of the time local candidates do not deal with pollsters, at least at the early stages of the decision-making process. The exception here is in mayoral races in major cities.

Geoffrey Garin has been a pollster with Peter D. Hart Research Associates in Washington, D.C., for more than 25 years. He said the first poll that is conducted for a prospective candidate is called a "benchmark poll" and provides a detailed analysis of "various important subgroups of the electorate." The initial poll usually keeps people on the phone answering questions for up to 25 minutes. The cost varies by the office being sought, the number of interviews conducted, and the area in which the candidate is running. "In a Senate race in California we are much more likely to do a larger number of interviews than we would in a Senate race in Rhode Island."

The benchmark poll for a potential Senate candidate in California would run around $40,000, according to Garin. A benchmark poll for a U.S. House candidate in northeast Florida would carry a price tag of around $20,000. While the price is steep, in terms of the total cost of a campaign it's a good investment. Professor Larry Sabato, director of the University of Virginia's Center for Politics, noted that in the 1996 Senate race in Virginia the two candidates spent a combined total of nearly $18 million.

"For somebody who is not an incumbent, we would be one of the first consultants to be involved just to help them think about the viability of the race," said Garin. "It's not completely knowable in advance whether somebody's going to win, but it's usually knowable whether they have a chance to win. So, very early on people will hire us for that purpose. Often it's a year and a half out."

If it looks as if a candidacy is viable for a major office—president, senator, governor, representative, and even in some big city mayoral races—a second group of consultants may be hired at this point, according to Sabato: "research specialists to do a full-scale investigation of their own candidate." The simple fact that this is becoming commonplace underscores the nature of political campaigns at all levels. They are often gritty and brutal.

"They do this very early in the process," said Sabato. "They do it for two reasons: One, they assume the press is going to find out information that the candidate's forgotten or won't tell the campaign manager and the pollster, and so on. And second, they assume that the other candidates are going to do negative research, opposition research, into their candidate. They want to know what they're going to be dealing with. And these professional managers have learned that they can't always trust the candidate to tell them the full truth. So sometimes with the candidate's permission and sometimes without, they commission 'oppo' researchers to do a very thorough—occasionally two- or three-inch-thick—research analysis of their candidate."

It is at this stage that the potential candidate and his or her closest friends and advisors start making decisions. The threshold decision is whether to run or not. Other decisions include who will be the campaign manager, press secretary and campaign treasurer. (Most states have election rules that require someone other than the candidate be in charge of the campaign's money.) If it is a major office, the state and/or national party may recommend professionals for the jobs. If it's a state or local office, it's very often a friend or even the spouse of the candidate.

Once the decision is made, the proper paperwork must be filed. After that there is usually some kind of formal announcement. In the case of statewide offices the formal announcement may be made in several places around the state to maximize publicity. In the case of local offices, the announcement can be as simple as holding a campaign kickoff barbeque or picnic where the announcement is made and some money can be raised at the same time.

In the case of presidential candidates, locations are scouted with the precision of a Hollywood production. Hometowns are always popular. GOP candidate Bob Dole went back to his hometown in Kansas to make his 1996 announcement.

Once the campaign has begun, the process involves an almost nonstop series of campaign events. Some are public and reporters are welcome. Some are private. Many times fund-raising events are closed to the news media, although it's never too hard to find out what went on by talking to people who attended the fund-raiser. Most of the time reporters can keep track of where a candidate is going and what's on the schedule by talking to the candidate's headquarters or press secretary. Very often, however, a candidate's schedule can change at the drop of a hat.

I was covering Jesse Jackson's primary campaign for president in 1984 in North Carolina. While the campaign rolled nonstop from morning to late at night, reporters periodically dropped off to file their stories. I dropped off to file one afternoon following a couple of events and planned to catch up with the campaign again around dinnertime. While I was filing, the campaign decided to drop one event and add another. Since I was not in contact with Jackson's staff, I found myself quite alone at the event site where I planned to rejoin the campaign, and never did find Jackson and his people until the next morning half a state away.

Helen Dewar of *The Washington Post* had a similar experience covering the last campaign of Sen. Jesse Helms (R-N.C.). "He ran in this monster bus. But he would never tell the local papers—because he was mad at them—what his schedule was until the last minute. And out-of-towners? He'd never bother with us. So you'd have to go out and find the bus and latch onto the bus and just follow it. Or stop and ask, 'Have you seen Jesse Helms's bus go through?' That was how you covered the campaign."

6.2 Who's in Charge?

The key players in any political campaign are the candidate, campaign manager and press secretary. Sometimes the titles vary. Press secretaries are sometimes called communications directors. Campaign managers are sometimes called chiefs of staff. In major campaigns, the candidate's pollster may be a key aide. Other strategists and advisors may be critical to the campaign organization. While a campaign treasurer is a legal requirement virtually everywhere, that person may or may not be an important advisor to the candidate.

Campaign managers are basically in charge of everything. They are deeply involved in campaign strategy, issues management, the candidate's message, the candidate's image and scheduling. The campaign manager is also in charge of paid staff and volunteers. The number of each depends on the nature and size of the campaign. Some campaigns for local office have no paid staffers, including the campaign manager. In presidential campaigns, the number of paid staffers can be in the hundreds.

Campaign managers often hire or recruit the press secretaries, media specialists, pollsters, opposition researchers, schedulers and other staff members. Journalists and political pros will often refer to the people closest to candidates as their handlers.

Historically, political campaign organizations have changed. Stephen Hess, senior fellow at the Brookings Institution and author of several books on the subject of politics and the press, said, "If you went back 50-plus years ago, you'd find that the people sometimes called handlers were amateurs. They were the friends of the candidate. They were the local political clubs. They were also part of a community that expected to get something if the candidate were elected. They were lawyers and insurance people and others who might be able to get contracts if the candidate were elected. But they weren't professionals. Between elections they weren't involved in politics."

The advent of professional campaign managers, press secretaries and consultants has not improved the quality of campaigns, said CBS News's chief Washington correspondent Bob Schieffer. He noted that this "cottage industry" has changed the tone and nature of campaigns because the professionals are not connected to the local community. When an election is over, the professional "takes his money and goes to the next town and gets ready for the next election."

Once the team is assembled, most candidates for mid- and upper-tier offices then find some place to use as a campaign headquarters. Lower-level candidates often work out of their homes. Some campaigns start working out of the candidate's or campaign manager's home and later move to external quarters.

In some campaigns, the press secretary or communications director is responsible for dealings with the news media as well as overseeing campaign advertising. More often than not, campaigns hire specialists in both areas. For reporters, the campaign manager and the press secretary are critical contact points in any campaign. Obviously, the best contact point is the candidate. But there are myriad times when a reporter can't get directly to the candidate. Candidate access diminishes in direct relation to how close Election Day is.

Important players in most campaigns are the candidate's speech-writers. The candidate's speeches are the basic unit of delivery for the candidate's message. In contests for local offices, the candidate is often the primary speechwriter, too, in conjunction with the campaign manager and/or the press secretary. In major campaigns, there can be several speechwriters. Hess was a speechwriter for President Dwight Eisenhower back in the 1950s. "It's incredible now," he said. "Presidents have eight speech writers. We had two, and we weren't all that busy."

Hess said that when he wrote speeches for Eisenhower during the 1958 non-presidential election campaign, the average speech would be about 25 minutes. Most campaign speeches today are about 15 minutes and will usually contain the two or three sound bites that the campaign wants to emphasize on that particular day. Most campaign speeches—stump speeches—contain the same basic messages and themes. Nonetheless, reporters need to be listening for what's new, what's different, what wording has been changed, added or dropped. The campaign speech is where reporters will often get their first hint that something in a campaign has changed or is different.

Reporters must never lose sight of the fact that in every single campaign, the entire campaign organization exists to promote and support the candidate. Reporters may know and like the press secretary or the campaign manager, but they are not there to provide journalistic information. They are there to get the most favorable, positive coverage of their candidate as they can. "I made one commitment to myself," said Michael Freedman, former press secretary to Rep. David Bonior (D-Mich.) and now vice president of communication at The George Washington University, "I would never lie." He conceded that not all press secretaries follow that guideline, although he noted that a press secretary who lies damages his or her own credibility and thus impedes his or her ability to help the boss.

For most press secretaries, "getting out the message—whatever message had been formulated—and spinning that message" is the essence of their job, said Freedman. Reporters must "distill from those messages that which is worthy of print or air and match that with a sense of fairness from whatever the opposing side is." Fairness, of course, is not what the campaigns want. If a reporter finds that one campaign likes his or her coverage and the other does not, that's a red flag and requires some introspective analysis.

Since 1984 C-SPAN has asked candidates in various races to wear microphones as they went about their day-to-day campaign activities.

"The closer they get to the big day, the less likely they are to wear the mikes. The less popular they are, the more likely they are to wear the mikes," said C-SPAN's president Brian Lamb. "It's inversely proportional to how much value a candidate thinks this kind of thing will have to them. You can chart it. Candidates who wear the mikes today will say 'let's skip it' in six months. The frontrunners are less likely the closer it gets to the actual election. They want to control everything that comes out of their mouth, because they think that one slip of the tongue can sink them."

Security is always an issue in campaigns. The higher the office sought, the greater the security around a candidate. Obviously security is a paramount concern around presidential candidates. (Sitting presidents are guarded by the United States Secret Service. That agency is also responsible for security around major party nominees for president once they've been picked.) Many veteran political reporters have observed a cozy relationship between candidates and their security force that goes beyond candidate protection.

"There are security matters that determine how far back you're going to be from the candidate," said CBS Radio News correspondent Bob Fuss. "Those are manipulated all the time. When a candidate has something that he wants to say, suddenly it's perfectly fine to have the reporters within five feet of him. When there's an embarrassing story that morning in the paper, suddenly security requires reporters to be 30 feet away."

Campaigns and the people who run them reflect the candidates who are running. Campaign coverage can be highly unpredictable and idiosyncratic, depending on the personality of the person being covered. Veteran *Washington Post* reporter Helen Dewar related an incident involving former Republican Sen. Bob Smith of New Hampshire.

"Smith was angry with the national news media in general, and specifically at us [*The Washington Post*]," she said. "So I had a great deal of difficulty in arranging an interview. Finally I arranged one at a place where I had to drive, as I recall, 65 miles fairly early in the morning to cover the event—which I wasn't much interested in—but to get the interview. I go to the event and cover it. It's an incredible heat wave in New Hampshire. And he jumps in his car and drives away." Dewar threw up her hands and laughed. "I'm running down the street waving my notebook at him. After many more phone calls I finally got to talk to him. But you have to be prepared for the unexpected."

While it is necessary for reporters to understand how each campaign is organized, that is seldom a story in itself. Understanding what's going on behind the scenes in any campaign can lead to great stories. Some specific things that reporters need to watch for are signs of friction within a campaign organization. Are the campaign manager and the press secretary on the same page or is there any indication of a disconnect? Is there discontent among staff and/or volunteers? Is there a shift in who has the candidate's ear? Is the candidate running the campaign or is the campaign manager or a consultant pulling the strings?

When there is discord in a campaign it often signals problems for the candidate. If information about the discord comes to you from the opposing campaign, it must be checked very carefully. It may well be in the interest of the opposition to promote tension in the opposing camp and they may be using you, as a reporter, to generate it. "Some stuff can be very helpful," said Dotty Lynch, senior political editor for CBS News. "A press secretary for one candidate can give you some negative information about another candidate. Again, you don't go right from there to air. You've got to check it through. But the tips that you get when you're covering a campaign will often come from one campaign trying to do damage to another."

In addition, if you sense discord or friction in one campaign the other campaign may be able to tell you why—a slump in the polls, a decline in campaign contributions or some other reason. Sometimes this can generate a news story, but other times it's inside baseball and is of interest only to political junkies and insiders. If you unearth this kind of information two criteria can help in determining its newsworthiness: What, if any, impact it may have on the voters and what, if any, impact it may have on the ultimate outcome of the campaign.

6.3 The Power of Incumbency

Campaigns in which one of the contestants is already in office are notoriously and traditionally short on news. Everybody knows how they're going to turn out and so there's usually not much there to cover. Political science professor Larry Sabato of the University of Virginia acknowledged the decision-making process that goes on in all news organizations. "Where do the resources come from? You have to pick a certain number of contests in advance to focus on." Noncompetitive races generally do not make compelling stories.

Occasionally the candidate's positions on key issues are of such interest that the race may be worth a story or two, even if it's deemed to be noncompetitive. Once in a while, the personalities of the candidates or people within the organization are so compelling that it's worth putting in the newspaper or on the air.

In 1996, I covered the reelection bid of House Speaker Newt Gingrich (R-Ga.) even though there was little doubt that he would win. The race had a lot of national interest. Gingrich was a high-profile, controversial figure. The opinions about him were strong even in his own district. His challenger was an independently-wealthy business mogul who was pouring a lot of his own money into the campaign. The story was interesting, even though, in the end, it was no contest and Gingrich was easily reelected.

For political reporters the fact is that nothing is a better bellwether of how a political race is going to turn out than incumbency. Incumbents, unless they are temporary appointees, have been elected to the office at least once. They are known to their constituents. They have a track record. They have existing organizations that can be transformed into the core of a campaign structure fairly easily. They have a fund-raising base. They usually have major party support. While many political science professors will say every race has the potential of an upset, an analysis of post-election voting data shows that incumbents—for virtually every office at every level—enjoy a commanding advantage.

For U.S. House seats as well as seats in the state legislature, the cards have been politically stacked against challengers. Every 10 years, when the state legislatures redraw district boundaries for the U.S. House and the state's legislative districts, the American tradition of gerrymandering usually comes into play. The fact is that, more often than not, redistricting protects incumbents, especially if the incumbent is in the same party as the majority party in the state legislature. "People's party affiliation is still the best predictor of how they're going to vote," said pollster Geoffrey Garin of Peter D. Hart Research Associates. "If you've got a district that has 60 percent of the people who habitually vote one way or the other because of their party affiliation, it's very hard to break through." Gerrymandering works to maintain that advantage.

As a result of gerrymandering and the concentration of political party loyalty, only a handful of races every cycle are even remotely competitive when there are incumbents running for reelection. Challengers are disadvantaged in every way in virtually every kind of race.

Professor Sabato uses physics as the way reporters can spot potential anomalies in the form of vulnerable incumbents' "Politics is like inertia: Objects in motion tend to remain in motion; objects at rest tend to remain at rest. And if a state has been competitive in the past it's likely to be competitive in the future. If a state is totally one-sided in its politics it's likely to remain there." He also noted that challengers who have managed to raise a large amount of money or those with personal fortunes have a greater chance of successfully challenging incumbents than those without significant funding or personal wealth.

Occasionally a reporter can find a way of reporting this phenomenon. If nothing else it serves to educate voters about what's really going on in the realm of representative and electoral politics. "I saw a good story in which a reporter basically said this is a 'no choice' election," said former network news correspondent Deborah Potter, executive director of NewsLab, a TV news research and training center. "There was one candidate who was going to win in a walk and he [the reporter] did a story about how all of these people are really disenfranchised because they don't have a choice. It was good reporting. He came at it from a voter's point of view." Such stories are exceptions.

6.4 The Oval Office Factor

If incumbents enjoy an enormous advantage in general, no incumbent enjoys a greater advantage than a sitting president. "The president and the White House and all of the resources that go with that can overwhelm," said *The Washington Post's* veteran political columnist David Broder.

Even when he is traveling as a candidate, the president of the United States flies on Air Force One. He uses the White House fleet of armored limousines. He is accompanied by a battalion of Secret Service agents. He is supported by the vast White House transportation and logistics operation and the White House communications office. Even though the incumbent president's political party or campaign organization pays for the non-official elements of a trip, the fact is that a great deal of the daily business of a sitting president—even when he's campaigning—is official.

A presidential visit is always a public spectacle and it is made even more so when the president and his staff want the public's and, more importantly, the media's attention. Every location is scouted in advance. Where will the president stand? What will the backdrop be? What will the television pictures look like? Will they project the dynamic image that the president's image-makers want to project? Nothing is left to chance. Reporters, especially local reporters who don't cover the White House or the president regularly, should be aware of the fact that even when something looks spontaneous, it probably isn't.

In addition, a popular incumbent president very often has "coattails." The political coattail effect occurs when a popular candidate can help pull other candidates to electoral victory if they grab onto his or her coattails. The 2000 presidential race was so close that neither candidate—Republican George W. Bush or Democrat Al Gore—had coattails at all.

But in 2002, after 9-11 and the war in Afghanistan, the dynamic had changed significantly. President Bush rode a wave of extraordinarily high approval ratings in virtually every public opinion poll and he and his staff decided to use his newly developed coattails in the 2002 non-presidential elections. The strategy proved very successful. Not only did it help the GOP regain control of the U.S. Senate and keep control of the House, it positioned Bush as a formidable force in anticipation of his own reelection in 2004.

Broder related an example: "I covered a race out in northern Indiana, a very competitive race. It was an open Democratic seat that the Republican won. And I was talking to him [the winner] after the election. It was one of the places Bush went during the final week of the campaign. And I said how much did Bush move your numbers, and he said 16 or 18 points. And I said, 'That was the day after he was there?' He said no that was the day before, because the local paper and television the day before had nothing but stories about the 'president is coming to South Bend.'"

New broadcast technology, including expanded use of digital video and satellite uplinks by local and national television, is serving to reinforce and strengthen the advantage possessed by incumbent presidents. Presidential events result in saturation coverage, not just in the local market where the president is visiting, but statewide and regionally. "What you're seeing now with the technology is that a visit by the president to Charlotte, North Carolina, on behalf of a statewide candidate, not only gets coverage in Charlotte, North Carolina, as was the case in 1976 or 1980, but it gets coverage in all of North Carolina and probably all of South Carolina as well," said Tom Mattesky, deputy Washington bureau chief for CBS News.

Mattesky explained that the White House is able to skew political news coverage through the use, if not manipulation, of local television. "You're seeing saturation coverage by local stations that now have multiple ways of transmitting from multiple locations. And they use those, not just for scheduled newscasts, but throughout the day. A presidential trip, albeit a political one to their city, gets coverage outside of the traditional news cycle. . . . It's not uncommon for local stations to broadcast the president's arrival, to broadcast his visit to a school, to broadcast his meeting with local national guardsmen, as well as to broadcast his speech. Years ago you might have the speech broadcast live and then you would see coverage in a packaged form on the 6 o'clock news and the 11 o'clock news. Now you see it across the board."

The impact is multiplied when every station in an area is doing the same thing. "So anybody who turns on not just one local station, but any of the local stations, they'll see the president of the Unites States and the candidate he's there campaigning for," said Mattesky.

6.5 Campaign Mileposts

The most important day in any political campaign is, of course, Election Day. That's the Super Bowl, the World Series and the Stanley Cup all in one. It's when all the work, sweat, effort and expense of the race for public office ends—and the voters get to decide.

The run-up to the general election, however, has several points of interest for political reporters. Each milepost can and often does generate some kind of fodder for a good political story. Reporters need to be cognizant of whether they've reached a milepost or whether it's something less significant. *The Washington Post's* David Broder observed, "What there's too much of—and I'm as guilty as anybody—is we tend to focus too much on day-to-day incidents of a campaign, the gaffes, the petty controversies."

Campaign mileposts do not happen at predictable times, nor do they take uniform shapes. The good political reporter will recognize them.

Usually the first milepost is for a person to decide to run. For most incumbents the decision to seek reelection is almost automatic. In fact, it is a much more significant milepost when an incumbent decides not to run again.

Once the candidates in a particular race have been identified, many news organizations will run candidate profiles. Wally Dean, senior fellow at the Project for Excellence in Journalism, noted that there is often a large amount of information presented by the various news media about candidates for the major offices—president, senator, governor, representative. "There's not very much information about a city council or county board or register of deeds or state treasurer—important offices which people have to make decisions about. And what they're getting from the journalists is biographies, which are handed out by the candidates. They're not learning anything about their character."

Dean posed a question for reporters and news organizations: "Is there an efficient way for journalists trying to cover a large number of races to give them something about the candidate's character that takes us beyond the bio?"

Candidate profiles tend to come very early in the campaign cycle. News organizations "want to be first, to kick the thing off," said University of Virginia political science professor Larry Sabato. "There's just one problem with that. Nobody cares, at that early point in time, maybe 15 months ahead of the election. Is there any written rule in journalism that prohibits them from reprinting some of this stuff? Or airing [it] right before an election when average voters are focusing?" Sabato suggests that political reporting often fails to generate much public interest because of timing and that "just because you published it or aired it 15 months ago doesn't mean that you can't revisit the same information again," updated with any new information that happened in the interim.

Mileposts during a primary election campaign include candidates who drop out before the primary. Look for the reasons, beyond what the candidate says when he or she makes the announcement that it's the end of the trail. Talk to people close to the dropout. Talk to the opposing campaign(s). What does this mean for the election overall?

It is always a good story if there are signs that a challenger may upset an incumbent in the primary election. It's an even better story when it actually happens, but it increases the credibility of a reporter within a news organization to be onto that story as early as possible.

The primary election itself is a milepost, always worth coverage, even in years when there isn't much electoral excitement or competition among the candidates.

At any point in the process—in the primary or general election campaign—campaign trouble and candidate mistakes can be mileposts, although as Broder observed reporters need to separate the mundane from the significant. The inability to raise money is often significant. Why is the candidate having trouble raising money? Is it public perception that he or she can't win? Has the candidate said or done something to discourage contributors? Is it the candidate's stance on some controversial issue? Is it something in the candidate's background? Bob Schieffer, CBS News's chief Washington correspondent, said people in a community usually have a pretty good idea about who's running. "The local people on the scene knew about candidates who had secrets in their past, who committed scandals, and those candidates were selected out early in the process."

As the race toward the general election kicks into high gear, usually a few weeks in advance of the election, stories abound. So-called horse race stories (who's ahead and who's behind if there's been polling done in connection with a race) are the subject of lively debate among political reporters. The fact is they can't be ignored completely, although if that's all a reporter is doing it tends to turn off readers, viewers and listeners. *Newsday's* Elaine Povich said, "Horse race stories are hot and cold. Some people love them; some people hate them. Who's in, who's out, who's up, who's down? I kind of like them because they give you a feel for how the thing is going." But she warned against letting them become a crutch.

If a reporter has developed good enough sources within the various campaigns it is possible to get a handle on the endgame strategies of the candidates. If that involves a change of game plan, a new approach, something radically different than what's been done to this point in the campaign, that can be a milepost that highlights the final push toward the general election.

A Conversation with Jamie Dupree

News director: Cox Radio, Washington Bureau

Very few reporters know the ins and outs of the U.S. Capitol as well as Jamie Dupree. He knows what's down every back corridor, whose hideaway office is where, and what all the arcane and indecipherable legislative language means. This tall, handsome journalist has been there since he was a congressional page in high school.

When Congress and national politics became my beats in 1989, it was Dupree who helped me find the kind of insight some reporters never do find. He showed me the subtleties, how to watch what was going on behind the scenes in order to understand what was really going on, how to read the body language, or sense the way the political winds were blowing.

One day we were standing in the Speaker's Lobby, the ornate room directly outside the chamber of the House of Representatives. It is as wide as the chamber itself and is directly behind the Speaker's chair. On spring days members take the sun and view Washington's famous cherry blossoms from the balcony overlooking Independence Avenue. Only members, staff and credentialed news media are allowed into the Speaker's Lobby and it is one of the best places on Capitol Hill to buttonhole members and their key aides.

On this particular day the negotiations were intense on a particular bill. Democratic Rep. John Dingell of Michigan was the chairman of the House

Energy and Commerce Committee at the time. He's a large, often gruff, shambling man who strode through the assembled aides and reporters, leaving a wake as he passed through the ornate wood and glass doors onto the House floor. "Come here. Watch this," whispered Dupree.

The scowling Dingell made a beeline for a young congresswoman standing next to the rows of seats on the Democratic side of the aisle and draped an arm around her shoulder. "That's a single Dingell," Dupree said in my ear. "That means he's putting pressure on her to vote with him on this. If he puts his other arm on her other shoulder that's a double Dingell and then you know things are really serious."

I asked him about the genesis of his love affair with Capitol Hill and politics:

J.D.: "My parents both worked on Capitol Hill for members of Congress and I was around it for most of my life. I was a page in the summer of 1980 for Congressman Dan Rostenkowski [D] of Illinois. In [19]81 he became chair of the Ways and Means Committee and he put me in the cloakroom. And then in '82 I was an intern for the Ways and Means Committee, when he was chairman as well. So I got a pretty good grounding in my high school years in backroom politics.

"I always wanted to be a sports reporter. That was my dream. And I'd still love to do play-by-play sports. That's what I wanted to do when I went to the University of Florida and I got into the program. I loved radio right off the bat, maybe because it's all you. If you don't get the story in radio, it's your fault. In TV sometimes the video didn't come out right or the font didn't come up on the screen right. But in radio it's just me. So I got into sports as well as news in Gainesville. But I knew right away when I was doing sports broadcasting that I didn't like coming up with 18 different words for 'defeated.'

"So I came back here to D.C., and news and politics were my big interests. I got a job at a little AM radio station out in Rockville, Maryland, and then came down to the Hill and worked for a group called the Berns Bureau. Part of my job was selling news and part of my job was covering news. So that was the beginning of '87, the latter part of the Reagan Administration. I worked in that job until late '88, freelanced on my own for a couple of months and got this job in January of 1989.

"I always loved the inner workings of the House, especially since I worked there. But I've really come to like the Senate. And then I've been able to get out on the campaign trail as well. So it's two different ways of political reporting: the machinations of this place, Congress, the nuts and bolts of it, but there's still a lot of politics in it, and there's the campaign trail and the conventions, which I really enjoy too."

R.A.: *You service local stations. Is that like doing local news from a national perspective?*

J.D.: "I try as hard as I can to localize the story. I take the national story, say, the House approves the president's tax cut plan, and I try to put their local member of Congress into that piece. That's the localizing of it. For Jacksonville, I try to put their members of Congress or their senators on. For Atlanta, the same thing. . . . But, say the mayor of Orlando shows up here. I have an Orlando station. So I'll go cover the mayor giving testimony before a House or Senate committee. You have lots of local-type stories and then you can localize a national story.

R.A.: *Are you ever looking for local issues within a national story?*

J.D.: "Sure. One of the big stories lately has been medical malpractice insurance and the stations will tell me 'we're having a big protest tomorrow or something is going to happen. Can you find an angle?' And I'll go find a story. Here's another example. The head coach at the University of Georgia basketball team got into all kinds of trouble recently. And I said to my news director in Atlanta that I'll bet I can go and find [Sen.] John McCain [R-Ariz.] and get him to say he's thinking of holding hearings on troubles in collegiate sports.

"So I went down to the Ohio Clock [an area right off the Senate floor]. I found McCain and not only did he say yes, he's looking at holding hearings, he said they were going to be meeting with the new NCAA [National Collegiate Athletic Association] president in a few weeks. And he and his staff were not only talking about the Georgia situation, but gambling allegations against a former quarterback at Florida State. So it quickly rolled into a story for several stations."

R.A.: *How much input do your stations have with regard to what you cover. Do they call you and say 'we want you to cover this or that?' Or do you call them and pitch stories?*

J.D.: "We've pretty much gotten to the point that I tell them what we're going to do. If they have a specific story they would like covered they call me or send me an e-mail. I've worked with them for so long that we've gotten in this rhythm that they know that I will cover what they need.

"Sometimes a station will ask for something and I just can't get to it because we've got a major story happening. I can't get everywhere. But you'd be amazed at how many hearings are carried on the [in-house] cable system. You can cover so many stories at once. Most of the time if they want it I can get to it."

R.A.: *Do you get the feeling from your news directors that they're looking for the sensational, the scandalous, the sleazy and that they really don't care much about issue stories?*

J.D.: "It used to be that way. They'd say, 'You want to cover that political stuff and that's just not going to get on the air.'

"Luckily I came on board about the time that Rush Limbaugh really began. These conservative talk shows are very issues-oriented. And you can say what you want about Limbaugh, but he talks about issues a lot of the time, things that are happening in Congress. And I found that we could get all those political stories on the air because it was what people were talking about on that station.

"I have a much better chance of doing a story about internal dissent among Republicans or troubles in Congress for the GOP in a newscast at 4 p.m. because in another minute Sean Hannity is coming on the air and talking about that exact same thing. When I first started there was a reluctance to do the political stuff, but when I showed them that we could go on the road to New Hampshire, to the primaries, to the convention and we could do daily live shots and daily talk shows then they warmed to it.

"I don't do politics just for politics' sake, but when we've got a big story going, then they love it. I'm always surprised by the insider questions I get about this stuff when I'm on the air."

R.A.: *Getting pols to talk is no problem. . . .*

J.D.: "The easiest thing I do is to put a microphone in front of members of Congress. They all want to talk."

R.A.: *But they all want to spin you? Manipulate you?*

J.D.: "Absolutely. You regard almost everything with a bit of skepticism about what you're hearing. And after a while you just know when somebody's giving you a bunch of partisan garbage. That's fine. It's like that's what I would expect. I remember there was a congressman from Ohio, Bob McEwen [R], and I'd interview him right outside the chamber of the U.S. House. He would give me the most outrageous statements you can imagine, likening Democrats to the coming of the plague. And he would get done with his great sound bites and he'd stop with this big smile and he'd look at me and say, 'Was that good enough?'

"It was like covering Bob Dornan [R-Calif.], the former congressman. You knew that Dornan was going to say something outrageous. And how, as a young reporter, do you realize that's what's going on? You've got to do your own homework to know the issues behind the story. One of the hardest things always is to come into a story cold. But you've got to read up and know what you're asking, and know what side A is going to say and what side B is going to say, and find a way to get underneath that.

"We're always looking for little changes in language, you know, the use of a word or a verb here and there. Many times the little things indicate a big change and a big story."

R.A.: *What's the best part of the job?*

J.D.: "Being here to watch things get done. I hate gridlock, I hate it when things are nothing more than the Democrats getting up and screaming and the Republicans getting up and screaming and everybody pointing their finger at each other and a bill going nowhere. I really like it when things get done.

"On the campaign trail the best part, by far, is going to New Hampshire and then going to the [presidential nominating] conventions. Everyone who wants to cover politics should go to New Hampshire at some time in their life for a [presidential] primary. Those people take democracy more seriously than any other people in the United States. They know the issues in depth. They ask amazing questions. They are great to interview after they talk to the candidates. New Hampshire is like covering a hurricane. You're just running everywhere all the time."

R.A.: *Who's the most colorful politician you've covered?*

J.D.: "Colorful? That would have to be Jim Traficant [D-Ohio]. There's no other member of Congress who has put me in a walking headlock through the rotunda of the U.S. Capitol. There's no one who's ever tried to school me—quoting him—to 'kick people's ass after sundown' than Jim Traficant.

"Few people know that Traficant ran for president in 1988. He had a couple delegates from Ohio, including a woman who wore a gigantic fruit hat down on the convention floor."

(NOTE: Traficant was tried in U.S. District Court in April 2002 and found guilty on 10 criminal counts including bribery, racketeering and tax evasion. He was subsequently expelled from the House—only the second representative kicked out for criminal conduct since the Civil War—and jailed.)

R.A.: *Any others that jump out?*

J.D.: "Two people that I would pull out right away. I've been just amazed to cover John Lewis [D] of Georgia. The guy is a civil rights icon and he calls me 'sir' and 'mister.' I finally had to stop him. Every time I see pictures of the Civil Rights marches I see pictures of him. I'm almost in awe of covering him. And that may sound silly, but he's really that amazing.

"And the other guy was Tony Hall [D] from Dayton, Ohio, who went on a hunger strike one time. And I remember going over to interview him and he was so committed [to what he believed] that he went on a hunger strike. I always found him to be extraordinary."

7

The End of the Trail

Most news organizations pull out all the stops for primaries and general elections. Primary elections are like the playoffs. The general election is the biggest of the season's big games. At the network and national newspaper level, planning for election night coverage begins a year or more in advance. At the local level, most newspapers and stations start planning several months in advance. Everything will be plotted, from set design to special edition layout to deployment of troops to how much money is in the budgets to spend on the coverage.

General election night is the most important night on the political calendar for news organizations. It's the night when the winners and losers are decided. It's the night on which all the elements that have come to represent the American form of representative democracy come together. For political reporters it is the ultimate night in their field of specialization.

Every two years on the first Tuesday after the first Monday in November (and on other selected dates in cases where municipalities hold elections other than in accordance with federal election law) newsrooms are abuzz. From the giant networks and major newspapers like *The New York Times* and *The Washington Post* to local radio and television stations and the smallest of dailies, it's the same story. In reality, it's a 48 hour day that starts on Monday morning and ends on Wednesday.

7.1 Endgame Coverage

Most news organizations ramp up their political coverage during the last week or two in October. If there is a correlation between the level of viewer and/or reader interest and the volume of political coverage, it generally manifests itself in the last few weeks of an election cycle. This is especially true if something has happened during the campaign to capture the attention of the voting public. Sometimes it is the result of what's perceived to be an extremely close race. Sometimes it's the result of what has gone on during the campaign—scandal, personal attacks, dirty tricks, a clash of ideologies or values. Sometimes it is an issue or series of issues that are of concern to a particular electorate.

Contested races almost always generate news coverage. For reporters preparing endgame stories it is important to analyze why a race was close, remembering what was on the minds of the voters. Using the information gathered in those early forays into neighborhoods and examining voter concerns in swing districts or precincts will result in better stories than simply quoting the candidate and reporting the horse race. What turned the election? What moved undecided voters?

Most news organizations have limited resources even when planning endgame coverage. There are only a finite number of reporters, photographers, videographers, column inches and air time. In the days leading up to the vote, the best news organizations usually will make an effort to present at least minimal coverage even of seemingly noncompetitive races.

The decision-making process in the exercise of news judgment affects all organizations based on resources, space and time. Even C-SPAN, which is devoted to providing as much political information as possible, is forced to make decisions, according to chief executive officer Brian Lamb. "We try to get all the candidates but there are times when you say 'that person doesn't have a chance.' We might let them have the opportunity to speak, but it's clear that they're not raising money, they don't have a following, they're not campaigning, they don't have an organization."

Until the extraordinary presidential election of 2000 that wasn't decided until more than a month after election night (see chapter 3.3), most reporters considered everything on election night, save for reporting the winners and losers, to be on autopilot. That is not to suggest that it's easy, but once reporters have been through the campaign, election night reporting generally is a rehash of what's gone before, aside from the vote tabulation itself.

In the case of television, networks and stations will have set up their graphics, plotted their live shots and planned their coverage format. Newspapers will have assigned reporters to write the stories of various races and the attendant sidebars; the art departments will have dummied up their graphs, charts and maps.

For a political reporter it's always more fun to cover a winner. Covering a loser is akin to covering a funeral or a wake. The winner's election night headquarters is always a party; for the loser it is always a difficult night after months of seriously hard work.

Election night 1992 in Houston was not easy. I had traveled with President George H. W. Bush since the primary season, literally hundreds of thousands of miles. To those of us in the press corps it was apparent in the final days of the campaign that he was not going to pull off a win, even though I was told by several people close to him afterward that Bush believed he would stage a miraculous comeback right up until the exit polling data started coming in around midday on Election Day.

It was obvious that the Bush election night victory celebration, as it was billed, was that in name only. The body language of everyone present was testimony to the fact that the game was over even as early returns started trickling in. The inevitable conclusion was underscored as Bill Clinton's Electoral College margin started mounting. Once the polls closed on the West Coast, Bush delivered his concession speech. Tears flowed. And the party was over.

7.2 Forests and Trees

After a political reporter has followed a campaign, or several campaigns, it is only natural for that reporter to consider him- or herself something of an expert. In most cases that's true. After all, the reporter knows the candidates and those people around them. (See chapter 5.1.) The reporter knows their strengths and weaknesses and in many cases their public personae and their private peccadillos. The reporter has contacted analysts, pollsters and experts on all sides. The reporter has been into the community and taken the pulse of the voters. (See chapter 8.3) The reporter knows the issues.

As a result, it is not unusual for reporters to make predictions or offer analysis about how the election will turn out. For some it is part of the job description. "Twenty-five years ago political reporters saw themselves differently," said Stuart Rothenberg, political analyst and editor of the Rothenberg Political Report. "They saw themselves as being there to get the hard information, put it out in a story. They wanted to report what the candidate said. Now some political reporters have master's [degrees] or doctorates and they see themselves more as analysts."

In 1994, I started covering the highly charged congressional election campaign from early spring when House and Senate Republicans, led by House Minority Leader Newt Gingrich of Georgia, unveiled their "Contract with America." I watched as they stood on the west steps of the Capitol looking down the Mall. In speech after speech they declared that they would run on that contract and take control of both the House and Senate. I reported what they said and I reported the scornful derision with which the prediction of victory was met by congressional Democrats. That baleful skepticism was shared by most of my journalistic colleagues.

The chatter in the House and Senate Radio and Television Galleries (where broadcast reporters who cover Congress work) was scathing. "Those guys have been inhaling," quipped one reporter—a reference to candidate Bill Clinton's statement in 1992 that he had tried marijuana but "didn't inhale."

Nonetheless, the GOP "Contract with America" did not vaporize or self-destruct, as many veteran political reporters thought it would. As the summer lapsed into the fall and the campaign moved into high gear, several facts became obvious. First, the Clinton Administration's failure to come up with a national health insurance plan, coupled with several other legislative missteps, had created problems for Democratic incumbents. Second, Republicans were staying on-message, portraying the Democrats as fiscally irresponsible, "the tax-and-spend party." The Democrats never mustered a unified response. Third, history indicated that the party that controlled the White House seldom picked up congressional seats in midterm elections and often lost seats. Fourth, as analyst Rothenberg pointed out on my radio program, vulnerable Democratic incumbents were not gaining much, if any, ground in the public opinion polls by late September and early October. By late October, many were actually slipping.

Several days before the election, I filed a story analyzing the lay-of-the-land as the nation approached the midterm voting. In that story, based on several interviews with key players and experts along with analysis of all the polling data I could collect I said, "Unless there's a last minute sea change, it appears distinctly possible that the Republicans could take control of both the House and Senate."

I was castigated. Several of my reportorial colleagues suggested that I was about one Bud short of a six-pack. Most were speculating that one chamber, the Senate, might change hands. Very few thought both would.

Nonetheless, Nov. 8, 1994, turned into Black Tuesday for congressional Democrats. The news turned bad for them virtually as soon as the polls closed on the East Coast. My CBS News colleagues and I could see the trend by 9 p.m. and shortly thereafter I went on the air to report that, indeed, the House of Representatives and Senate, for the first time in two decades, would be in the hands of the GOP. By midnight, the last nail was pounded into the Democrats' collective coffin when the incumbent Speaker of the House, Thomas Foley, lost his bid for re-election from the state of Washington to the upstart Republican George Nethercutt.

This was not the only recent election that did not go as the majority of media pundits and analysts predicted in advance. The 2002 midterm congressional election confounded the experts and left many veteran political reporters scratching their heads. Going into the election, Republicans held the House and Democrats controlled the Senate—both by razor-thin margins. Through the summer most national political reporters, supported by public opinion polls and the historical precept that the party holding the White House, in this case the GOP, seldom gained seats in midterm elections, were reporting that it seemed likely things would remain *status quo*. Wrong again!

Several factors came into play that blindsided many journalists. First, a very popular President George W. Bush invested a tremendous amount of his personal political capital by campaigning tirelessly in states where GOP candidates faced tight races. (See chapter 6.4.) Second, Democrats were unable to develop a cohesive, unified message in the wake of the terrorist attacks on the United States on 9-11. Third, the preelection polls reflected a fairly evenly split electorate but proved to be a less reliable barometer than reporters thought.

Finally, the perennial crutch of political journalism—conventional wisdom—turned out to be seriously off the mark.

- Conventional wisdom says endorsements don't work. It turned out that the endorsement of a president who enjoyed a 60-plus percent popularity rating going into the election did work.
- Conventional wisdom says the president's party usually loses seats, especially House seats, in midterm elections because weak candidates often win in presidential election years by latching onto the

coattails of the White House winner. There was virtually no coattail effect in 2000, and in fact George W. Bush lost the popular vote. As a result the GOP congressional winners in 2000 were well-positioned to hold onto their seats by themselves.

- Conventional wisdom says reporters can drop into and out of campaigns and still produce accurate stories. If the 2002 elections proved anything conclusively it is that there is no substitute for spending time in communities and getting close to campaigns and the people running them. Two cases illustrate the point. Republican Sonny Purdue won election as the first GOP governor of Georgia since 1872. Among his issues was one that figured prominently in his phone and direct-mail operations. He pledged to let the voters decide on the fate of the Confederate Battle Flag in the state. The issue was not heavily played in radio and TV ads, nor did it figure prominently in much news coverage, but it resonated with voters. In Florida, Democrat Bill McBride had a proposal for cutting class sizes and paying for it by a 50-cent per pack tax on cigarettes. But the math didn't work and time after time when citizens asked McBride about it, he had no comprehensive answer. As a result, what reporters were calling a neck-and-neck race that would go right down to the wire, turned into an easy victory for Republican Jeb Bush.

Political reporters must look beyond conventional wisdom. While they can't simply dismiss such analytical tools as historical models, public opinion polls and surveys, expert input and one-on-one interviews, they should never lose their journalistic skepticism.

7.3 Election Follow-Up

The morning after a general election is characterized by the euphoria of victory or the hangover of defeat. In some cases, often where the race itself was not much of a contest, there's not much need for more than one follow-up story, for example, that the incumbent was re-elected and pledges to continue what he or she has been doing.

In other cases, there are natural follow-ups. Unexpected events, unexpectedly close races, upsets or historic firsts should generate follow-up stories, often more than one. For example, when Democrat Douglas Wilder of Virginia became the first African American to be elected governor of a Southern state since reconstruction, the day-after follow-ups turned into a week's worth of stories. The same situation prevailed when former pro wrestler and Independent candidate Jesse Ventura was elected governor of Minnesota. (See chapter 2.4.)

The focus of election follow-ups are directed by the circumstances that dictate the story. They can be event driven, issue driven or anecdote driven. Some news organizations that downplay the importance of political coverage generally try to get away from political stories as quickly as possible.

Once in a while, something so out-of-the-ordinary happens, even in a runaway election, that it merits coverage. That's what happened the morning after Democrat Walter Mondale was drubbed by incumbent Republican President Ronald Reagan.

Mondale and the press corps that followed him throughout the campaign were about to leave St. Paul, Minnesota, bound for Washington. Mondale's son came on the intercom in the chartered press plane and told the reporters to put down their cameras, microphones, tape recorders and notepads because his father wanted a few minutes "off the record." A moment later, Walter "Fritz" Mondale came through the plane and shook hands with every reporter, producer, cameraperson and photographer on board. He knew almost every name and he thanked everybody for their coverage of his campaign. It was one of the most unusual moments in my political reporting experience. In keeping with my tacit agreement to go off the record, I reported the incident, much as I have related it here, without using any of the quotes or banter that took place on the plane.

It lives on as one of the classiest things I've ever seen a big-name politician do.

7.4 After the End of the Trail—Governance

Win or lose, as soon as the election is over, political campaigns—paid staff, volunteers, facilities, offices—close up faster than a cheap lawn chair in a hurricane. One or two people, usually including the campaign treasurer, stay around long enough to pay the final bills. And then that part of the political process is over until the next campaign, the next race, the next election cycle.

Nonetheless, the political process continues. The second step in American politics is governance, doing something for the people who elected you. This is the heavy lifting of politics. It is compromising, maneuvering and navigating the reefs and shoals of making government work.

As in almost any walk of life, there are obstructionists. My reportorial colleagues often called them "porcupines." No matter what the issue, they would roll up into a ball, stick out their sharp quills, and say "no" to everything. The porcupines do not want to govern. The reality is that porcupines are rare, primarily because the American people, generally, do not elect politicians who are not for something. Since 1992, when I covered President George H. W. Bush's reelection bid against Bill Clinton, I have believed that one of the primary reasons he lost was that he was not as skillful as Clinton in articulating what he favored. Every speech was loaded with what he was against. But when one analyzed the content, there wasn't much there that defined what he was for.

So after the election comes the business of doing something, or at least giving the appearance of doing something. For reporters, "one way or another, it's all covering politics," said *Newsday's* associate editor James Toedtman. "These people want to make sure they get reelected."

Governance is not a word you hear average people using. It's a word that politicians love. It creeps into the vocabulary of political journalism. But civilians look at you like you're some kind of wonk if you start talking about governance. Nonetheless, it's the substance and end result of the American political process. For reporters, it's where what was said, proposed, supported, rejected and/or promised during the campaign is tested.

Once the process has moved from the vote-getting business to the governing business, the playing field changes. This is where journalists start charting and comparing what was said during the campaign against what actually takes place. As the Rev. Jesse Jackson once said, "after they talked the talk did they walk the walk?" The office involved doesn't matter. President, members of Congress, governors, members of the state legislatures, mayors, city council members, county commissioners, school board members and every other elected official in the country is involved in governance. Virtually every time a reporter covers something before one of these officials or bodies, he or she is covering politics.

Newsday's Toedtman observed that electoral politics and the politics of governance "easily morph into one another." He used the example of Sen. Max Baucus (D-Mont.). "He's got a bunch of timber farmers in his state, and he's preoccupied with making sure they're not undercut by the timber industry in Canada. Now is that governance or electoral politics? He needs the votes of the timber workers and he needs the money of the guys who run these giant lumber companies. But it's also governance because he's beating on the door of the U.S. trade representative saying watch out for these interests."

Toedtman noted that whenever a reporter analyzes an issue, both sides of the process—electoral politics and the politics of governance—are in play. "Same way with steel or tobacco or textiles. The congressmen and senators all have the interests of their states and the industries that are in them at heart. So it's governance for sure. But I'm not sure where to draw the line because there are also a lot of voters who are dependent on these industries."

The more a reporter covers an elected official or group of elected officials, in most cases, the better the coverage gets. CNN's senior political correspondent Candy Crowley said, "After a while, if you've covered them long enough, you can read them. That was the fun of covering the White House. You knew when a guy was ticked off. Or you knew when something got shaded a little differently that something was going on with policy."

On the other hand, covering a newly elected official can be both enjoyable for the reporter and elucidative for the readers, viewers and listeners. Are they doing what they promised? Are they dodging what they promised? Are they getting bogged down in the process? Are they learning the ins and outs of governing? What are the reasons for their actions or lack of action? Reporters, however, must not be enticed into getting drawn into the internal working of the process. The consumers of news, for whom the reporter is writing or broadcasting, are less concerned with how something gets done than with what the end product is or is likely to be.

Washington Post reporter Helen Dewar covers the U.S. Senate as well as electoral politics. She says she approaches governance from a slightly different perspective than she does the campaign trail. "You need to familiarize yourself with all the nuances of the bill," she said. That means more than just reading it. It means talking to as many of the people—elected officials, staff, outside groups—as possible. It also means finding out exactly what the legislation, resolution or ordinance will do and will not do.

In the end, Dewar said reporters must remember their primary function: "You're still trying to write a compelling story that reaches readers directly, as opposed to writing it in governmentese. You're trying to wrap in all the political assessment of it as well."

That takes the reporter back to the electoral process. CBS News's chief Washington correspondent Bob Schieffer says politicians make many promises to many different interest groups in order to raise money, get votes and be elected. Politicians who disappoint the people who give them money can become endangered. He used one hypothetical example: "To raise money if you're in Fort Worth, say, you have to go to the goat-ropers' association and say, 'Folks, I want you to know that any issue that comes up that involves goat-ropers I will be with you morning, noon and nighttime too.' If you send out that letter, you'll raise some money from the goat-ropers.

"If you send out a letter that says, 'I want you to know that if I get to Washington, any time an issue involving you comes up, I'm going to give it my best judgment.' If you say that, you won't raise enough money to pay for the postage. You have to say, 'Goat-ropers, I'm your guy.' And then you have to send another one to the welders' union and another one to the people who belong to the country club.

"What happens is you have to sign off on so many issues in order to raise the money, that by the time you get to Washington, your positions are set in concrete. You cannot compromise. It is one of the reasons it is so difficult now to reach any kind of compromise on whatever issue. These people have signed off on the issues before they get to Washington and put themselves in the situation where they cannot compromise."

Tracking the money (see chapter 13.1) and who donated it to the elected official when he or she was a candidate can help lead reporters to the reasons behind the positions the official takes on various issues. To expand on Schieffer's example, how much money did the goat-ropers—collectively and individually—contribute to that Texas congressperson?

Public opinion polls on a wide range of subjects and in a significant number of different locations indicate that voters do not like legislative gridlock at any level. Sometimes reporters close to a legislative body are drawn into a stereotype of gridlock when legislation or other action moves slowly. The 1996 Telecommunications Bill had its roots at least four years earlier. The legislation was moving, but at a glacial pace.

The key is for reporters to have the depth of knowledge to be able to explain the difference between the sometimes agonizingly slow process and the real condition of legislative gridlock. Toedtman said gridlock is a story when "Congress is hopelessly bogged down and hopelessly overwhelmed by partisan politics or hopelessly confused." And he added that there's a dual purpose in reporting such a story. One is to tell the voters what their elected officials are failing to do and the other is "that congressmen also read your stories. And if you can show them how silly and stupid they really are being, then, in one small way, you can help them keep from doing what they're doing. You can help them be a little more honest and hold their feet to the fire. There's no question that politicians read what's reported about them."

How reporters cover governance influences the public perception of what government is all about. Unless you're working for a highly specialized news organization, reporting that gets mired in process is simply bad reporting. Larry Sabato, University of Virginia political science professor, said that it comes down to fundamentals. "The average young reporter ought to remember that most people are interested in politics because of the issues, and the issues that affect their lives— health care or the building of a new road or improving education for their kids or whatever it may be. They're interested in that." They are less interested in such mechanical issues as scheduling the legislative agenda, behind-the-scenes arm-twisting, and back-bench maneuvering aimed at obstruction.

In addition to the public perception of governance, the way reporters present their stories has a profound impact on how the public views their elected officials. CBS News's senior political editor Dotty Lynch chided reporters and news organizations that overlook the reality of what's taking place in favor of scandal or personality conflict. Just reporting about "the politician who screws up, doesn't show up, who lies—when they're there [at work] until 3 o'clock in the morning working on legislation is an incomplete picture."

She said the public perception of politicians is different than the perception of the journalists who cover them. "A study done for the Pew Foundation several years ago shows reporters actually see politicians as harder working than the general public, because reporters tend to know the good as well as the bad. . . . It was a really interesting finding that reporters were less cynical about politicians than was the general public."

8

Roadmap for Reporters: The Campaign Trail and Beyond

Politics and government used to be staples of American journalism. In recent times, however, many consultants have been advising radio and TV news directors, and to a lesser degree newspaper executives, that people don't care about politics and therefore it's ratings poison to do political stories. In March 2003, the *American Journalism Review* published an article by Dave Iverson, director of Best Practices in Journalism, and Tom Rosensteil, director of the Project of Excellence in Journalism. The two, in concert with the Pew Research Center for the People and the Press, conducted a survey examining what media consultants normally ask about political stories in their surveys.

The consultants ask if people are interested in news reports about government and politics. An overwhelming majority say no. Asked more specific questions, such as whether they are interested in seeing reports about how government can reduce health care costs or improve public safety, the answers are exactly opposite.

While news executives are still listening to their consultants, reporters often can sell political stories if they can persuade their bosses that such stories are interesting and important to their audience. Some reporters have gone so far as to call them something other than "political" stories.

"Politics is really about how things get done for people," said Deborah Potter, executive director of NewsLab. "So it's important for reporters to cut to the chase as much as they can and figure out what's really important in a campaign. What are these two or three or more candidates suggesting, promising, proposing, that will affect people in their daily lives? How can you then report on that in such a way that people understand that there's a clear choice to be made?"

8.1 Jump-Starting Your Coverage

Only a few political reporters, mostly those working for networks or large newspapers, have the luxury of being able to devote full time to the beat. Most have other day-to-day news- gathering responsibilities. It is fairly common for news organizations to dovetail certain non-campaign beats, especially those related to government, with political reporting—city government, county government, Congress and the statehouse all work well with political journalism. Acknowledging the time demands of day-to-day news coverage, reporters who want to cover politics should try to cover as many preliminary political events as possible as early in the cycle as possible. It is likely you'll cover many events that won't produce stories at this early stage of the process, but the advance work will prove to be extremely useful. Good political reporting does not begin when a campaign is in full swing.

Many reporters devote some of their personal time to this kind of advance work. Often the preliminary water-testing or early campaign events are held in the evening or on weekends in order to maximize the number of people attending. These kinds of events afford the opportunity for you to make yourself known to the candidate. Let the candidate know what news organization you work for. Exchange business cards. Most political reporters keep an extensive file of business cards.

Getting in on the ground floor will allow you to see the development of the campaign organizations and the people around the candidates. This type of advance coverage cannot be done by phone or Internet, but it is extremely valuable.

"There's no substitute for being there and covering something directly and alive," said Helen Dewar of *The Washington Post.* "The more things you can cover directly—and see and feel—the more alive your story's going to be. . . . One key thing is talking with the candidate so you can see how he or she responds to a question. And you can satisfy direct questions without going through press secretaries and campaign managers and spinmeisters."

Who the candidate picks for the campaign staff and why certain people are being picked are important early questions. Are they kindred political spirits? Do they offer unique skills such as fundraising, media savvy, past political experience? Are they old friends or classmates of the candidate? Have they been recruited to the campaign from constituencies the candidate hopes to reach? Are they the children, spouses or other relatives of big contributors or people the candidate would like to be big contributors? Have they been imposed on a candidate or campaign by the national or state political party? These questions will help you analyze why a candidate or campaign is doing things or not doing things as the race progresses.

I covered Arizona's Bruce Babbitt when he embarked on his unsuccessful bid for the 1984 Democratic presidential nomination. He attended several very low-key events in Manhattan in late autumn 1983 and I tagged along. This was so early in the campaign that Babbitt often traveled alone, by taxi. He'd show up at somebody's door or be announced by a doorman, go into an apartment and talk to 15 or 20 people. He talked about his vision for the country. He answered questions. He'd stay about an hour and head off to the next event. There were seldom more than two or three reporters there. I was sometimes the only one. It gave me a very good impression of the man as well as the candidate.

Several months later, when he was besieged by the battalion of newspeople covering the Iowa caucuses, he'd look for familiar faces, reporters that he recognized from the early days, and we could usually get a question or two to him. He'd stop and talk for a moment.

The hard reality of a political campaign is that after all the time, effort, energy and money is expended, somebody is going to win and somebody is going to lose. Babbitt came in near the bottom of the crowded field that year in Iowa. I ran into him in a hotel lobby the morning after the caucuses and asked him the inevitable question about his future. He told me enough that I knew what was going to happen. "When?" I asked one of his senior staffers, who I had also known since those early days in Manhattan. "Later today or tomorrow morning," was the answer, accompanied by a telling sigh and unhappy look. I was able to file a story saying Babbitt was going to call it quits, and within 24 hours he did. A little bit of early effort paid off in getting a leg up on the competition.

8.2 Doing Better Interviews

Getting politicians who are running for office to talk to you is never very hard, although it becomes increasingly difficult as campaigns move toward Election Day and demands on the candidates' time increases. Access generally diminishes the closer you get to Election Day. The level of difficulty involved in getting interviews is also related to what office is being sought. It's always easier to get a county commission candidate to give you an interview than a candidate for president. Nonetheless, as with almost everything else connected with covering politics, the amount of advance preparation the reporter does will have an impact on the quality of the stories ultimately produced. Interviews are no exception.

Young reporters tend to make two basic mistakes. They have a tendency to go into interviews with a list of questions and they often do not listen carefully to the answers as they are given. This is sometimes the result of nerves, sometimes the result of inexperience, sometimes a combination of both. The result is often an interview that could have been better or an interview that could have produced a better, more interesting story if the reporter had only listened to what was being said and pursued it.

The best interviewers tend to be the best listeners. Listening is not just hearing the sounds the interviewee is making, but understanding what's being said and what's not. Good listening will lead the reporter to what's being avoided, what's being spun and what's being massaged by the politician. Listening will tell a reporter when a question has been sidestepped or ignored altogether. Listening leads to follow-up questions.

Such seasoned political interviewers as CBS's Bob Schieffer, CNN's Candy Crowley and Fox News's Brit Hume note that they do not write down specific questions, but go in with a list of subject areas about which they want to ask. Schieffer called it "a game plan" and added, "The secret to interviewing is not the questions, but listening to the answers. The second question ought to play off something that the guy said when you asked the first question. That's where you get the news. Why did he say it the way he said it? Why did he put emphasis in one area when you might have thought he'd put emphasis some place else? The best follow-up question you can ask is, 'What do you mean by that?'"

Schieffer said that politicians will often want to recite a list of talking points and be done with the interview. Asking that question— "what do you mean?"—will force the candidate or politician to reveal whether they have anything more to offer, whether they've given the issue serious consideration or whether their position is superficial.

"The best questions are usually the most obvious," said Schieffer. "Short questions are better than long questions. They're the questions your viewer or reader wants answered. What does this mean to me? Why should I care about that?"

Young reporters often are timid about challenging older individuals. Get over it. It is entirely appropriate for reporters to ask for clarification and expansion in follow-up questions. It is also appropriate—even though politicians hate it when it happens—that reporters challenge inconsistencies and contradictions.

In some ways interviewing incumbents is easier than interviewing challengers. Incumbents have a record that reporters can check before asking the questions. Incumbents made promises during their previous election campaigns that can be included in the interview preparation.

Challengers often adopt a two-pronged strategy: Lay out what they object to in the incumbent's job performance and offer a plan for what they will do if elected. "How is that going to work?" is often a question that will get the challenger to expand on a proposal. It can also expose any gaps in the candidate's own preparation. If the answer is vague or incomplete, the reporter ought to follow up with a request for further explanation. If the challenger is making an assertion about his or her opponent that doesn't square with the record compiled by the reporter, then ask about it.

When politicians throw out statistics and numbers, do some arithmetic to make sure they are accurate and add up. Statistics can be manipulated. Beware of the ways in which statistics can be skewed. If a politician, for example, starts talking about what the "average person" is going to do, get, obtain in benefits or otherwise amass from a certain program or proposal, consider the nature of the demographics in question. Is a disproportionate number of people within the universe being considered in any given category that may create a false impression of what "average" is? Is the area in question extremely affluent? Extremely poor? Well educated? Undereducated? Ask the candidate who he or she considers an "average person" within this context.

Every journalism professor in the country says it, but as a matter of practical application, it is absolutely true: The more homework you do before an interview, the better that interview and the subsequent story are going to be. Political journalism requires constant attention. Jamie

Dupree, news director for Cox Radio's Washington bureau, said keeping up with the news starts early in the morning and goes right up to lights-out. "At night before I go to bed, I always check the wires and the major newspaper web sites just to make sure I'm not missing anything. I even check [Matt] Drudge [the on-line gossip columnist who often deals with politicians and political scandal] just to see what's going on. It's constant. You've got to do it all the time or you'll end up falling behind."

Michael Freedman, vice president for communication at The George Washington University, saw it from the other side when he was press secretary to Rep. David Bonior [D-Mich.]. "I'm thinking, as a press secretary, why aren't they asking better questions? Why aren't they fleshing out the issues?"

Freedman said skilled press secretaries and campaign message-meisters would often supply questions for local reporters, like authors' publicists who hand out questions for interviewers too lazy to read the book. Freedman said that he was "embarrassed" for those reporters who just read the questions verbatim.

The campaign trail is loaded with potholes. Among presidential campaigners, Ronald Reagan and Bill Clinton were among the best at what the political pros call "staying on message." This is the political term of art that means the politician is going to say what he/she wants no matter what the questions are from journalists. In Clinton's 1992 campaign the message was, "It's the economy, stupid!" And he stuck to it religiously. Reporters feel they are getting stiffed by a candidate staying on message. No matter what question the reporter asked, Reagan and Clinton would answer what they wanted.

The goals of reporters and the goals of politicians are often at odds. Reporters want news; politicians want their face and their message to be in the news, but only in a light that is flattering and in a context that is controlled. Reporters want clear answers; politicians want to stay on message. Reporters want to be able to tell readers, listeners and viewers how certain proposals will work and how the proposals will affect them; politicians do not want to be so specific during a mid-campaign interview that it will come back to haunt them later. Reporters want something spontaneous, fresh and new in their interviews; politicians work very hard to repeat their campaign themes, to stay on message and to provide reporters with as little fresh material as possible save for what veteran reporters call the "sound bite du jour."

That's the daily quote that's inserted into the stump speech to provide reporters with something that seems new. It's always a well-considered, well-tested quote that will be helpful to the campaign, designed to enhance the "message" without changing the message or detracting from it.

It is not at all unusual to see or read news stories in which several reporters have had interviews with a candidate and to see or read the same quote in each account. Politicians routinely do that, in case the reporters missed the sound bite du jour in the stump speech.

Young reporters are appropriately taught to ask open-ended questions in order to obtain the most information. They are trained to work from the general to the specific and to ask closed-ended (yes or no) questions when they need to pin somebody down on a very specific point. Politicians train themselves to provide reporters with "the quote" or "the sound bite" no matter how bad or how obtuse the question is. Top notch pols occasionally go so far as to rehearse their answers with key staffers before they ever face a real reporter. "The politician is there to deliver a message," said CBS's Schieffer. "The reporter is there to get to the truth as closely as he possibly can."

There are times when a trained politician simply will not provide specific answers no matter how reporters frame the questions. A Washington, D.C., criminal investigation provides an extreme example. In the summer of 2001, Chandra Levy, a young intern in the office of Rep. Gary Condit (D-Calif.), mysteriously disappeared. Foul play was suspected. It was widely reported that the 50-something congressman and the 20-something intern had a romantic relationship. Reporters had been chasing Condit through the halls of the Capitol for weeks, but he refused to answer questions. At the height of the investigation Condit agreed to a prime-time TV interview with journalist Connie Chung. Two key questions were: what was the nature of Condit's relationship with Levy and what, if anything, did he know about her mysterious disappearance?

Despite dogged questioning by Chung, Condit stuck to what, in effect, was a script. He would not deviate from it. He would not expand on it. He would go no further than what were obviously prepared and well-rehearsed answers. He refused to discuss his relationship with Levy and he repeated over and over that he knew nothing about her disappearance. The short-term result was heightened public skepticism and the long-term result was political disaster. Not only was

Condit not reelected to another term in Congress, he didn't make it past the Democratic primary.

Aspiring political reporters should be cognizant of the fact that good, professional campaigns, even for local or state offices, know how the news business works. (Political pros often call it "the care and feeding" of the press. The connotation is less than flattering.) For example, it is not unusual for a candidate to agree to an interview seemingly at the spur of the moment. This is seldom as spontaneous as it may seem and is often close to the reporter's deadline, and with the specific intent of preventing the reporter from being able to balance it with the other side.

Reporters can reduce, if not eliminate, the effectiveness of the tactic by making a last-minute phone call, even with a deadline looming. Opposing candidates and/or campaign organizations will usually go out of their way to provide some kind of response, lest the other side hog the spotlight.

8.3 Detours from the Campaign Trail

"When you're on the [candidate's] airplane you develop what I call the aluminum tube syndrome," said CBS's Bob Schieffer. "You're inside this airplane. You travel with these other reporters. They're your competitors but they're also your friends. You become part of the entourage of a candidate. And if you talk only to the candidate and his spinners you just don't get a balanced view of what's going on. There were reporters on the McGovern plane in 1972 who were absolutely convinced that McGovern might pull an upset. Of course, we all know that didn't happen. All you had to do was stand back a bit to understand that was not going to happen."

"The worst place to get the story is on the candidate's airplane," he added. "The best place to get the story is on the ground. Talk to the voters. Talk to people in the community. See what kind of an impact that the candidate and the campaign is having on the people."

When reporters are either following a single candidate or covering a campaign with multiple candidates, it is easy to be seduced into covering only what is being said on the trail. It's an easy type of coverage. The sound bites and quotes are there for you every day. The events are easily accessible. The sound bite du jour and event du jour are elements of the political process, but not the only elements.

"Part of our job is basically to describe what's happening out there," said *Washington Post* columnist David Broder. "So some of our coverage is driven and should be driven by what the candidates choose to talk about. But we can't be deaf and blind to other things that are going on. And that's why I think it's useful to get away from the bus or the plane from time to time and bounce what's happening in the campaign off the voters and see what they're making of it. And finding out what questions they have that are not being answered."

Broder's technique is legendary. He targets ticket-splitting precincts and knocks on doors, engaging voters in "conversations." His goal is to find out what the voters have on their minds, so he doesn't color his conversations with anything from the campaign trail. (See *A Conversation with David Broder,* following chapter 4.)

Reporters need to step back from the campaign itself and analyze the impact of what the candidates are saying. This is the time to call on your contact list (see chapter 5.1) and talk to people outside of the process as Broder does. Include academic analysts, interest groups and citizen groups, as well as individual voters. If your news organization conducts polls or there is a new public opinion poll regarding the race you're covering, that is often a good peg for this type of off-the-campaign-trail story.

Look beyond the horse race and produce a story that deals with the impact of what the candidates are saying, or not saying, about certain specific issues or subjects. Look at both the narrow impact on the campaign and the broader impact on the voters. In order to vary campaign coverage, some news organizations make it a point to do these kinds of analytical stories from outside the campaigns several times during the primary season, and several times again during the general election race.

"A lot of political writing and coverage is pretty mediocre," said Wally Dean, senior fellow with The Project for Excellence in Journalism. "It tends to be one-dimensional. It tends to be all the same. You hear from the same kinds of characters, usually middle-aged white guys in ties and business cards who work in government buildings, who speak one kind of language. They speak in terms that the public doesn't use. You need to use reporting tools that are useful to the receiving end of your journalism not to the producing end of your journalism."

One of those tools involves looking beyond the sound bite and the quote to what your readers, viewers and listeners care about. What matters to them? It is often something different than what matters to the political pros. A smaller number of slightly longer interviews with a few more questions seeking depth will produce a better journalistic product than racing in and doing a whole lot of one- or two-question man-on-the-street interviews that will likely yield little substance.

Broadcasters often are guilty of exploiting this hit-and-run technique. They string together three or four fast sound bites, often without even naming those people talking, and say they have taken the pulse of the community. They haven't. That kind of reporting gives viewers and listeners very little of substance regarding the candidates or the issues. It also reinforces the public perception that radio and television provide only superficial content—because it is superficial.

Two longer sound bites (in which the individual voters are named and which express contrasting points of view) provide the basis for better, more thorough, and ultimately more responsible campaign coverage. Two longer sound bites may not have the MTV-style flash and flair that some consultants say viewers want, but they provide more useful information than the flash and flair, without consuming any more airtime.

While talking to voters and seeking out experts, interest groups and others not directly involved in a campaign often make for good journalism, there are many examples of good campaign stories that are out in the open, but not in the realm of traditional candidate coverage. The best political reporters keep their story sensors finely tuned to what's going on literally outside the bus window.

"The '92 campaign, I covered Clinton," said CBS Radio News correspondent Bob Fuss. "When we left New York on the first of his bus trips, there was an extraordinary story there that convinced me, and a lot of other people, that he really had a good chance of beating President [George H. W.] Bush. It certainly didn't look that way going into it. But the story was what you saw from the bus along the roads. We would be driving on these back roads in rural areas and there would be thousands of people lining the roads. We'd pull into a town with a population of 15,000 and there would be 20,000 people there who'd come in from all the surrounding areas."

Fuss provided another example of a campaign story that could easily have slipped under the radar. "Traveling on the Gore campaign [in 2000] you would not get from the speeches any notion that gun control was important." Fuss said the only way to find that story was to go outside the "bubble" that surrounds a candidate and talk to people who attended an event. "I remember asking one local politician in

West Virginia why he [Gore] wasn't doing better there and the answer was 'gun control.' There's a lot of under-the-radar stuff in campaigns that can be hard to find. For example, the Reagan campaign in 1980 started using a lot of Spanish-language radio ads and very few people caught on to it. There was a story there about some of the very specific kinds of demographic targeting."

Newsday's Elaine Povich said, "The job of the reporter is to go underneath the blanket and find out what's really there. It may be a really pretty blanket lying there in the park, but what's under it? A log or an alligator? You don't know until you lift it up." She recalled an incident during the 2000 George W. Bush campaign in which his media people had devised a setting to highlight a trade issue. Bush would deliver his speech against a backdrop of shipping crates. "They had these crates stacked up and they all said, 'Made in the USA.' It made a great television picture. It took some enterprising reporter on the scene to pull back the label and see that it covered up 'made in Taiwan.'"

8.4 Drive Carefully on the Infobahn

The Internet, the information superhighway, the worldwide web! This may be the greatest journalistic tool since the telephone. But every reporter needs to approach it with skepticism. Information on the Internet is both abundant and easy to access, but not all of it is accurate. In fact some of it is patently false or misleading, potentially libelous and journalistically dangerous.

Reporters who use information from the web without verifying it do so at their peril. Legitimate web sites can be tainted. Even items that seem beyond reproach need to be double-checked. When my research assistant, Dawn Rogers, digs up a legal case or official document for me, I require her to find it in two places and compare the two versions, lest one or the other be contaminated by tampering. If hackers and those who would do mischief can get into the NASA computer system or shut down the computer network of a major corporation, it follows that they would have little difficulty in getting into other web sites and tinkering with the data just for the fun of it.

Reporters have no way of knowing if information obtained on the Internet is legitimate without cross-checking and verifying. Just because something says it was written by David Broder or Bob Schieffer doesn't mean it was. Just because the web site appears to be that of a legitimate agency or organization doesn't mean that it is.

"I'm dealing with the Internet a lot now and the standards on the Internet just aren't as great as they are in print and in television. People throw stuff up there," said Dotty Lynch, senior political editor for CBS News. She said some of her interns and entry level people have not been trained in double- and triple-checking the accuracy of information. "They 'Google' something. When you ask them for information they do a 'Google' [search] and they assume the first thing they get is factual." Using a search engine such as Google is fine, but not all information that pops up is equal. "The relative value of a particular source that they find on Google needs checking and rechecking," said Lynch.

There are several warning signs for journalists when they encounter information on the web. If you find an article, say, by David Broder somewhere other than on *The Washington Post* web site or on the web site of a Washington Post News Service subscriber, be wary. The same thing applies to all unsigned articles or information for which it is difficult or impossible to find the source, author or links to other sites where the information can be verified. Beware of postings that have no date or that originated on a single-posting or personal web site. If it looks too good to be true, it probably is. For the most part if you find one of these problems with Internet information it's a good idea not to include it in your story, even with appropriate attribution.

When reporters determine that a web site is legitimate and that the information is accurate, they must attribute what is obtained from web sources. It is no different than using information from books, magazine articles, newspapers and/or any other non-web source. Foremost, it prevents the reporter from being accused of plagiarism. (See chapter 12.1.) Secondly it allows the reader, viewer or listener to assign a value to the information, especially if it comes from a political source, corporate source or interest group that may have a vested interest in getting out their particular spin on an issue. Knowing the source of information is necessary to knowing how valuable, accurate and relevant the information is.

"I find that some of the young people who come in don't understand the need to attribute," said CBS's Lynch. "I keep saying, that's stealing. We didn't get that on our own. Where did you get that? Oh, you read that in *The Boston Globe*? All you have to do is put 'according *The Boston Globe* and you're fine.'"

A Conversation with Brit Hume

Managing editor and chief Washington correspondent: Fox News
Host: *Special Report with Brit Hume*

What you see on television is exactly what you get when you encounter Brit Hume. He is witty and articulate, always impeccably dressed. I knew him during his 23-year tenure as an ABC News correspondent and covered the 1992 campaign of President George H. W. Bush with him. I've always considered him smart, but it wasn't until I interviewed him for this book that I realized how much he had thought about and analyzed the relationship of the news media and politics.

When Hume left ABC to join Fox in 1996, many people in the industry were predicting failure for the fledgling network. When I sat down with him in May 2003, the Fox News Channel was riding high in the ratings and Hume's nightly Special Report was enjoying enthusiastic critical and popular support.

His awards include an Emmy for his coverage of the 1991 Persian Gulf War. He is the author of two books.

I asked him about his show and its role as a vehicle for political coverage:

B.H.: "If you're doing what I do, which is a cable show, you don't have quite the same obligation that you have with a broadcast show where you're reaching for a mass audience. I was asked to do an hour show, out of a 24-hour schedule, with a focus on politics. It was never going to be pure politics in the sense that CNN's Inside Politics was pure politics and dealt only with issues that affected the next election, the world of electoral politics, the world of consultants and primary campaigns and so on.

"I always believed that the political story is the struggle for power that at times is engaged in running for election, but most of the time it's a struggle for power by people who are already elected who are fighting it out to get the upper hand on given issues. Sometimes the story that affects politics the most is happening in another country, as in Afghanistan or Iraq. I was always looking for the story that people in Washington weren't thinking or talking about.

"At the end of the day, I was blessed to be able to do a show for people who like politics, instead of trying to do what the networks are trying to do all the time, which is trying to do politics for people who don't like politics. There was always going to be some ceiling on the audience. We're just not going to get a lot of people who don't care anything about politics.

"But with the half-hourly updates, we've tried to give people a sense that they can get their news here if they like our focus and not watch network news. I don't think we'll ever be able to wean people away from local [TV news], because nobody can. You can't give people their sports, can't give people their weather. You can't tell them what happened down the street."

R.A: *Give me a little of your background. How did you come to be a political reporter?*

B.H.: "I started out working as a general assignment cub reporter in 1965. I grew up here [in Washington, D.C.]. I never found the news in local communities where I lived very compelling compared to what I'd grown up around. Having grown up here, with all this stuff happening in your neighborhood, in your home town, didn't make the zoning disputes in Glastonbury, Connecticut, all that compelling. It was, ultimately, the raw material of the work I was doing, but I always wanted to get back here. I mean, if the president's here, how excited can I get about the mayor?

"To me the correspondents I looked up to were the people I saw from Washington. So I always wanted to be here, partly because it was home and partly because it was news Mecca. I always thought the ultimate stories were elections and conventions and presidents. That seemed to me to be historic and more important than anything else."

R.A.: *What was your first campaign?*

B.H.: "You could technically say the first campaign I covered was the very, very brief campaign of [Republican] James Buckley for president in 1976. But the first campaign I covered as a reporter on the trail was George Bush, the father, in 1980. Then I covered Mondale in '84, then Jackson in '88, then Bush reelection, Clinton reelection and then in 2000 I was in an anchor chair."

R.A.: *Local news directors are constantly hearing from their consultants that politics is boring so let's not put very much of it on the air. Is there an argument against that?*

B.H.: "I think there is. You have an affirmative obligation as a journalist to do two things: be interesting and be fair, not in that particular order. If you can satisfy those demands I think you can succeed with almost any subject. If you go in as a journalist with the attitude that stuff isn't interesting, in and of itself, then you're going to have a terrible problem. If you think it's interesting and know what's interesting about it, then you have a real shot at making it interesting to other people.

"Politics, particularly campaigns, are compelling stories. There's a journey involved. There's a race involved. Somebody's ambitions are going to be realized and somebody's going to fail. There's a real human story there to tell. There's also a clash of ideas and ideals.

"We've had a tremendously positive response at Fox News, where we do a lot of politics. I think that maybe one reason that local news doesn't do a great deal of politics is that they're not very good at it. . . .

"I do think that there's a terrible dearth of political coverage, and once that starts it becomes self-reinforcing. If you're a successful news organization that people trust, when something's happening and they hear about it someplace else, they come to you. They want to hear what you have to say about it because they trust you.

"If your audience isn't hearing about politics anywhere else and you have to introduce them to it, then get them to care about it, and then deliver your version of the coverage of it, you've got a terrible burden to carry. So to some extent it's self-reinforcing. If nobody else is doing it, it means you've got to pick up the whole ball and carry the whole thing. You tell them here's who this person is and here's why you should care, and at some point you've got to get around to telling them what happened. [Shakes head.] That's a problem."

R.A.: *Let me deal with the issue of bias. Bernie Goldberg wrote his book alleging a left bias at CBS. Your network has taken criticism from the left for alleged right-leaning bias. Does bias exist?*

B.H.: "Yes. It's a very serious problem. And each day I don't know whether to fume about it or thank God for it. Bias has given us the professional opportunity and the competitive advantage that we have. There are a great many people out there who didn't like what they were getting from news because of their view that there was bias, or people who had completely given up altogether. They are, today, the bulk of our audience.

"I have thought a lot about bias. I used to think, back in the '70s when I was covering the news, that it was a canard that there was a liberal bias. And I came, eventually, to believe otherwise. . . .

"Most reporters that I know wouldn't be caught dead attending a political meeting other than to cover it. It just wouldn't happen. They're not consciously trying to skew the news to help one partisan over another. That's not how it works. People do carry a certain set of personal views with them. And purity of heart about bias is not enough.

"Bias is very insidious. Unbiased reporting, in my view, begins with a consciousness of bias. If you carry with you an awareness that the person you're covering or the news conference you're going to write about represent ideas that you don't agree with or do agree with, right away that ought to be a danger signal. And you should go into it with the notion that I need to be careful that my own views don't creep in here. I need to be careful about language. I need to choose my language very carefully.

"The political effect of words used by a reporter making sure not to be biased is very great over time. Let me give you an example. Years ago I did a piece for one of the opinion journals about one of the political struggles that was going on in Washington. I said, quite accurately, that the Democrats wanted to raise taxes. At that point the Democrats were pushing to increase taxes. The editor of the publication, who may have been more favorably disposed to the Democrats than I was at the time, changed the wording to 'the Democrats think we need a tax increase.' That's also equally true, but far more benign in the way it sounds.

"Both approaches are true. Both are defensible. Arguably, you can say both are biased. But it constitutes a wonderful example—without ever straying from fact, there's nothing extreme about the language, there's nothing overtly pejorative or favorable. But I cite that as one example of the impact of language. And it's the kind of thing that a reporter in a hurry, banging away on the keyboard, has not got time to guard against unless he or she is very conscious of it and very conscious of where sensitivities exist on issues. And if you are, and you're good, you can weed that stuff out. . . .

"Rob, if I were putting this in a way that I thought was a particularly good way of teaching this, I would almost want your textbook not to be widely circulated. I don't particularly want my colleagues who don't get this to get it. Because their failure to do so constitutes our competitive advantage at Fox News, where we've tried very hard to get it.

"Now at times, people have said of us that we've strayed too far in the other direction and where the other media are positive we're negative or vice versa. That's something we have to work on, something we have to worry about. But we do worry about it."

R.A.: *How should young people prepare for a career in journalism?*

B.H.: "Don't major in English. Don't major in philosophy. Don't major in psychology. Don't major in physics. Major in history. The most useful thing for you to know if you're a journalist is history. And any practical experience is better than almost anything."

Section III
Nuts and Bolts

9

Gadgets, Gizmos, and Cyberspace: Technology on the Trail

Nothing has changed the face of politics and political journalism over the last half century as much as technology. It has changed the way candidates stage, shoot, edit and package their campaign ads. (See chapter 10.3.) It's changed the content of the ads. It's changed the way candidates solicit money. It's changed the way journalists research, cover and report. It's changed the way newspapers are published and radio and TV news is presented. It's also changed the way in which the American people receive much of their political information.

In the 1950s, television news was in its infancy, radio provided rudimentary political news mostly in the form of headlines, and most people got their serious news from newspapers. By the 1970s, Americans were riveted to live television coverage of such epoch political events as the Watergate hearings. The number of daily newspapers in America was on the decline. News had ceased to exist on many local radio stations. By the mid-1980s, there was news on the Internet. And by the early 2000s people were able to get news headlines and breaking stories using their computers, palmtops, cellular telephones and electronic pagers.

9.1 From Apples to BlackBerries

When I first started in the business in 1967, television news was shot on 16mm mag-stripe film, radio news was covered with heavy portable reel-to-reel tape recorders, newspapers were produced in hot type, and every newsroom had at least one clicking and clattering teletype machine that delivered the product of a wire service.

"Newsrooms were noisy places," said Deborah Potter, former CBS and CNN correspondent and executive director of NewsLab. "Everybody was banging on manual typewriters and shouting at each other. Everybody smoked. I sat across from [the late CBS News correspondent] Dallas Townsend and watched him consume three packs of Camels, not in a day, in a shift. We used pay phones with dimes. We dictated scripts to people who cut them into stone. I worked at a [TV] station where things would get lost in the soup [film processor] or come out various rainbow colors but not the ones you shot them in."

In those days computers were room-sized behemoths at places like M.I.T. and Cal Poly, almost exclusively the province of research scientists and the military. Personal computers, laptops and palmtops were the stuff of science fiction, like Dick Tracy's two-way wrist radio. There was no Internet. Nor were there cellular telephones, computer typesetting and layout, digital audio or video recorders, videophones, satellite transmission and distribution, virtual video generators, digital manipulation of video and still photos, or e-mail.

Today, reporters and politicians use all of these tools and more. Even old-timers who at one point cursed the newfangled machines as progeny of the devil have come to recognize them and rely on them as indispensable. But the technology is a double-edged sword. Most journalists in all media concede that technology has both improved things and made them worse. They say there's better access to more information, more sources of information, better communication and better delivery systems for getting news to the public. At the same time, they say there's too much information to process, problems with the accuracy and quality of much that's on the Internet, too many systems for delivering news which dilute quality and too little time for the kinds of reporting that produces stories that connect with readers, viewers and listeners.

There is little doubt that the new technology is here to stay and, in fact, newer, better, faster technology with more capabilities than ever is making its way to the market every day.

For years, reporters used to travel with portable Olivetti typewriters in little blue cases. Most of them put something distinctive on their case to distinguish it from every other reporter's little blue case. Around 1980, Radio Shack introduced the TRS-80, a portable computer, and the news business was changed forever. (We irreverent reporters called them "Trash 80s.") They worked on double-A batteries and by today's standards were only a small step above the old Olivetti typewriters. The memory was extremely limited and they were slow.

The modem was a pair of rubber cups that fit over the earpiece and mouthpiece of a telephone.

Fox News's chief Washington correspondent Brit Hume said the TRS-80 transformed how he and his producer did their jobs on the 1984 campaign when he was with ABC News. "The producer found that it was a great logging tool. And we even had a little miniature printer back then that printed out stuff on paper about the width of a cash register receipt. But you could do logs [of videotape] on it. So we'd go to an event and run an audiotape recorder. We'd get out of the event and into the car or the bus headed to the airport or to the next event and he'd be doing the verbate [verbatim transcript]. . . . He'd print out a copy for him and a copy for me and by the end of the day I would have in my hands everything the candidate said that day.

"He was then able to feed the log into the mainframe computer system at ABC. So when the tape came back, the log would be printed out and put in the box with the tape and then put into the library. This was incredible. Up to that point, stuff like this couldn't be done from the road. Somebody would have to log it all at headquarters. [Now] it meant that if we were going to do a great big piece—where we'd want to pull together lots of stuff from many different days—we could go through our logs, which he pasted into notebooks, pick the stuff we'd want, call New York, identify the tapes, and have the stuff sent to some feed-point somewhere. It would be there when we got there and we could do a great big long piece on day-of-air. We did that more than once. It was a tremendous breakthrough."

In addition, the word-processing capabilities of those crude computers were little short of a miraculous improvement over the old method of scratching margin notes in your script or story or physically cutting and pasting pieces of paper when the story changed or you got some late information or quotes.

Within that same decade, the 1980s, the Internet started to become a powerful weapon in the reportorial arsenal. But just as the chainsaw replaced the handsaw and made the job of cutting trees faster and easier, there were also unintended consequences. With chainsaws they included more injuries, mistakes and unregulated clear-cutting. While the Internet gave reporters faster access to more information than they ever had before, it was far from perfect. Information often was posted that was wildly wrong. Without double- and triple-checking facts and sources, reporters run the risk of going on the air or into print wrong. (See chapter 8.4.)

Nonetheless, most reporters agree with Cox Radio's Jamie Dupree: "I don't know how I did my job without it."

"When I first started doing this, certainly in the '70s, we used to depend on clips from Congressional Quarterly to build our research," said CBS News's senior political editor Dotty Lynch. "That would come in a week or 10 days after an event. With *Hotline* [a daily political newsletter with transcripts of what the major news media were saying] that started in '87, suddenly you could find what *The Des Moines Register* said within four or five hours of when it was on the stands in Des Moines. If you were covering the Iowa caucuses, what happened there yesterday was suddenly very easily accessible. Now that we have the Internet you don't have to wait for any intermediary. You just go directly to *The Des Moines Register* and see what happened. So the speed of getting information and the amount of information that's available is dramatically different."

David Broder of *The Washington Post* agreed that the Internet is a fine tool, but he cautioned, "You have to remind yourself now, because there's so much on the web, that the real job is still to go out and report the story. There is a temptation to just wait until the text comes up or go to a web site on the subject—particularly in this town where there are so many think tanks. It's tempting to just sit at your desk and think that you're doing your reporting. But in fact you're not. You still need feet and eyes out there to have some sense about what is going on."

Nonetheless, Fox's Hume says some things are possible today only because of the Internet. "I do a feature called The Grape Vine, which is a compendium of usually four items that somebody else has done but which I think are interesting and likely not to have been nationally distributed. . . . We're scavenging in newspapers for interesting items that would not have received widespread attention. They all come from the Internet. It's all surfing and searching. This feature wouldn't exist without the Internet. It wouldn't be possible."

Many college journalism schools are now requiring students to take courses in Computer Assisted Reporting. CAR, as it's widely known, provides students with a general understanding of the computer and Internet as journalistic tools. CAR is fundamentally a three-pronged process: finding the information and/or data, managing it and using it. Put succinctly, if a reporter finds the stuff but doesn't manage it (file it, organize it, synthesize it, catalogue it), it is difficult or impossible to put it to use.

Hand-in-hand with the rise of the Internet is the widespread use of e-mail. In political journalism it's a two-way conduit through which reporters can communicate with candidates, campaigns, experts and other sources and through which all of those people can reach reporters. "I get so many e-mails a day you can't imagine it," said Cox Radio's Dupree. "I hated the old fax machines. They took forever. Somebody would say, 'I'll send it to you' and 40 minutes later it wasn't there. I went away for four days and I had more than 600 e-mails when I got back."

CBS Radio News correspondent Bob Fuss said e-mail permits more complete campaign coverage. "It used to be very difficult. If I was traveling with the Democrat, the Republican candidate would physically send people to the press area to hand us things. . . . Sometimes they'd come to the hotels and stick things under the doors at night trying to get information to us. It's much easier now. [In 2000] I was traveling with Gore and I'd get e-mail from the Bush campaign or they'd call me or I could call them. So I could get an immediate read on their responses to what Gore was saying or the campaign was saying."

"E-mail is also a wonderful new tool because you can engage in conversations all over the world," said James Toedtman, associate editor of *Newsday*. "I've done stories where I've talked to people by e-mail on all continents. You still need to be aware of time zones, but not like you used to when you were making telephone calls. If you send an e-mail to Tanzania, they're already in bed, but when they get the message you'll have a response by the time you get to work the next morning."

Nonetheless, Toedtman conceded that the downside is being inundated with various types of communications. "It comes at you from so many directions. We've got faxes. We've got e-mails. We've got phone calls. We've got people mailing stuff. Every morning it takes me an hour just to get through the e-mail that's accumulated overnight."

"We're in a new world, even more than campaign 2000. E-mail and Internet are the way everybody is communicating now. It's faster. The interaction that you can have in e-mail in some ways is better than phone, where you don't miss each other or have to call back five or six times," said CBS's Lynch.

You no longer need a computer to send and receive e-mail. In fact, the rage among Washington journalists and politicians is a wireless e-mail transmitter and receiver called a BlackBerry, the product of a Canadian company. (As this book goes to press several other companies are introducing e-mail devices similar to the BlackBerry.)

"Wonderful thing happened the other day," said Lynch. Connecticut Democratic senator and presidential candidate "Joe Lieberman's press secretary, very funny young guy named Jano Cabrera—he was Vice President Gore's press secretary—does everything by BlackBerry. We were on this small plane going down to South Carolina [for the first 2004 Democratic presidential debate]. There were about 36 seats—all political reporters and four senators and their aides. So Jano gets his BlackBerry out and writes a note to his e-mail list of maybe about 90 people: 'Am sitting next to Senator Bob Graham [D-Fla.] on the plane and I have no clue what to talk to him about. Any suggestions for small talk?'"

Lynch said there is a downside to the new technology as well: "When you're having lunch now with a press secretary for a campaign they're half talking to you and half looking at e-mails from other reporters and people on their campaign. It's very distracting."

Almost every newspaper in the country now has a web site. So do all the television networks and many radio and television stations. Those web pages provide an additional source of news for the public and allow the organizations that own them to promote their other news delivery platforms. They have also increased the workload on journalists and news organizations.

"We have two news holes," said *Newsday's* Toedtman. "We have the shrinking news hole [in the regular newspaper] and the news hole without walls. I had a story in today's paper that was limited in size, but we produced the larger version of it, with charts, on the web site. And as more and more people are getting their information on the web, that remains a viable option."

Broder added, "We have deadlines all the time now. Instead of worrying about where your story's going to be at 6:30 in the evening, you have to worry about where it is at 10 o'clock in the morning, because if something has happened they want it on the web. More people read *The Washington Post* on the web now than read it in the old format. It's absolutely changed our lives."

In some cases the new demands require newspaper reporters to stop reporting long enough to file and/or update their stories once or several times during the day. In the old days, with one deadline, that was not the case.

Television and radio are impacted as well. CBS News's deputy Washington bureau chief Tom Mattesky explained, "In effect, we are now serving all of the traditional broadcasts we've always served but we are also paying very close attention to what we are putting on-line and what we're putting [on radio] in the cars with people driving home from work that they can be teased a little bit, intrigued a little bit with what we've been covering so that they will then want to tune in that night to the Evening News or to watch an in-depth story we'll be doing in prime time on one of the magazine shows."

9.2 The Wireless World

The first time I used a cellular phone on the campaign trail was covering the Iowa caucuses in 1984. It was about the size of a sewing machine and was incredibly heavy. When I got about two miles outside of Des Moines, service vanished. I was in a cell-free zone.

Today, virtually no reporter leaves home without a cellular telephone.

The old days on the campaign trail look like Conestogas and smoke-signals compared with today. "When we talked about filing, we looked for the F sounds—food, phones and facilities," said *Newsday's* Elaine Povich. "Food, because you didn't know where your next meal was coming from. Phones, because nobody had one. And facilities, for the obvious reasons. Now, with a cell phone, you can report and file from virtually anyplace anytime."

For broadcasters, especially radio broadcasters, the cellular phone means there are few, if any, places where a reporter can't bring the news to his or her audience. "I remember in California I covered the campaign for proposition thirteen [the 1978 ballot initiative that limited the state's ability to raise property taxes]," said CBS's Fuss. "There were no cell phones. . . . You could only file a story when you could get to a physical telephone. That meant that you'd often go a fair amount of time between filing stories. That was a disadvantage in some ways and an advantage in others. There was time to think about your story and figure out what you were going to say when you next got to a telephone. When cell phones were created it meant your bosses could instantly reach you and you could go on the air anytime anyplace, except airplanes. And now even airplanes have air-phones that are sufficiently good to broadcast from."

Not only has the rapid expansion of wireless communication helped newspaper and radio reporters file their stories faster and from far-flung places, television is also reaping the benefits of technological advances. During the wars in Afghanistan and Iraq in 2003, the nation was provided real-time coverage from some of the world's most rugged, remote and inhospitable terrain thanks to videophones, satellite phones, night-vision lenses, laptop computer transmission and wireless technology. Yes, the pictures were often grainy and pixilated but they were a breakthrough. CBS's Mattesky said it is only a matter of time before people will see similar coverage from political campaigns. "You don't necessarily have to bring in satellite trucks any more, or for that matter you don't have to make a production facility available to put speeches or other political events on camera."

He noted that high-tech firms are working to improve miniaturization, transmission quality and ease, and to make the pictures and sound better. "I think what we saw during the Iraq War was that if there is a desire for something, to see it as it happens, people will accept the quality that's available to them. They've also become somewhat used to that. I don't think for major presidential speeches, for major candidate speeches, you'll see that kind of technology used, but I do think you'll see some experimentation with lower-level candidates or those that rank slightly lower in the polls than the front-runners."

What used to be the stuff of science fiction is rapidly becoming reality for political journalists. Wireless connection to the Internet is expanding with the improvement in digital cellular telephone quality and reliability. Laptop computers with internal cellular phones have moved beyond the prototype phase of research and development. A reporter can exchange e-mail, check facts, access the news organization's relational database and feed a story—radio, television or print—from virtually anywhere in the world.

9.3 It's a Long Way from Gutenberg

Technological developments of the last decade and their ongoing evolution have transformed the way journalists gather and report the news. The transformation of newspapers is an example of the pace of change. Gutenberg developed movable type around 1450. Broadsheets and the precursors of the modern newspaper appeared in early colonial America in the early 1700s. Newspapers were abundant in Revolutionary times. Until well after the Civil War, in the 1870s, newspapers were composed and printed by people placing the type into forms, one letter at a time, inking the forms, and printing one page at a time, not much different from the way Gutenberg did it.

The industrial revolution saw the development of hot type and Linotype machines that dramatically increased the speed and volume of newspaper composition and production. That was the norm until the 1960s when cold-type layout was developed and newspaper production became even faster and easier. Today the turnaround time from reporter to reader is measured in minutes.

Newsday's James Toedtman said he can now spend more time than ever before gathering facts, adding late developments and honing his stories. "It's given me more time because the production of our newspaper is so much more efficient. We used to have 7 o'clock [p.m.] deadlines and the presses didn't start until 7 o'clock the next morning. It would take a couple of hours for the stories to be transmitted from Washington to New York, then work their way through the copy desk, then be put into the Linotype in the composing room, then laid into page forms and then matted and cast and put on the presses. The presses started at 7 o'clock in the morning. That's 12 hours. Now, we can finish a story at 11 or 11:30 [p.m.] for a press run that starts within an hour."

For television, the technology has changed the coverage landscape. CBS's Mattesky: "Everything now is live. It doesn't matter if it's a presidential speech on an aircraft carrier or if it's a campaign stop in Yellowstone Park. It's now something that we see instantly. And the equipment necessary to do that has changed remarkably. The digital technology has allowed us the flexibility of taking very small equipment into very remote areas. It also allows us to set that equipment up very quickly and easily and with very few people. It has allowed us—from a broadcaster's perspective—to put things on television or radio instantly, from wherever in the world we need to."

Network TV news is highly competitive and technology is providing the weaponry with which many of the competitive battles are being fought. That is true at the local television station level as well. In addition, local TV stations in many markets are trying to put on as many hours of local news programming as possible.

For most television stations, local news programming is the station's profit center. It's relatively cheap to produce local news programming, and the station owns all of the commercial time in those local programs. Commercial revenues are not shared with networks or program syndicators. Many stations are trying to fill much of the non-network broadcast day with local news because of its profitability. Yet to be competitive, those stations cannot merely rely on studio presentations, recorded and edited packages from field reporters, and national and regional clips supplied by a host of news services to fill their news programs.

Because of the increasing number of national TV news sources, local stations can't afford to look like "news for hicks" and expect to attract a significant audience and thus attract significant advertising dollars. Local stations are using the same technology and techniques that the networks use to make their product look slick and hip. Live shots are a staple of local news, along with a battery of sophisticated virtual graphics, animation and character-generation to help improve production. Local stations also routinely use satellite and microwave transmission to provide live coverage. Many are embracing the speed and flexibility of digital video and editing to increase their news inventory and make their programming look good.

The production values and presentation of local television news, along with hours and hours of broadcast time devoted to local news programming, does not substitute for news content itself. "There's a lot of product out there and I'm not sure that in every market there is enough news to fill it," said Deborah Potter, executive director of NewsLab, a nonprofit research and training organization that works with local television news departments. "At the local level you have stations putting on news eight hours a day and some of them producing additional newscasts for some other station across town with their own staff."

Weak stories, poor reporting and bad writing do not produce the kind of television news that will grab and hold an audience, regardless of the technology being used to package and deliver it. In some cases the volume of stories needed to fill the programming schedule—and the workload that accompanies reporting and producing all those stories—results in journalistic mistakes and sloppiness. Reporters required to make several live appearances within a short period of time often end up sacrificing such fundamentals as double-checking facts and assuring a fair, balanced presentation.

Rather than addressing the amount of news that may or may not be taking place in a market, some local stations are relying less and less on hard-news coverage, and turning instead to local features—health, lifestyles, entertainment, food, home improvement and the like—to fill their newscasts. As a practical matter, this makes it even harder for reporters to sell political stories to their producers and news directors.

In addition to demands for more journalistic output from reporters, broadcast and cable news organizations are trying to maximize coverage while minimizing cost. "In terms of politics, we will begin to see some efforts in the next campaign [2004] to cover things a little differently," said Mattesky. "You will begin to see fewer people dispatched to remote locations, and yet you will get the same amount of material back live, and for that matter perhaps even more material back as a result of the technology and equipment changes."

Mattesky explained that the networks have developed a system of "pooling" video, thus eliminating the need for each network to send a camera crew to each event. Instead of one speech being recorded by five different cameras, as was the standard practice for decades, that same speech is now fed live by one camera to five different networks. "In the 1996 campaign we were dispatching our own crews, our own satellite trucks, to every location that candidates were traveling to. In 2000, we found ourselves in a situation where, in cooperation with ABC and Fox, we would split up the transmissions of the speeches. If there were three speeches by George W. Bush in a day, ABC would cover one and transmit it to all three of us, CBS would cover one and transmit it to all three of us, and Fox would cover one and transmit it to all three of us."

The goal, he said, is to cover everything, yet reduce the cost of coverage. The networks, however, still send their own editorial personnel—producers or off-air reporters—to events with pooled video coverage. That gives each network its own editorial perspective on the speech, the story or the event. If there is an opportunity to question the candidate, each network has its own person there to do it.

Local television stations—in some cases as cooperative ventures and in some cases as the result of duopoly—also are expanding their use of pooling, although some are pooling reporters as well as video, which results in less editorial independence and fewer reportorial eyes and ears on-scene. Many journalists and academics are concerned that the net effect is potentially one-sided or unbalanced coverage. Reducing the number of editorial perspectives and independent news judgments minimizes the public's ability to draw independent conclusions from the composite journalistic product.

Some station owners and news directors are seriously wrestling with the issue of how to contain the costs of news coverage while not jeopardizing the product. (See chapter 15.2 and 15.3.) Others are willing to sacrifice the quality of the news at the altar of boosting profit.

9.4 C-SPAN

Few technological developments have had as much impact on political journalism in America as the evolution of the Cable Satellite Public Affairs Network. Just about everybody knows it as C-SPAN. It started in 1979 as a single cable channel that carried the proceedings of the House of Representatives and grew to become the robust enterprise it is today—with C-SPAN 1, 2 and 3, C-SPAN radio, XM and Sirius Satellite radio, and 10 web sites. C-SPAN has become an indispensable tool for political reporters and political professionals. Today C-SPAN not only covers the House, it covers the Senate gavel-to-gavel, along with most other major briefings, news conferences, speeches and political debates both in Washington and around the country.

"We call it America's town hall," said C-SPAN's chief executive officer Brian Lamb. Some of the coverage is done unilaterally by the network but much of it comes from other sources. The cameras in the House and Senate, for example, are owned, controlled and operated by the two chambers of Congress. That is why viewers seldom, if ever, see a senator giving a speech to an empty chamber or a House member sleeping through a portion of debate.

Lamb explained how C-SPAN could provide extensive coverage of local campaigns without expending a prohibitive amount of money. "What we did in the 2002 campaign was 130-plus debates that were created by other organizations. We love the fact that other organizations create events and we cover them, or they create events and we carry them. The broadcast stations in this country have been very cooperative with us, more often than not giving us—it's rare that they charge for it—access to a debate for a Senate or House race or gubernatorial race and letting us run it after they've run it. Sometimes they even let us run it live. Very few broadcasters in this country say no to us when it comes to running debates."

The C-SPAN channels reach about 87 million households. Of that number about 10 percent are regular viewers, 30 percent are occasional viewers and 60 percent don't watch at all, according to Lamb. He also points out that C-SPAN's own demographic studies show that C-SPAN viewers both pay attention to what they are watching and vote.

C-SPAN allows a reporter to witness more political events and hear more politicians in a week than that one reporter used to be able to see and hear in a month. CBS's Dotty Lynch says it has made her life easier and at the same time more productive. "I used to travel a lot more than I do now, because I couldn't see any of these meetings in any way other than going to Des Moines [Iowa] or Manchester [N.H.] or anywhere else the candidates were. Now C-SPAN covers everything. So I can see these meetings and candidate forums starting a year and a half or two years out. That's a technological change that's improved things. If I can see a forum on C-SPAN in my office or in my home then I've saved two days of travel time and expense, which is an issue that matters a lot in television these days."

Newsday's James Toedtman said it almost allows him to be in two places at one time. "They hadn't finished their voting on the tax bill I've been covering when I came to meet you today. But I can go to the Internet and I can see what the final vote was and who voted which way. And I can go to C-SPAN, click on the icon, and I can see the rebroadcast of the last 15 minutes of debate and the voting and the rhetoric and so forth. And all of that comes through the little display tube on my desk."

Some editors and news directors believe that all a reporter really needs today is a phone, Internet access and C-SPAN. Stephen Hess of the Brookings Institution was among many journalists and scholars interviewed for this book who think that is misguided and shortsighted. "You can cover almost anything by tuning in to C-SPAN. The State Department, the White House briefings are all on C-SPAN. In one sense it's efficient and on that level you can be quite accurate. You've heard and recorded the president speaking, the candidate speaking, the spokesman for the president speaking. It gives you the headline, the top of the news. What you miss, of course, is the nuance. Putting a reporter on the campaign trail will tell you what makes the candidate tick."

"You absolutely have to have reporters on the ground to tell people what's going on," said Lamb, noting that there are a lot of things that go on outside camera range. In addition, he said, there are things the camera is not permitted to see. "Here's an example. When Jim Wright was Speaker we asked to take our camera into the Speaker's offices. We were turned down. He didn't want the country to see what the Speaker's office looked like because it's very expensive looking."

Political analyst Stuart Rothenberg warned that politicians are very skillful in circumventing tough questions by using C-SPAN. Candidates often use it "to bypass reporters, especially national reporters, and take their message right to the people. On the other hand, a lot of voters want to get it from the horse's mouth. It's not a bad thing for voters to see a candidate campaigning in Iowa. But they need to know that it's not the whole world. There's more going on than what that one camera sees."

C-SPAN's value to political reporters is a very important tool in the chest, but it is only one tool provided by technology. It's hard to build a house without a hammer; it's impossible to build a house with a hammer alone. The analogy is true for building political journalism with C-SPAN alone.

A Conversation with Brian Lamb

Chief executive officer and founder: C-SPAN

His office overlooks Washington's historic Union Station and Senate Park. Two walls are glass; two are lined with books. The man is part visionary, part executive, part teacher, part scholar and part performer.

Brian Lamb is not exactly a TV star, but he is certainly a cult figure. For people who watch C-SPAN, he's a part of their lives. For many he is C-SPAN. On screen he is low-key, laid-back and almost taciturn. In person, one quickly senses his energy and enthusiasm. Lamb was the driving force behind the development of C-SPAN and has presided over the expanding empire since the day it was launched in 1979.

Today it is C-SPAN, C-SPAN2, C-SPAN3, C-SPAN Radio, 10 web sites and XM and Sirius satellite radio.

His broadcast career began in Indiana where he did everything from spin records to sell air time. During a hitch in the Navy he worked in the Pentagon public affairs office during the Vietnam War and he returned to Washington when he got out of the Navy to work as a news reporter, Senate press secretary and as a member of the White House telecommunications policy staff.

R.A.: *Did you really host a show in Indiana called Dance Date?*

B.L.: "Great name, isn't it? About as good as C-SPAN. I invented both of those names and never liked either one of them."

R.A.: *How did C-SPAN come about? It started with coverage of the House of Representatives, didn't it?*

B.L.: "It started when technology changed dramatically, through the use of a satellite to deliver television programs to cable systems. The actual satellite was launched in '75 and HBO started using it first. Then everybody else started to get into the game on an incremental basis. We were the sixth new kind of service provided to cable systems. The first five were Home Box Office, channel 17 out of Atlanta, channel 27—which turned into the 700 Club—out of Portsmouth, Virginia, the Madison Square Garden Network, and Showtime. We were number six.

"At that time the cable industry was looking for programming ideas. Most people thought it was a joke. They didn't think it was important. They didn't think it would go anywhere. It's typical of new technology. People always pooh-pooh it when it comes out, because the vested interests help that. They don't want anything new to succeed, because then they lose market share and the big networks have lost a tremendous amount of market share. It's human nature.

"So it took a long time for anybody to recognize what was going on and we sneaked in early. It's cooperative, nonprofit, supported by the cable television industry. We get all of our money per subscriber. There's no advertising. And it was just another programming service to this developing cable industry, and that's why it worked. I made the proposal in '77 and it took us until '79 to get on the air. They liked it because it was different and it wasn't going to cost a lot."

R.A.: *From those early days, when you were just doing gavel-to-gavel coverage of the House, C-SPAN's become a real political tool, both for political junkies and for the average citizen who wants to get a little more depth. How did that evolve?*

B.L.: "We are exactly the same today as we were in the beginning. Our mission statement is the same. We, internally, consider ourselves every bit as much a journalist as anybody else in the business. Some journalists don't think that. I've heard some of the biggest television journalists say out loud that you don't practice journalism when you just point a camera in a certain direction and pick up an event. My quarrel with that analysis is that every day we pick what we cover. We pick the time of day we put it on the air.

"We started with the House, but our main mission today is so much broader than that. It is to capture as many political events, cultural events related to politics, and let the public see them in their entirety and make up their own mind and never worry about the ratings. That's what makes us the oddest place in all of television. We don't worry about the ratings. We don't know if there are a thousand people watching us at any one time or a million. That is much different than every other place because they're driven to have to deliver eyeballs to advertisers. We don't have to do that."

R.A.: *How do you make those journalistic decisions about what stories you're going to cover, what stories you're not going to go to? How do you decide?*

B.L.: "The same way any other editorial board, group or editor does. Except we have a mission here that if we cover the Israeli side, we want to cover the Palestinian side. We may not do that tomorrow, but when they come along and have a news conference a week or so later, we'll go cover that because a week or so earlier we covered the other side.

"That would be difficult to do if you were always worried about how many people were watching, because sometimes these events are not very exciting. They're entirely too long. They don't say anything. Anybody that watches knows that they're getting the company line. We realize that. But, again, that's what journalists have done over the years. They go to these events and decide what, inside these events, they want to pass on to their audience. This allows the public to be a part of the process. There's no other way to describe it. We make decisions, editorially, the same way any other news organization does, but without the pressure of ratings."

R.A.: *Am I correct that C-SPAN reaches about 90 million households?*
B.L.: "Close. It's about 87 million."

R.A.: *Any idea of actual viewership?*
B.L.: "Yes. We've done demographic studies every four years. I don't like to sell it too hard, but it works out to about 10 percent of the public that watches us on a regular basis. What is regular? We can show from our studies that it's daily. What does that mean? Do they click through? How much do they watch? We do know that 10 percent, one in 10, are regular viewers. Three in 10 are sometime

viewers. Six in 10 never watch. That shouldn't surprise anybody be-cause five out of 10 people don't vote in presidential elections, so why would they watch C-SPAN? And only a third of the population votes in off-year elections. So it gets to be a fairly identifiable group that would be our market out there. And 90 percent of our viewers vote.

"At least when you speak to our group, either on a call-in show, a book show, or in a forum that we're doing, you're reaching a sizable au-dience in the thousands, probably on rare occasions in the millions. People will fly for four hours, across country, to speak to an audience of 300 people, so why wouldn't you come to a studio to talk to thou-sands of people who vote?"

R.A.: *When I was covering Congress and did C-SPAN regularly I was al-ways amazed at how many people would stop me in a restaurant or in a store and say "I saw you on C-SPAN." You must get that a lot?*

B.L.: "All the time. I'll tell you what I think it is—people who watch entertainment television are entertained and it just goes into a big black hole. It's just a moment for them. I go to movies a lot. I don't watch them on television. I go to the theater. And I tell you most of the time I can't remember the movie the next day. I go just for the pure raw pleasure, or sometimes displeasure, of the two hours I'm in the movie.

"People who watch C-SPAN are there for a reason. They're trying to improve their knowledge level. They want to be there. They're not just floating by. And if they didn't want to be there, they'd go somewhere else. They've got 200 choices these days."

R.A.: *In researching this book I have unearthed what I might call "the C-SPAN dilemma." Editors and news directors are telling reporters—you've got the Internet, you've got the phone, and you've got C-SPAN. You want to cov-er politics? Cover it right here from the office. How do you respond to that?*

B.L.: "I don't buy it. You can say sometimes we're going to cover something on C-SPAN. But there's a lot of peripheral vision when you're on the spot. There is no peripheral vision on television. You can't describe the smell in the room. You can't describe whether it's hot or cold. You can't describe an aide sitting off to the side making gestures to a candidate.

"I once had a United States senator appear on one of our call-in shows and he had three aides sitting out in front with big chalkboards and every time a question would come in these aides would write the answer on these chalkboards and hold it up. I truly felt bad about not being able to say to the audience this bozo is being fed every answer by three intelligent aides sitting out in front of him. He's not here anymore. But I call that peripheral vision.

"But you don't have to be out there for every event. It happens in this town every Monday when print journalists report about what happened on the Sunday talk shows. They watched TV."

R.A.: *Why wouldn't you either tell the audience or flip a camera around and show those aides writing the answers?*

B.L.: "Because of the way the game is played, which I hate. The game is that the member comes in and sits in the chair on the set and you just don't do that. We don't have that happen very often, and in fact it couldn't happen today because of the way our cameras are set up. That's where the public is shortchanged.

"As a network we have tried to show that stuff as often as humanly possible. But you can only take that so far and in that case we didn't do it. The truth of the matter is if we'd done it he wouldn't have come back. I'm not sure he came back anyway. That's the power of the person being covered—the president, the Speaker [of the House]. It's the power of access.

"Why do certain people go to certain organizations to talk? We've never in the history of this network had a secretary of state agree to come and take questions from the audience. We've had two secretaries of defense come and take questions. That's all, in the history of the network. I can't remember ever having a secretary of the treasury come and take questions. I think we had an attorney general, but not very often. They won't do it. They won't take the chance. They don't want to have the possibility of saying the wrong thing on a call-in show. We've never had a president do it.

"We've had a vice president. George [H. W.] Bush did it once. Al Gore did it once. Al Gore came on once in '93 and never came back. Never would come back and take questions. I've always thought there were two reasons. One, we couldn't show him the numbers [of viewers]. And two, he just didn't want to be hassled by the calls. . . . We take the calls at random, just as they come in, with no protection. Sometimes we're part of it, journalists are part of it, letting them get away with this control thing without letting the audience know about it."

R.A.: *Your questioning and interviewing style have shown up in a number of articles. It's very terse, very tight. You ask five- or six-word questions. Did you develop that technique yourself?*

B.L.: "It's absolutely me. The reason I say that so strongly is I copied everybody in my early years. I wanted to sound like David Brinkley or Chet Huntley. There came a time, and I can't remember who told me this, but it was early, when I was in my late teens—this person said, 'Will you stop being everybody else and be yourself. You either have a style or you don't. You either have a voice for this business or you don't. Stop trying to be like anybody else.' And I did.

"It also tracks with our mission. What we do should not be about us. It's about the guest, and when a guest is there the questions are meant to get the guest to talk. The more I argue with the guest, the more I become the issue and the more the public takes sides. If they like the guest, their reaction is, get off his or her back. If they don't like the guest they say, go get 'em. There's a place for that in journalism. But we're on a different kind of mission."

R.A.: *How do you describe that interviewing technique?*

B.L.: "Minimalist. Open questions. Basic questions. That's it. Assume that the person watching your interview knows nothing. And so you start from the basics. Who are you? Where are you from? Where did you go to school? Where have you worked? All those simple basic questions that you're taught in journalism school will never do you in. They'll always work for you.

"Open questions are absolutely paramount. If you ask a question as a lot of people in our business do that says, 'Don't you think that Washington, D.C., is a wonderful place in the summer?' you have tried to put words in the other person's mouth. You've given them very little room to work in. The pros know how to get around that. Sometimes all you get is yes and no. If you ask somebody, 'What do you think about the weather in Washington in the summer?' it's open. They have the opportunity to say what they want. We try to train all of our people to do that. It's basic. It's back to the '50s. This is nothing new.

"The business has changed in the last 20 years. It's all personality driven. I have no interest in being a personality. I have no interest in watching them. But we do our thing and almost everybody else does the opposite."

R.A.: *How do you prep for an interview?*

(Lamb hosts two shows a week: a live call-in show on Friday mornings and a pre-recorded weekend show called Book Notes.)

B.L.: "If it's an interview on the morning show, I do very little prep. My objective is to get the basics out of the guest and get the phone calls going. We have a quota here of the number of phone calls that every host has to take, because if you don't put a quota on them, they'll ask questions. And if they ask questions then it's not a call-in show. Every morning for three hours there's a quota of 60 calls. So get the basics. If somebody's well-known you don't need much. If there's a cabinet officer on, just open up the phones. If it's the secretary of veterans affairs or secretary of the interior, they're ready for them. They're out there and they've been wanting to talk to them for years.

"On the book show that I do, it's a whole different environment. It's quiet. It's an hour. And the way I prepare is to read the book. Period. It's that simple."

R.A.: *Exactly the opposite of Larry King, who says he doesn't read the book?*

B.L.: "Larry King's success is in the fact that he has a contract that pays him seven million dollars a year or more. Enough people watch him and enough advertising is sold—last figures I saw, that show generates 25 million dollars a year for that one hour a night and he's paid something like seven [million]. That's a pretty good profit even when you add in all the other costs in there. They're probably making a 50 percent return on their dollar. It doesn't matter what anybody thinks in our business that Larry King says he doesn't read the books.

"I don't read them to impress the other people. I read them because I want to learn something. If I read a book it's a much different interview than if I don't. You can do it the other way successfully. But if you read the book, there's all kinds of stuff hidden in those books that most people don't see. It often generates some of the best interviews. [Gestures to his book-lined walls.] In here are all the Book Notes books. The first one up here [points] was Neil Sheehan, *A Bright Shining Lie.* Over there, with the yellow cover, was the last one. Over seven years that's about 750 books."

10

Money and Manipulation

Politics and money have been dirty dancing for as long as there's been politics and money. In the court of England's King Henry VIII, citizens would give expensive gifts to courtiers with the expectation that those courtiers would appeal to the king on behalf of the gift-bearing citizens. By the mid-1800s lobbyists representing powerful political interests would deliver bags full of money to members of the United States Congress in exchange for political favors.

Money is so important to the electoral process in America that those rare few who successfully run for office without much money usually merit news stories for that reason alone. They are simply a modern political rarity. When the late Democratic senator from Minnesota, Paul Wellstone, first ran for office, he did so in a dilapidated bus, using small contributions from average citizens. At first, few political pros or national journalists gave him much of a chance. After all, he was campaigning on a shoestring, not playing the game by traditional rules. He had very little money and couldn't afford such standard campaign accoutrements as TV and radio advertising, top-of-the-line pollsters, expensive campaign consultants and an advance staff to plan his every campaign stop down to the second.

What Wellstone did, and that he won doing it, became a major news story. A no-frills, no-money campaign for the U.S. Senate was extraordinary. The reality of American politics is that it is expensive to run for virtually any public office, from president down to the school board in a rural district.

Regardless of the issues raised in the campaign, regardless of the personalities of the candidates, and regardless of the horse race aspects of the contest, political reporters must always keep one eye on the money. How is a candidate raising it? Who is contributing it? What promises is the candidate making in order to raise it? And how is the candidate spending it?

10.1 Harvesting the Dollars

Most politicians will tell you that they do not particularly enjoy raising money. They all do it because they have to. Some are particularly good at it, whether they like doing it or not. Former Democratic President Bill Clinton and his successor, Republican President George W. Bush, were both gifted fund-raisers. Other politicians at all levels concede privately that it makes them uncomfortable to go up to strangers and ask for contributions.

The best way for a candidate to run for office and not have to raise campaign funds, and thus be beholden to the people who make campaign contributions, is to be independently wealthy. CNN's senior political correspondent Candy Crowley said the parties are all looking for "a bunch of billionaire candidates." Independent wealth also eliminates any problems connected to campaign finance regulations and frees the candidate to focus only on the job of getting elected.

When Democratic Sen. Herb Kohl of Wisconsin first ran for office, he did it mostly with his own money. He was a wealthy businessman, owner of Kohl's Department Stores and the Milwaukee Bucks NBA team. Some of my Capitol Hill colleagues thought he should have adopted the campaign slogan "I'm So Rich I Can't Be Bought."

Unfortunately, there are far fewer independently wealthy people who want to run for political office than there are political offices in search of candidates. The majority of people who seek public office are faced with the reality of having to raise the money to finance their campaigns. Once they've made known their intentions to run, they can start the process of raising money. In most states, running for office requires the establishment of a campaign bank account separate from the candidate's personal or business account, and the appointment of a campaign treasurer who is responsible for the money. (See chapter 4.2.)

The first place most candidates turn is to their political parties at the local, state and national levels. Political parties, however, do not have unlimited funds and, while they pay lip service to supporting all their candidates, the amount of dollars actually invested is directly related to whether the candidate in question is seen as having a chance to win. The challenger to an entrenched and popular incumbent is not likely to get much financial help from his or her political party.

Whether the party chips in or not, the candidate will need to seek contributions from other sources. (Political contributions are not tax deductible and there are limits on how much individuals and corporations may give to candidates.)

Some local races can be financed by contributions from donors solely within a certain geographic area. The higher the level of the office sought, the wider the circle that must be drawn in the quest for money. In some major Senate and gubernatorial races, it is not unusual for a candidate's fund-raising operation to solicit contributions from known political contributors (often gleaned from national party contributor lists) all over the country. These campaigns also tap corporate, union and interest group contributions because if the candidate is elected, he or she will have a policy impact on issues of concern to those organizations.

The mechanics of fund-raising involve an array of standard techniques including holding events like picnics and barbeques, golf and tennis tournaments, parties and gatherings in private homes, dinners and banquets, concerts, speeches and other presentations. Direct mail and telephone solicitations are also common. During the run-up to the 2004 Democratic presidential primary season, former Gov. Howard Dean of Vermont tapped the Internet as a way of raising campaign funds. It turned out to be a brilliant and successful fund-raising tool.

Politicians have tried just about everything. They've set up information/solicitation tables in shopping malls and on street corners. They've passed the hat in churches and at public events. They've shamelessly stopped passersby on public streets and asked for money like itinerant panhandlers.

Sometimes, politicians and their handlers actively seek news coverage of these fund-raising enterprises. Other times, they are private and closed to the news media. Whenever a fund-raising event is closed, political reporters' antennae should go up and they should start asking questions. Why is the event closed? What's going to be said in there that you don't want the voters to know about? Is the politician going to make promises he or she doesn't want on the public record?

While the McCain-Feingold Campaign Finance Reform Bill (see chapter 3.5) limits unregulated "soft money" and restricts the ability of interest groups, unions and corporations to spend unlimited campaign dollars, the quest for that money goes on. "You knew the minute that campaign finance reform was passed, they were trying to figure a way around it," said CNN's Crowley. "These are very clever people."

CBS News's chief Washington correspondent Bob Schieffer believes the omnipresent money chase has helped spawn a degree of partisanship at the federal level that in some cases has made legislation and political compromise all but impossible. He used the powerful fundraising record of the National Rifle Association as an example and added: "Let me tell you something, the people on the other side of the issue, the gun control folks, they use this issue to raise money for their side," he said. "Every year in Congress you'll see three or four votes on gun control. It's a fund-raiser for both sides. You'll see a vote every month or so on abortion in some manner because it's a fund-raiser for people on both sides of the issue. These issues, I call them perennials, are fund-raising devices for people on all sides of them. And as long as this continues you'll see this kind of partisanship."

The most noble politicians will tell you that they engage in the process of raising money in order to have an impact on the public policy agenda and to help the voters of their district, state or country. They will say that they are in the business of politics to appeal to people's hopes, goals and desires. The less noble politicians use the system in order to appeal to people's fears, prejudices and hatreds.

Schieffer cited the late Republican strategist Lee Atwater, who played a pivotal role in the campaigns of Ronald Reagan and the first President George Bush. One Atwater technique was to exploit and capitalize on so-called wedge issues. "Lee Atwater wasn't looking for issues people could agree on," Schieffer said. "He was looking for issues that divided people. And he knew that if you could figure out the best way to stick that wedge in, the better the chance of getting your people elected."

10.2 Spending the Dollars

The higher the office sought, the more a candidate will have to spend. Some candidates hire professional fund-raisers to help in raising money.

Polling is often the first major campaign expense and sometimes is done even before a candidate makes a formal declaration that he or she is running. For major state and national offices, people considering entering the race may commission a benchmark poll. (See chapter

6.1.) In major races, polling not only tells the candidate how he or she is faring with the voters, it helps the candidate determine what issues are resonating, and where the opposition may be vulnerable. It also plays an important role in the financial operation of campaigns. (See chapter 11.2.)

"As campaigns get bigger and bigger and more and more money is spent, polling is really a tool to make sure the money is being spent as well as possible and as effectively as possible," said pollster Geoffrey Garin of Peter D. Hart Research Associates. "So as campaign budgets go up and the media budgets go up, the polling budgets go up partly as a tool of accountability and efficiency if nothing else."

Once the decision to run is made, the campaign manager is often the first paid staff member, although in some local races the campaign manager donates his or her time to the process. First-time candidates often pick a relative or close friend to manage the campaign.

Office expenses are usually, but not always, a campaign expense. Some candidates seeking local offices will run their campaigns out of their homes or businesses. Candidates seeking major offices almost always have an office they call "campaign headquarters." It is generally the least expensive office space available. Controlling office expenses leaves more money for other, more important, campaign expenditures. For major offices, such as governor, U.S. senator and U.S. representative, a candidate may have offices in several places within a state, along with staff members in each.

Depending on the campaign, other key personnel who may or may not be paid include the campaign treasurer, press secretary, scheduler, office manager and coordinator of volunteers. All polling costs money, whether a pollster is hired as a part of the campaign or as an outside consultant. Other campaign consultants are usually paid fees for their services, although a few consultants dealing with specific issues may work for free if they are committed to the position of a particular candidate. Depending on the newsworthiness of the race, this can occasionally be an interesting aside for reporters to check—who's being paid and who's working without pay? If it doesn't make a whole story itself, it can be an element of a bigger story.

Other campaign costs can include travel expenses to get the candidate from one place to another. In a senatorial or gubernatorial race in a big state like California or Texas, that means air and ground transportation, hotels, meals and the like for the candidate and the traveling staff. In small states, such as Rhode Island or Delaware, those expenses are considerably less because the candidate will travel almost everywhere by car and will seldom spend a night away from home.

Planning and staging political events has become a cottage industry within the business of politics. Elaborate staging started with presidential candidates and has now extended down the ladder to candidates for senator and governor. Tom Mattesky, deputy Washington bureau chief for CBS News, likened it to the creation of political theater. "There are professionals out there now who are like advance men for the circus. They are out there scouting locations days or weeks in advance, looking for that perfect backdrop, courting the local television stations. . . . What you're getting are these really well-structured, well-financed advance units that are out there with the sole purpose of getting coverage of a political visit on local television."

The biggest campaign expense by far, for almost every modern campaign, is advertising. This includes everything from lawn signs and bumper stickers to billboards, from pamphlets and fliers to newspaper and magazine ads, from telephone campaigning and direct mail to radio and television commercials. Candidates are even using the Internet both as a fund-raising tool and an advertising medium.

Some campaigns employ the services of professional political advertising agencies and/or consultants as they are needed. Others have political advertising experts on their staffs. The importance of advertising in political campaigns, at almost all levels, has become so critical that it requires candidates to seek professional help. For major offices, the advertising agencies and/or consultants work closely with the campaign's pollster, campaign manager, press secretary and other key aides, operatives and advisors to hone and refine each ad.

It is an important part of overall campaign strategy that goes on 24 hours a day, seven days a week as Election Day approaches. The closer to the end of the campaign, the more frenetic the advertising activity and the more likely it is to generate news stories. The advertising—especially the radio and television advertising—is often changed, tweaked, adjusted or modified on a daily basis. While this has a strategic purpose, changes and adjustments also drive up the cost to the campaign.

Political reporters must be aware of the various campaign costs. How and where campaigns spend money (or cut back campaign expenditures) during the race can be telltale signs of either problems or a shift in momentum for a particular candidate.

A campaign that undergoes a shift in spending patterns should raise reporters' interest and promote questions. It is not always a sign that something newsworthy has happened, but it can be. For example, if a national party viewed a U.S. House race as noncompetitive at the beginning of the cycle and suddenly decided the challenger had a chance of winning, there would likely be an infusion of dollars from the national party. How does the candidate spend that money? If it's spent on advertising, what is the nature of that advertising? Is there a shift in message, tone or focus of the advertising? Does the campaign turn to negative ads? If so what's the nature of the negativism? Is there a change in those people pulling the strings (has the national party sent in experts or advisors and changed the dynamics of the campaign organization)?

Campaign staff will seldom talk about such internal matters, especially the allocation of campaign funds, but outside consultants, political analysts and even opposing campaigns—that are always attuned to what's happening on the other side—often can provide some insight. A good question for reporters to ask campaign press secretaries at regular intervals is: "What do you hear about what's going on with the opposition?"

10.3 Political Advertising

As television emerged as the country's favorite delivery platform for news and entertainment in the 1950s, it was soon clear the new medium would play a pivotal role in politics. Gen. Dwight Eisenhower was the GOP presidential candidate in 1952. He became the first presidential candidate to use television for political advertising, although his opponent, Democrat Adlai Stevenson, ultimately responded with ads of his own. The Eisenhower campaign recruited people from big ad agencies on Madison Avenue. Stephen Hess, senior fellow at The Brookings Institution and a former Eisenhower speechwriter, reflected, "They didn't know much about politics, but they knew something about advertising. And actually, it didn't work very well."

Those early ads were stiff and stilted, grainy black-and-white film footage, more an experiment than the kind of slick, highly produced, carefully honed commercials of today. In addition, Eisenhower was not a particularly telegenic figure. In a series of question-and-answer ads, actors would pose carefully scripted questions. In one, an African American asked, "General, the Democrats are telling me I never had it so good?" The question was edited to Eisenhower's answer, which was clearly delivered from another location at another time. The sound quality did not match, the editing was rudimentary. But the ads did serve to show the public what Eisenhower looked like and sounded like, and they hammered home the theme, as Eisenhower said that "it's time for a change."

Today campaign ads and the people who make them are a major subset of the business of politics. There are Republican ad agencies and Democratic ad agencies. There are GOP and Democratic producers and directors who script, shoot and edit the commercials. "The most expensive and serious part of the campaign is the commercials," said Hess. "They spend more time to make a commercial, spend more money to make a commercial. A national commercial is a pretty finely wrought piece of 30-second film."

Those early TV campaign commercials were designed to let the public see and hear the candidate saying something about his or her agenda. Today, campaign ads employ all of the technology and creative skills available. Production values weigh heavily—location, framing, editing, lighting, sound, pacing. Content is critical. Is the ad expository? Persuasive? Confrontational? Comparative? Positive? Negative?

It took only a dozen years, from the Eisenhower campaign's tentative steps into TV advertising, for the genre to take a singularly newsworthy turn. The 1964 presidential campaign pitted Democratic incumbent Lyndon Johnson against Republican Sen. Barry Goldwater. Goldwater had, at one point, suggested the use of tactical nuclear weapons as a way of ending the war in Vietnam. Johnson's campaign moved to turn that against Goldwater in the form of a classic political commercial that is known as "the daisy."

The ad opens with a picture of a little blonde girl plucking petals off a daisy with birds chirping in the background. She was counting as she went, hesitating at six and seven. Her voice fades out and is replaced with a raspy, nasal male voice counting down—six, five, four—to a nuclear explosion as the camera zoomed in to the iris of the girl's eye, forming the dark backdrop for the blast. The nuclear mushroom cloud is seen and Johnson's voice is heard, saying, "These are the stakes. . . ."

The age of negative political campaign advertising was born. It would take no time for the political pros to expand its use with greater sophistication of both message and technique. In 1968, Democrat Hubert Humphrey's campaign aired an ad that belittled Republican Richard Nixon's vice presidential running-mate, Spiro Agnew. Agnew's picture appeared and a man broke into laughter. That's it. Simple production; simple message.

The 1988 campaign saw an extensive use of negative advertising. Democrat Michael Dukakis attacked Republican George Bush's selection of Dan Quayle, a young, relatively unknown Indiana senator as his vice presidential choice. But the brunt of the negative campaigning was used by Bush against Dukakis. One ad showed Dukakis driving a tank, looking silly in a tanker's helmet, suggesting that Dukakis would be a laughingstock as commander-in-chief of the nation's military.

Another ad featured the ominous-looking image of an African American murderer named Willie Horton. An announcer said, "Dukakis not only opposes the death penalty. He allowed first degree murderers to have weekend passes from prison." The voice describes Horton's escape and subsequent stabbing of a young man and rape of his girlfriend. "Weekend prison passes . . . Dukakis on crime," concluded the ad.

There is a range of opinion among political pros, scholars and journalists about the effectiveness of negative advertising. CBS's Bob Schieffer said, "Negative advertising works. It works in the short run. It doesn't make things better, overall. And it's much easier to use 30 seconds to attack someone else than it is to lay out your own qualifications. The result of that is we have sort of degraded the whole process." He added that it does not make covering a campaign pleasant or rewarding. "You get to the end of these campaigns and you're not glad because your candidate won or sad because your candidate lost, you just want to go take a shower."

On the other hand, an academic paper entitled "Effectiveness of Negative Political Advertising," published in 1998 by Professor Won Ho Chang of the University of Missouri School of Journalism, Jae-Jin Park, a public relations specialist with the LG Corporation of Seoul, South Korea, and University of Missouri graduate student Sung Wook Shim, contends that negative advertising is only marginally effective. The study, based on telephone interviews, concluded that negative political advertising appears most effective with lower-income people and less effective with women and older people. While some other studies suggested African Americans were more likely to believe negative ads than non-African Americans, this study did not support that conclusion.

The Chang-Park-Shim paper also chronicles a steady growth in campaign spending on broadcast advertising, along with the evolution of the technique. The authors noted, "Although there exists no rule in using political advertising, prior to the 1980s candidates usually used issue or image ads at the beginning of a campaign to establish their positive image and then used negative ads at the end of the campaign to attack the opponent. . . . In today's political campaign, candidates, either challengers or incumbents, use negative ads from the beginning." (The entire study may be accessed at www.scripps.ohiou.edu/wjmcr/vol02/2-la-B.htm.)

Not all political advertising is newsworthy, but it can't be ignored. Many major news organizations believe that campaign advertising is worth the time and expense to track it, monitor it and archive it. When campaign advertising becomes negative or highly confrontational, it often becomes a story. This is a problem for political reporters. Often one of the worst places to judge campaign advertising is as a reporter covering a campaign. Veteran CBS Radio News correspondent Bob Fuss refers to it as being inside the bubble. "A huge part of American politics, from the voters' point of view, is the TV and radio ads. And when you're in this bubble . . . you're not seeing or hearing the ads. So, to that extent, you are separated from a big part of the political story."

Many large news organizations reserve the analysis of political advertising to sub-specialists, reporters who are trained in analyzing political ads, and who operate away from the day-to-day coverage of campaigns. Hess noted, "Some newspapers have something they call 'ad watches' in which they deconstruct the commercials for you. They point out what's true and what's not true in the commercial. This is why he said what he said and this is why they used this particular shot."

Occasionally network television news provides this kind of coverage, but for the most part it is reserved to newspapers because it is expensive, time-consuming and requires a commitment of resources that many local TV stations simply do not have or wish to expend.

Campaigns use the same techniques as Madison Avenue to test their ads. They use focus groups and instant-response testing to measure the effectiveness of them. (See chapter 11.5.) In addition, pollster Geoffry Garin of Peter D. Hart Research Associates noted a new trend, "Increasingly, the Internet is being used to test advertising. You can stream commercials over the Internet and then invite certain kinds of people to look at them."

10.4 Free Media

While campaign advertising is critical to virtually any candidate, free media is essential. Free media ranges from news stories, interviews on radio, TV and in print, profiles, debates, speeches, general appearances—anything that gets the candidate's face and message in front of the public. The better known a candidate is, the greater the chance of getting elected.

There is nothing a candidate likes better than to get his or her face or voice on radio, on television or in the newspaper, especially if it is accompanied by favorable coverage. An interview with a disc jockey who knows nothing about politics or the issues of the campaign is considered a bonanza. If the candidate doesn't get outright favorable news coverage, neutral coverage is the next best thing.

Despite the fact that politicians will often address the importance of a free and unbridled news media, they don't really like critical coverage. Do not be surprised if you, as a political reporter, report something critical and have somebody from the campaign confront you about it. If you have done all of your journalistic homework—double-checking your sources, quotes, documents and data—stand your ground. Your job is not to curry favor with a campaign. It is to seek and report the truth fairly and honestly.

"Now the press gets a lot of criticism because we sometimes reveal these personal things about people," said CBS's Schieffer. He blames the elevation of state primaries at the expense of local caucuses and state conventions for creating the conditions that engender heightened media scrutiny later in the cycle. "That's weakened the parties," he said. "It's really taken people out of the process. Under the old way, people in the community knew if a guy was a run-around. And if they knew that, they probably also knew enough not to take a chance on him, so they'd pick somebody else. Now we don't find out about these [personal] things until we get to the national level and the press gets blamed for spending too much time worrying about people's personal lives. In fact this is the first time that most of these people undergo any kind of scrutiny."

At all levels, political reporters must be aware of the issues that concern various communities and the positions of the various candidates. This argues in favor of news organizations assigning reporters to cover politics, even if it's only for the campaign season. A specialist will bring a depth of knowledge to the campaign story that a generalist—somebody who covered the cops last week, the zoning board yesterday, the candidate's appearance today and a labor negotiation tomorrow—will not.

"It's very easy for any reporter to base his or her story on the speech of the day, the campaign stop of the day, the theme of the day. But a reporter also has to identify what the crucial issue is in the campaign and press the candidate to talk about those issues," said Tom Mattesky, deputy Washington bureau chief for CBS News. "We don't have to look at politics as evil or candidates trying to deceive us as journalists, but I do think we have to be careful that we don't allow them to identify the agenda. We have to, as journalists, identify what's important and ask questions that touch on issues or explore issues that the candidates don't want to talk about."

It is not unusual for campaigns and candidates to adopt deliberate and well-orchestrated campaign plans based on avoiding very much direct contact with reporters. Few will shut out reporters completely, but they are not above making decisions based on who they perceive as friendly to the campaign and who they perceive as unfriendly. Presidential candidates, for example, will often devote significant time on a daily or regular basis to do one-on-one interviews with local TV anchors, while circumventing the national news media. The assumption on the part of the campaigns is that the local anchors will not ask questions that are as tough or probing as the national news media. Unfortunately this is occasionally true. Shamefully, some local anchors have even allowed campaigns to provide questions and used them.

"There's constant tension, over access and so forth. And it changes over the course of the campaign. During the primaries there's lots of access. They'll let you talk to them. As the campaign goes on it gets harder," said CBS Radio's Bob Fuss.

Veteran *Washington Post* reporter David Broder noted that lower-level candidates are more reluctant to appear to be dodging direct questions. "By and large if somebody's running for a statewide office or a local office you can get some interview time with them. They're not quite so arrogant that they think they can just sort of blow you off. But the presidential candidates feel perfectly free to do that."

Politicians like circumstances—and actively seek to create them—in which the news media have no option but to cover a campaign speech or appearance as the political story of the day. The candidate thus gets to control what he or she says and effectively limits the investigative or inquisitive role of reporters. The later in the campaign process, the less likely it is that a reporter will get to ask questions of the candidate. Leading candidates or those candidates locked in close races often deliberately try to avoid direct contact with the news media for fear of making the kind of mistake that can change the course of an election.

10.5 Media Manipulation

Access to candidates is just one form of the not-so-subtle campaign practice of attempting to manipulate the news media. Politicians want to control what is reported and thus control what the public sees, hears and reads about the candidate. It works the same way once candidates are elected and are involved in governance, but it is especially intense during an election campaign. Candidates believe that the better their press secretaries, the more they will be able to control the media.

CBS Radio's Fuss said it is constant. "Everything that's done is an attempt to manipulate you. Where you're standing, in terms of what you're going to see, is planned by somebody. The picture you're going to be looking at is designed to put the candidate in the best light." He added, "If there's a heckler in a crowd the handlers will often go to great lengths to keep you from finding out who that person was and what got them upset."

Seasoned reporters understand that the politicians and their aides want to use, manage and manipulate them. The reporter's task is to avoid it, but that's not always possible. For example, when a major candidate—for president, U.S. senator, or governor—is involved in a campaign event, the news media often have only two options: cover the event as it's presented or don't cover it at all. When manipulation is heavy-handed or when there is a repeated pattern of denying access to a candidate, many reporters include that information as a part of their stories.

Manipulating the news media takes on many forms. "The political forces do use the press for trial balloons. It's a time-tested and well-used strategy to find out whether an issue . . . is going to fly well with the public," said Michael Freedman, vice president of The George Washington University and former congressional press secretary. The big problem for political reporters is when a trial balloon is floated, usually by someone who will do so only on the condition of anonymity, the candidate can back away from it or disavow it in public and on the record, leaving the reporter looking foolish. (See chapter 12.5.)

Sometimes it is obvious that you're being used as the vehicle to launch a trial balloon. It is imperative to examine, test and analyze trial balloons before going into print or on the air with them. Is this really the candidate's position? Does it represent a policy change? Who has a vested interest in getting this information out? Why is this being given to me? Ask outsiders, other insiders and even the opposition about the information. Many veteran reporters who suspect they're being used for the launch of a trial balloon will find a way to tell their audience about it somewhere within the story.

Skilled politicians and their press secretaries make it their business to know and understand how the media operate and what they want and need. Part of the game of manipulation is to provide reporters with something new to report. CBS News's senior political editor Dotty Lynch called it the message of the day. "The savvy campaigns know how to write a 15-minute speech with three good 10-second quotes in it, and they know that's what will be picked up. They know how we work and usually you end up falling for it because those are the only interesting things in the speech."

10.6 Spin

On Oct. 13, 1988, the second debate between Republican presidential candidate George H. W. Bush and Democratic candidate Michael Dukakis took place in the Pauley Pavilion on the campus of UCLA. It was a warm, pleasant evening in Los Angeles. I was seated in the "radio ghetto," in the balcony about a mile from the stage, anchoring the

CBS News radio coverage of the confrontation. Most of my colleagues covering both campaigns viewed it as a make-or-break event for Dukakis. From a promising beginning, his campaign had stumbled and stuttered several times, and he went into the evening trailing Bush in most polls.

CNN anchor Bernard Shaw was the debate moderator and opened with a direct question to Dukakis, who had been damaged by Bush's allegations that he was soft on crime and by the Bush campaign's Willie Horton ad. (See chapter 10.3.) "Governor, if Kitty Dukakis [the candidate's wife] were raped and murdered, would you favor an irrevocable death penalty for the killer?" asked Shaw.

It was red meat. I expected Dukakis to grab it and show some passion and fire in his answer, something that had been lacking on the part of the Massachusetts Democrat throughout much of the campaign. (I found later that most of my news media colleagues had exactly the same expectation.) For the next two minutes, Dukakis gave a tepid, passionless answer that sounded more like a disinterested professor lecturing on the gestation period of a moth than a guy talking about the rape and murder of his wife. Dukakis restated his opposition to the death penalty, cited the drop in the crime rate in his state, and called for a hemispheric summit to fight a war on drugs. He never really addressed the personal issue of the hypothetical involvement of his wife.

Afterward, top staff members and campaign surrogates—Dukakis's spin doctors—fanned out among the reporters to say what a wonderful job their man did in the debate and how he took tough questions like the one asked by Shaw and demonstrated real leadership and courage.

It was classic spin.

Every journalism student in the country has heard the word, but there is often confusion about what spin really means. For the most part, spin is presenting information that is most beneficial to a candidate, politician or organization, and/or that makes the most positive presentation possible on behalf of the person or issue being discussed. It is not necessarily lying, but it often involves recasting the truth. Spinmeisters tend to use only facts that are beneficial, order information in a way that is positive and omit facts or information that may be negative or damaging.

On that October evening in Los Angeles, I asked one of Dukakis's spin doctors about the candidate's answer to Shaw's opening question. The response was that it was a terrific answer and clearly laid out his position on crime. There was no allusion to the candidate's lack of passion or dull recitation of facts. I asked the same question to one of Bush's spinmeisters and was told that Bush had again clearly defined the differences between his "values" and those of his opponent. The Bush camp had made a deliberate decision that less was more. Their spin could do no more harm to Dukakis than he had done to himself.

In retrospect, most political analysts believe that Shaw's question and Dukakis's answer were turning points in the waning days of the campaign and Dukakis did not rise to the challenge. No measure of spin could change what took place on the Pauley Pavilion stage that night.

For political reporters, spin is a fact of life and they have no choice but to learn how to deal with it. It is actually not very hard. If the reporter presumes that there's more than one side, he or she can treat the issue fairly despite the spin. If you're spun by one side, you have an obligation to get the spin from the other.

"There's no question you're being spun," said James Toedtman, associate editor of *Newsday*. "The problem is to keep your gyroscope running so you can fend it off."

"You need to resign yourself to the fact that you're going to be spun, you're going to have people every day of the week trying to send messages to you that they would like to have delivered to a mass audience," said former press secretary Michael Freedman. "You're going to have to distill from those messages that which is worthy of print or air and match that with a sense of fairness from whatever the opposing side is. But it is the job of some people to spin and try to persuade you that a certain story is worth putting on the air or in the paper; and there are going to be other people who are going to try to convince you otherwise."

Veteran *Washington Post* reporter Helen Dewar noted that one area in which campaigns tend to spin relentlessly concerns the meaning and significance of the votes cast by incumbents in the process of governance. In some cases, what's being said doesn't square with the facts. "I see very often that local papers will accept, without challenge, what a candidate says about the real meaning of his vote, for a tax increase or whatever, when it's purely made up," said Dewar, adding that the ball is then in the court of the reporter. "Press the candidate. Press the campaign. Ask them for something in print saying the senator really did lead the campaign for better treatment of animals or whatever. Ask for documentation and then get on the phone again. Check interest groups that worked on the issue."

As a reporter, being spun is to be expected. Buying the spin without checking and cross-checking the information will result in flawed and unfair news stories.

10.7 Dirty Tricks

Modern politics has moved a long way from the noble concept of public service envisioned by the Founding Fathers when they conceived of a representative form of government for the brand new United States. Running for office not only involves long hours, deep commitment, grueling schedules, high tension, intense pressure, sometimes clashing personalities and a level of personal competition that rivals contact sports, but it often involves the dark business of dirty tricks.

University of Virginia political science professor Larry Sabato (and coauthor Glenn Simpson) revealed much of the seamy world of political dirty tricks in their 1996 book *Dirty Little Secrets* (Times Books). The authors suggest that dirty tricks have become so pervasive that there is a cynical assumption on the part of politicians, reporters and the public that everybody does it.

Some of the notion of dirty tricks is traceable to Watergate—not just the break-in, but the cover-up and the use of the CIA and the IRS by President Nixon to "get" his enemies. Watergate may well reign as the home-run king of dirty tricks, but there's more than enough evidence of other campaigns engaging in the practice.

Opposition research has long been a staple of the dirty tricks business. In fact, there is a subset of political operatives who specialize in digging up dirt (often in exchange for very big fees) on the opposing candidate, his or her family or campaign staffers. Opposition researchers seek to find out everything they can about the target's sex life, financial affairs, medical history, personal relationships, religious practices, friends, business dealings, drinking habits, drug use, social and private behavior, morals and family life.

Researchers talk to everybody who ever knew the candidate. If the candidate bloodied another kid's nose on the playground in elementary school, you can bet that they've found that kid and talked to him or her. Ex-spouses, neighbors, coworkers, bosses, subordinates and anybody who has an axe to grind against the candidate will be interviewed. The opposition research file can be thousands of pages. And campaigns then make calculated decisions about what will be ignored, what will be used, how it will be used and when in the campaign it will be used.

Leaks of damaging information to the news media are a very common way in which campaigns use their opposition research. While the information that's leaked often provides the basis for news stories, reporters have an obligation to examine why the information is being leaked to them and what the benefit will be to the person who's leaking it. Very seldom in the political arena is information leaked without an ulterior motive on the part of the leaker.

Using leaked information that is damaging as the foundation for a carefully researched and fair news story is legitimate. A reporter who lets him or herself be used by a campaign to cause damage is ethically challenged. Reporters constantly need to be aware that rumor, innuendo, half-truths and misleading information are all part of the arsenal of the dirty tricksters. The tricksters are under no obligation to tell the truth. Nor do they always operate within the law in obtaining their information.

A word of caution: If somebody leaks information to you that you know to have been obtained by illegal means, and you know who obtained it, there can be potentially serious legal consequences for using it. Third party intercepts, for example, where a third party records a telephone conversation of two or more other people, are illegal everywhere unless the intercept is done by a law-enforcement agency acting under the umbrella of a court order approving the wiretap. If you come into possession of such illegally obtained information, take it to your news organization's legal department before you air it or print it. There are circumstances in which using the material may be permissible (see *Bartnicki v. Vopper*, a case in which an illegal third party intercept was obtained legally and aired by a radio station). But err on the side of caution if you know or suspect that information you're being given was obtained illegally. In many cases you have an obligation to report such illegally obtained information to the proper authorities.

During the height of the Clinton-Lewinsky scandal, Linda Tripp—the woman who originally recorded her conversations with Monica Lewinsky about Lewinsky's relationship with the president—was indicted by a Maryland grand jury for making the recordings. Maryland is one of several states that requires the consent of both parties before a conversation can be recorded. Failure to do so is a criminal offense.

In most cases where information obtained from dirty tricks is leaked to a reporter, the reporter will not know or be made privy to how it was obtained by the dirty tricksters. In fact most campaigns will have several layers of insulation between the candidate, the press secretary, other top operatives and the dirty tricksters in order to allow them to deny knowledge of any illegal activities conducted by the tricksters on behalf of the candidate.

The menu of dirty tricks goes well beyond interviewing everybody who ever knew the candidate in order to dig up dirt. Opposition researchers often pick up the trash from a candidate's home or campaign headquarters, looking for anything potentially embarrassing or revealing about the candidate or the campaign. They'll comb through court documents, business documents, newspaper clips and public records looking for anything that might be damaging.

It is not at all unusual for one campaign to plant a "mole" in an opposing campaign. Campaign volunteers often rise quickly to positions of trust within a campaign organization and as a result are able to hear and see highly sensitive information. If the volunteer (or even in a few rare cases a paid staffer) passes that sensitive information along to the opposition, it can do serious damage.

Pranks and practical jokes are also done by one campaign against another. They are often more in the form of annoyance than serious political subterfuge, but occasionally they make their way into the news. One campaign ordering dozens of pizzas to be sent to the other campaign, or canceling hotel reservations for the opposing candidate and staff, are examples.

Professor Sabato said there's more in the realm of dirty tricks on the horizon. "The Internet. There are various ways of hacking into the e-mail system at other campaigns. That's been done and it's very difficult to detect. You actually have to have a specialist on board who can be monitoring your system."

One of the purposes for the bungled break-in at Democratic headquarters in the Watergate was to bug the office of party chairman Lawrence O'Brien. "Of course there's eavesdropping," said Sabato. "There are just a thousand advanced ways of doing eavesdropping . . . but you don't even have to break in any more. As long as they're meeting in a glass [windowed] office in a high-rise building, there's equipment today—laser technology and parabolic microphones—that can pick up what's going on from across the street."

Campaigns go to great lengths to keep their dirty tricks under wraps. They'll usually deny that any kind of dirty trickery is going on. But as Woodward and Bernstein did with Watergate, when a reporter uncovers it, it is almost always a news story. What candidates fear is that if dirty tricks become the story, that can cause serious damage and even supersede the newsworthiness of the campaign itself.

11

Taking the Public Pulse

Political journalists and politicians all use polls, surveys and other methods of public opinion research. It gives both groups insight into what the public is thinking, which issues raised by the politicians are resonating and which are not, and how a candidate stands in relation to his or her opposition.

Politicians use polls to help them decide whether to run, to frame their messages, to test their ideas, to determine where and how best to spend their money and to track the race.

Polling and public opinion research have been around for decades. The process has evolved. "It's radically different compared to when I started," said Geoffry Garin, a veteran pollster with Peter D. Hart Research Associates. "When I began at Hart Research in 1978, about half our research was conducted door-to-door, which was a wonderful way to do research. You could speak to respondents for a half hour to 45 minutes. You could use all sorts of visual aids. Now, 25 years later, zero percent of our research is door-to-door for a variety of reasons, having to do with cost and social changes. People are frightened to let interviewers inside their houses and interviewers are frightened to go into most neighborhoods."

Yet polls abound and, in fact, there is more political polling being done than ever.

11.1 Polling and the Press

Polls fall into two broad categories: private or proprietary polls that are done for a specific candidate or organization, and public or published polls that are conducted by and/or for major news organizations. Reporters use both.

The goal of public or published polls is to give readers and viewers a way of understanding why a campaign is unfolding the way it is.

"What are the trends and forces that tend to shape the dynamics of a campaign so that the public can have access to some of the same kinds of information candidates have when they're making decisions," said Garin.

The public or published polls often have similarities. They ask similar questions. The universe of potential respondents is the same. They are conducted over roughly the same time period. Common preelection questions include, "If the election were held today, which candidate would you vote for?" Reporters should not rely on only one poll if more than one is available. Comparing the information in two or more polls can reveal flaws or anomalies in the data, or it can reinforce and strengthen the findings. The key is that the polls were conducted on about the same dates, examining the same population, and asking similar if not identical questions. For example, most major news organizations sample national opinion about the president's job approval rating at regular intervals. These polls can be compared.

Most top political journalists believe that published polls are useful tools, but they are cognizant of the fact that overuse of them can turn them into crutches and diminish the impact of what they are reporting. "We have come to rely too much on polls and polling to drive our coverage," said NewsLab's Deborah Potter. "At the same time I'm not advocating that we ignore them. Some research we did in '96 shows that viewers, and readers, want to know the score, if you will. If you went to a basketball game you wouldn't want them not to have a scoreboard. You still want to watch the game, but you want to know how they're doing." The majority of political reporters attempt to strike a balance regarding when, in what manner and how often they use polls in what they report.

"Most national reporters use polling as a tool both to clue them in to why the candidates are doing what they're doing and also to understand major themes," said Garin. "Local and regional reporters way over-cover the horse race aspects of polls and use them to determine how much coverage somebody's going to get, or the type of coverage that somebody's going to get. So sometimes they cover somebody as a loser long before the election's ever held and the reality may be that the person has a good chance of being elected, but they don't get a fair shot from a reporter on account of being behind in a poll. That's not good for the political system and it's not good journalism either."

When a reporter is given information from a private or proprietary poll, the reporter needs to examine why the information is being proffered, who will benefit from its release and what the benefit will be. Questions need to be asked before the information is used. Nobody is going to let you see proprietary polling data because they like you. There is something in it that they want before the public. In these cases, it is essential for the reporter to source his or her information in as much detail as possible so the reporter's readers, viewers and listeners can draw their own conclusions about the validity and/or importance of the polling data. Even if the reporter agrees to provide the individual giving the information anonymity, telling the audience that it came from one side or the other or from an interest group is valuable.

Garin pointed out that there is an inherent danger if pollsters themselves leak inaccurate or faulty data. "Most polling firms that have been around for a while and hope to be around for a long while know that giving a reporter bad or inaccurate information is not good for your long-term reputation. Information is the currency of journalism and it is something you can trade with," he said.

Political operatives, handlers and staffers who leak proprietary polling information are not as constrained by concern over long-term consequences as firms like Hart Research, and as a result they will occasionally provide incomplete, flawed, misleading and even inaccurate data. Some have even, on rare occasions, doctored the numbers to make them appear more favorable to their candidate or unfavorable to the opposition. It's up to the reporter to check what is provided and not simply rush it into print or onto the air.

Some of the bigger news organizations do exit polling outside voting stations on Election Day. Staffers ask voters in selected precincts who they voted for and why. The results of the exit polling often weigh into election night coverage, and calling the various races on the part of broadcasters. For newspapers, the results of the exit polls play into post-election stories about why the voters voted as they did.

Broadcasters, in the past, have used the information from exit polling to extrapolate the race results and "call" races long before the raw votes themselves have been tabulated. It is especially controversial when broadcasters call races before the polls have closed elsewhere. The argument is that calling presidential races in the East, where polls have closed, can negatively impact the behavior of voters in the West, where the polls are still open. It is unlikely, however, that the networks are going to remain silent until the polls have closed on the West Coast or in Hawaii.

In 2000, the networks pledged not to call races until the polls had closed in any given state. In Florida, the polls close at 7 p.m. The networks, however, forgot that Florida's panhandle is in the Central time zone and blithely called the state (incorrectly) at 7 p.m. Eastern Standard Time. They promise that they won't do that again.

"Most campaigns pay for polling to affect the outcome of the election, not to understand the outcome of the election," said Garin. "Once Election Day has come, most campaigns say that I've spent all my money, my fate is in the hands of the voters. It's up to news organizations and universities to take it from there. And that's where most of the exit polling gets done. And it's a very important tool in understanding what happened."

11.2 Polling and the Politicians

"Most of the work that we do is done for the internal consumption of campaigns. They're for an audience of five or six people—candidate, campaign manager, media consultant and a few other folks who are spending the campaign's money," said Garin. "In politics you're dealing with two very limited resources—money and the attention of the voters. Our goal as researchers is to help candidates maximize both of those scarce resources." He noted that the pace of polling activity increases as the election approaches.

The first poll that's usually done for a politician is called a benchmark poll. That provides information that will be weighed in making a decision whether to run or not. The poll is taken to reveal whether the candidate has a chance of winning, the public's view of the candidate and what issues are of paramount concern to the voters.

During the course of the campaign, many candidates and their organizations rely on tracking polls, a series of polls conducted at regular intervals that chart movement on the part of the electorate or segments of the electorate. "Internally a tracking poll is designed to understand what's happening in an election at a point when the voters are paying attention to it," said Garin. "Or if you're spending a lot of money on commercials, are they working and, if not, it suggests that you probably want to do something different. Or if your opponent is spending a lot of money on commercials, are they working? Do you need to rebut them somehow?" He also said that tracking polls have an impact on cash flow within a campaign.

One critical use of polling within campaigns is to identify voters who will make the difference between winning and losing—ticket-splitting areas, uncommitted voters and undecided voters. Garin noted that when voters have expressed a party preference, that's usually a good barometer of how they'll vote. The battle is for those voters who are genuinely uncommitted. "The size of that group varies from election to election. It's usually somewhere between a quarter and third of the electorate. And that's what you're fighting over from the very beginning of the race. For the other three-quarters or two-thirds, their votes are almost entirely predictable based on their attitudes about parties and politics and government."

Once a campaign has identified uncommitted or swing voters, polling is used to help identify the arguments that will help move those voters toward voting for the candidate. "Then you target your advertising to those kinds of people," said Garin. "You know who they are demographically or through other kinds of characteristics, and you try to buy your TV time and focus your mail budget or your radio budget at those groups. So our market research is aimed at finding the most persuasive message aimed, targeted, to the people who are most likely to be persuaded by it."

Garin added that polling is not restricted to positive campaign uses. "It is perfectly legitimate if, for example, we were working against Rob Armstrong in a congressional race and we were going to run a negative commercial about Rob Armstrong. We would want to know which of four negative commercials would be most effective. So we would call up a random sample of voters in the district and say 'If you knew that Rob Armstrong did this, would that make you less likely to vote for him?' And we'd ask that about four different topics. We would know which of those topics we should make a commercial about."

He distinguished this type of research from push polling (see chapter 11.4), which is a telemarketing technique designed to sway voters away from or toward a particular candidate. In polling linked to negative commercials, "there is a research purpose," said Garin. "It's being conducted under legitimate research conditions—for example, do we have a representative random sample. It's not designed to convey the information but to find out what works."

Politicians also use polling once they're elected to test policy initiatives and find out what the public is thinking about various issues. Former President Bill Clinton certainly used polling as much as any recent politician. His one-time pollster Dick Morris once told the CBS News broadcast 60 Minutes that Clinton used polling "as often as he used respiration, as often as he breathed." That was an exaggeration. Nonetheless, CNN's senior political correspondent Candy Crowley said, "I think that President Clinton, in some ways, gave polling a bad name."

Crowley pointed to a trend among post-Clinton politicians. "I think there is a movement to appear not to be using consultants and pollsters as much as they have been. Of course, they may be using consultants and pollsters to tell them not to use consultants and pollsters."

11.3 The Mechanics of Polls

Most polling is now done over the telephone. A common technique for obtaining a random sample involves a process known as "random digit dialing." Pollsters will program a computer to dial numbers within certain area codes and using certain prefixes. The older method of picking numbers from the phone book at random did not account for cellular telephones and unlisted numbers. Even random digit dialing precludes participation in a poll by people who do not have telephones at all.

There is nothing scattershot about polling. While there are people who will try to tell you that the polls are wrong, inaccurate, unreliable and biased, that is not reliably the case when the polling is conducted using the accepted methodology of the American Association for Public Opinion Research (AAPOR). The mathematical conclusions are based on time-tested application of statistics and probabilities.

Reporters using polling data must remember that polls are a snapshot. They reflect one particular time period. What may have been an accurate picture a month ago may not be accurate today. Checking the date(s) on which a poll was conducted is essential.

If a poll does not provide such information as the sample size, the date or dates of the survey and the margin of error, reporters should be very wary about using the information. As a reporter I was always skeptical about polls with a margin of error greater than +/- 5 percentage points. At +/- 5, the range is 10 points and in the political realm that's so large that the significance of the results is suspect. (For example, in a poll with that kind of a margin of error, if candidate A is favored by 44 percent of those surveyed and candidate B is favored by 41 percent, with 15 percent undecided, it's largely meaningless, because within that margin the numbers could be reversed and still be accurate.)

For reporters who have not taken a course in research, the AAPOR has a detailed collection of standards and practices. The entire collection of documents can be accessed at www.aapor.org. The following is a thumbnail sketch of information that is particularly of interest to political journalists culled from AAPOR's "Best Practices for Survey and Public Opinion Research":

Have specific goals for the survey. The objectives of a high quality survey or poll should be specific, clear-cut and unambiguous. Such surveys are carried out solely to develop statistical information about the subject, not to produce predetermined results, nor as a ruse for marketing, fund-raising, changing voters' minds or similar activities. . . .

Select samples that will represent the population to be studied. A replicable or *repeatable* plan is developed to randomly choose a sample capable of meeting the survey's goals. Sampling should be designed to guard against unplanned selectiveness. . . . In a bona fide survey, the sample is not selected haphazardly or only from persons who volunteer to participate. It is scientifically chosen so that each person in the population will have a measurable chance of selection. This way the results can be reliably projected from the sample to the larger population with known levels of certainty/precision. . . . Virtually all surveys taken seriously by social scientists, policy makers and the informed media use some form of *random or probability sampling*, the methods of which are grounded in statistical theory and the theory of probability. . . .

Take great care in matching question wording to the concepts being measured and the population studied. Based on the goals of the survey, questions for respondents are designed and arranged in a logical format and order to create a survey questionnaire. The ideal survey or poll recognizes that planning the questionnaire is one of the most critical stages in the survey development process, and gives careful attention to all phases of questionnaire development and design, including . . . question wording and order. . . . Beyond their specific content, however, the manner in which questions are asked, as well as the specific response categories provided, can greatly affect the results of a survey. Concepts should be clearly defined and questions should be unambiguously phrased. Question wording should be carefully examined for special sensitivity or bias. . . .

Train interviewers carefully on interviewing techniques and the subject matter of the survey. . . . Good interviewer techniques should be stressed, such as how to make initial contacts, how to deal with reluctant respondents, how to conduct interviews in a professional manner, and how to avoid influencing or biasing responses. . . .

Use statistical, analytical and reporting techniques appropriate to the data collected. Excellence in the practice of survey and public opinion research requires that data analysis and interpretation be competent and clear, that findings or results be presented fully, understandably and fairly. . . . Findings and interpretations should be presented honestly and objectively, with full reporting of all relevant findings, including any that may seem contradictory or unfavorable. . . .

Disclose all methods of the survey to permit evaluation and replication. Excellence in survey practice requires that survey methods be fully disclosed and reported in sufficient detail to permit replication by another researcher, and that all data (subject to appropriate safeguards to maintain privacy and confidentiality) be fully documented and made available for expedient examination.

The AAPOR's own list of elements to be disclosed includes most things reporters should look for in assessing the reliability of polling data, including who sponsored the poll, the wording of the questions, the sample size and the universe it represents (is it a national poll, a state poll, a city poll), the estimate of sampling error and the date or dates when the poll was conducted.

When proprietary polling data is leaked or made available to a journalist by a campaign or other political organization, the reporter ought to ask those questions. Often the person or organization leaking the information will not provide it, and this should be reported.

Journalists using polling information have an obligation to report both what they know and what they do not.

In addition, reporters should be very wary of information obtained from Internet surveys, questionnaires in which respondents have the option to participate, man-on-the-street surveys and polls in which people are asked to phone in their votes/opinions. None of these fit within the criteria of scientific polling. Occasionally such information makes an interesting anecdote within a story, but only if it is reported as such and not represented to be a scientific poll.

11.4 Push Polling

Push polling is not polling or survey research at all. It is an underhanded technique of persuasion used by some campaigns and/or interest groups backing a particular candidate that is designed to push voters away from voting for one person and pull them toward voting for another.

From a journalistic standpoint, it verges on the dishonest. When a campaign or interest group engages in push polling, that may be newsworthy with regard to the ethical practices of the campaign or interest group, but the results of the poll should not be reported as anything but anecdotal to the practice. Unfortunately, some campaigns and interest groups provide push polling information to reporters and it regularly finds its way into print and on the air as unchallenged polling data. That it gets reported with such regularity is evidence that many reporters do not understand legitimate polling well enough to differentiate serious polling data from this illegitimate campaign tactic.

"Push polling is when you are trying to persuade people under the guise of polling. It is a way of conveying negative information under the guise of impartial research. And if you call up several thousand people, you plant an idea and they don't think it's campaigning because there's no attribution to the campaign. And you wouldn't call up any several thousand people, you call up the people you knew to be swing voters," said Garin.

The American Association of Public Opinion Research soundly condemns push polling. "Conducting a so-called 'push poll,' a telemarketing technique in which telephone calls are used to canvass potential voters, feeding them false or misleading 'information' about a candidate under the pretense of taking a poll to see how this 'information' affects voter preferences. . . . The intent is to disseminate campaign propaganda under the guise of conducting a legitimate public opinion poll." (The entire survey of "practices the AAPOR condemns" can be accessed at www.aapor.org.)

Garin and other legitimate pollsters also decry the practice. "It happens fairly often in campaigns and it's bad for us as pollsters. It's something that we don't condone or participate in. It is not legitimate in any way. We're in the research business. This is not research. It's persuasion."

11.5 Focus Groups and Instant-Response Testing

Focus groups are small groups—25 to 40 people—gathered in one place. A trained leader conducts the session or sessions. Focus groups can be used to test campaign messages, test a candidate's language (known as word testing), screen advertising and discuss issues.

Focus groups provide understanding at "a level of depth that you just can't get with a telephone interview," said Garin. "You can really understand the motivation that people bring to their political behavior. Polls very frequently tell you what people think. Focus groups tell you why they feel the way they do. Focus groups are very important to understanding the vocabulary and language of politics—what words are understandable and not understandable. What's the language that regular people use when they talk about issues."

The makeup of focus groups can vary depending on the purpose of the research. Sometimes a focus group will be made up of all Republicans or all Democrats or all independents; sometimes the focus group will be all supporters of one particular candidate; often the focus group will be a mix. Sometimes the focus groups are broken down demographically—all women, all men, certain age groups, racial and ethnic groups, religious groups.

Usually, focus groups are conducted in rooms with two-way mirrors so the gathering can be recorded without having the participants cognizant of the cameras and microphones. In some cases, people who participate in focus groups are paid a minimal amount for their time.

The interpretation of the information obtained through focus-group research is used by politicians to sharpen their message or change the language of their presentation. It tells them what's working and what's not. It also tells them why.

In addition, some researchers who conduct focus groups add instant-response testing to the mix. Instant-response testing allows researchers to use real-time responses to a speech, a commercial or some other visual presentation. Each participant is given a box about the size of a cigarette package. It usually contains a dial or a slide with corresponding numbers zero to +5 and zero to –5 or 1 to 10 with 5 representing the middle. As the respondents watch the speech, commercial or presentation they are told to gauge what they like and what they don't by pushing the slide up and down.

The participants usually are broken down into sub-groups—Republicans, Democrats and independents, for example—and their responses are measured by a moving graph or series of moving graphs representing each group, imposed over the speech, commercial or presentation by a computer. When there's a spike or a dip, the researcher can determine exactly what word, phrase, message, gesture or image is drawing the positive or negative response. In the case of multiple graphs, it also can tell the researchers where the groups are responding alike and where they are not. Adjustments can then be made in accordance with what the instant-response research has revealed.

There is experimentation underway to test campaign commercials through the Internet, allowing researchers to obtain the same kind of instant-response data without having to convene a focus group. It is entirely likely, if this proves successful, that the Internet will provide a platform for other kinds of instant-response testing.

A Conversation with Elaine Povich

Washington correspondent: *Newsday*
Author: *Partners and Adversaries: The Contentious Connection Between Congress and the Media*
  (Freedom Forum, 1996)

I never had to ask many questions when I covered the same Capitol Hill news conference as Elaine Povich. She always seemed to have my questions on her list. But as I discovered later, she had almost everybody's questions on her list. Research and legwork, I would learn, were her hallmarks. So were a keen wit and sense of humor.

It didn't take me long to encounter this energetic, hard-working, tenacious, smart young woman right after my beat became Congress in 1989. She was everywhere. "Who's that?" I asked a colleague. "Elaine Povich of the Chicago Tribune," *was the answer. "Great reporter." That was high praise in a press corps that included some of the best journalists in the world.*

Her coverage of President Clinton's national health care plan won her the Everett Dirksen Award for distinguished congressional reporting. She left the Tribune *in 1995 and became a Freedom Forum fellow, where she wrote her book. She joined* Newsday *in 1996.*

Newspapering is in her blood. Her great uncle was the revered Washington Post *sports columnist Shirley Povich. She got her first taste of real reporting while she was still an undergraduate at Cornell University.*

E.P.: "My first summer internship I'm in college and I was working at my hometown newspaper in Bath, Maine—just a little town on the coast. And I'm covering the school board. The president of the school board is the father of one of my best friends. So I cover the school board that night and went back and I wrote the story. And the next day I ran into the president of the school board on the street. I said, 'Hi. How are you?'

"He said, 'Oh, I'm okay. About that story. I used to know you. You used to be such a nice girl. What's happened to you?'" [Laughs.]

R.A.: *What was your first political story?*

E.P.: "I was with UPI and was directly involved in Jimmy Carter's 1976 victory. I was working in Jackson, Mississippi, at the time. And as you may or may not recall Mississippi was the state that put Carter over the top that year when he won. And it fell to us in the Jackson bureau to call the state, which is the old-fashioned way we did it. The wire services called the states.

"And I will never forget my bureau chief, Andy Reese, sitting there smoking pipe after pipe of tobacco and getting more and more pressure to call the state for Carter and him not wanting to do it. It was an old-fashioned way of doing things. We used to phone the precincts and find out how things were going. We had local reporters at various counties throughout the state telling us what the vote was in those counties. And he was getting tremendous pressure from New York to call the state and he wouldn't do it.

"So as the rookie reporter, it fell to me to answer the phones that night. And I answered the phone and it was the New York bureau on the line and they said, 'How come you haven't called goddamned Mississippi?'

"And I replied with no trepidation at all for a rookie reporter, 'Because we use goddamned paper ballots!' So they had to wait until all the paper ballots were counted. And finally Andy, may he rest in peace, called the state for Carter and thankfully Carter won."

R.A.: *What's the best part about political journalism?*

E.P.: "Learning about why people run for office, what makes them tick, why they want to put themselves out there. You know, it's not like being a car salesman. If I'm selling Chevrolets and I sell you a car and you don't like it, you blame Chevy, not me. If I'm selling myself as a candidate and I go out there and say something you don't like, you blame me. What makes a person want to do that to themselves. What makes a man or woman put themselves out there, in front of the world, and make all the mistakes that people make and say all the dumb things that people say? What's in it for them? Why do they do it?

"I think what I've found at root is most of them really like people. Not all of them. There are some notable exceptions. But most of them like people. They enjoy getting out there and seeing people. This may sound a little pollyannaish but they really like doing things for people. And to watch them as they try—cynically in some cases, sincerely in some cases—as they try to sell themselves to the public is worth the price of admission."

R.A.: *What's the downside?*

E.P.: "Having to hear the same speech over and over and over again in 17 different towns on 17 different days and never being able to turn your ears off totally, because that might be the one speech in which he screws up."

R.A.: *Does anyone stand out as most interesting?*

E.P.: "I'd have to say John McCain, hands down. Part of that had to do with access, being able to be on his bus and having him accessible to us, as reporters, made him more interesting simply because we knew more about him. He is a fascinating character. He's had many incarnations in his life and has learned from every single one of them. And he's retained that knowledge. It's shaped him and made him the man he is. He was endlessly fascinating."

R.A.: *Politicians love to talk. . . .*
E.P.: [Laughs.]

R.A.: *What's the trick in getting them to say something of substance, slicing through the spin?*

E.P.: "The more access you have to someone the more likely it is that you'll be able to get them to blast out of the mode of a stock answer to every question, and actually answer your question in a way that's unique, different and—God forbid—interesting. The one thing about McCain is that after a while you'd either run out of things to ask or he would run out of stock answers and start talking about things that he actually believed.

"Now that got him in trouble more than once. For example, one reporter asked him about what he would do if his daughter was pregnant and there was the whole abortion/anti-abortion thing. He actually sort of said what he believed. He said it would be her choice, which didn't make the anti-abortion people very happy.

"So I think you can get answers by continued access to people—the campaign plane, the campaign bus.

"Of course, many of the candidates maneuver mightily to keep you away and to keep you focused only on the story of the day. They want you focused on what that speech is against whatever backdrop it is. You know, the Busy Bee Restaurant event with—quote—real people, a camera story. But access is vital to getting them to say something."

R.A.: *Newsday's a big paper but it covers a very specific area—Long Island, New York. How much do you try to localize national stories?*

E.P.: "A lot. I have a much better chance of getting a national issue into the paper if I can localize the story in some way. I did a story just this week about citizenship for immigrants who serve in the U.S. military. The way I got that into the paper was to take a poor kid from the Dominican Republic who was killed in Iraq and write the story from that point of view. I told the story through his case.

"When he was killed his family decided they didn't want to ask for citizenship. They were so bitter about his death that there was nothing the United States could do. But two weeks later, after a bit of reflection, they decided that he loved this country and he died fighting for this country and perhaps he would have wanted citizenship. That opens up the larger political issue, a bill that's moving through Congress to make it easier for non-citizen soldiers and their families to become citizens. So I brought this whole national issue together, crystallizing it around this one guy."

R.A.: *You cover the governance side of politics as well as the electoral side of politics. Do you view the process as a continuum or do you treat them as separate entities?*

E.P.: "A little bit of both. A campaign is different than governing. There's a wonderful line from one of those movies when the president is elected and he turns to his staff and says, 'Now what do we do?' There's some of that.

"But it's also a continuum. Most people run for office presumably so they can take the office they seek. And presumably when they take the office they seek they can do something with it. Of course, that's not always the case. Some people get elected and disappear. They get elected to the Senate and you never see them again for six years until it's time to run again. That is a fatal flaw that can be exploited by their opposition.

"The idea is you persuade people that you should be elected to this office because you can do X, Y and Z. And once you're elected they fully expect that you will at least attempt to do X, Y and Z. Part of my job is finding out whether they attempt to do X, Y and Z, whether they are successful at doing X, Y and Z and whether it will give them something to run on next time."

R.A.: *So you take what they said during the campaign and see if they kept their promises?*

E.P.: "Sometimes when they're campaigning they don't know that it's pretty hard to accomplish X. They should know this but they don't, but they get to Congress and in the case of the House they're only one of 435 or in the Senate they're only one of a hundred and it's not always easy to fulfill what they've promised.

"It's very interesting to see whether they abandon it, try to weasel out of the promise, or whether they work within the system and settle for a [non-binding] sense-of-the-Senate resolution saying we believe in motherhood."

12

Ethics

Most serious journalists who have the commitment and drive to get into the business, and stay in it, do so because they believe that what they do is critical to the functioning of the American democracy. They are generally idealistic. They believe that good, fair, honest reporting will make society a little bit better and will help people.

While working political journalists don't spend a whole lot of time talking about ethics, most reporters, even young ones, have pretty finely tuned antennae for what is right and what is wrong. Whether they articulate them or not, most have strong moral and ethical values. Among reporters, it is common to hear discussions of issues and how they should be covered. While this is, de facto, the realm of ethics, many reporters relegate the word "ethics" to the province of journalism professors to be discussed within the confines of an academic setting.

As a matter of practice, most reporters have had somebody along the way, as I did, put it in a nutshell for them. "You won't have a problem in the world," said my mentor, the late Bob Martin, when I was just a kid in Denver, "so long as you just report what you know as gospel and tell the truth." Not bad advice. I always tried to do that.

Nonetheless, political reporters deal with ethical questions on a regular basis. One of the best ethical guidelines is for a reporter to examine and know the direction of his or her own moral and ethical compass. Even for veteran reporters, producers and editors, a little self-reflection and discussion with peers and colleagues is not a bad thing. For young reporters, it is essential.

12.1 Plagiarism and Journalistic Dishonesty

When I started work on this book, I had no intention of saying anything about plagiarism and other types of reportorial dishonesty. I did not think it was necessary. Every semester I would give a cursory warning to my students and leave it at that. After all, honesty, integrity and ethical credibility were hallmarks of good journalists.

I changed my mind and my classroom practice in April 2003, when Jayson Blair, the functional equivalent of a reportorial suicide bomber, blew himself up in the crowded marketplace in the village of journalism. Blair was a 27-year-old *wunderkind*, a rising star reporter at *The New York Times*. The slow motion detonation of his career began when it was exposed that he had lifted wholesale chunks of an article first published in the *San Antonio Express-News* under his own byline and without attribution.

There had been warning flags before, indications that some of his quotes and accounts that seemed too good to be true were, in fact, too good to be true. By the time the dust settled, the explosion laid bare a trail of made-up quotes, plagiarism and deception. He filed reports about things he did not see, from places he had not been, quoting people he did not talk to. Blair's journalistic career ended even more quickly than his meteoric rise at the nation's once- (and probably still) preeminent newspaper.

Jayson Blair is the undisputed poster child for ethically challenged reporters everywhere. His actions cost two of his superiors—executive editor Howell Raines and managing editor Gerald Boyd—their jobs. They resigned in the wake of the scandal. It tarnished the reputation of one of the world's greatest newspapers. It made a public that was already cynical about some news reporting even more so. The casualties were all over the village square.

Most of my former colleagues, those still laboring in the journalistic vineyards, have no sympathy. Unbelievable. Incomprehensible. Stupid. Appalling. Just a few of the expressions that accompanied even oblique references to the Blair case.

Put as simply as possible for journalism students and working journalists: Plagiarism, making up quotes, embellishing facts—the type of journalistic dishonesty embodied in what Blair did—is a career-ender. Finito! Kaput! Journalism students caught engaging in such practices should be flunked and expelled. In the real world, working reporters know that such conduct will get them fired and will leave such a bad smell around them that it is highly unlikely that they will ever work in the news field again. Nor should they.

12.2 Conflicts of Interest

In 1993, my wife, Barbara Stafford, was appointed deputy assistant secretary of commerce for Anti-Dumping and Countervailing Duty Investigations. That made her a senior official in the Clinton Administration, charged with investigating allegations of unfair trade practices leveled by U.S. industries against competing industries in other nations exporting to the United States. It was a very active and very important position. International trade and unfair trade practices were big news.

As a CBS News correspondent, I went to my bosses when her appointment became likely and told them that in order to avoid any actual or perceived conflicts of interest, I thought it best if I recuse myself from covering any stories involving her area. My bosses agreed and, during the time of her government service, CBS News assigned other reporters to cover stories involving anti-dumping regulations, countervailing duties and unfair trade practices. When she became involved in reforming U.S. law and writing the implementing regulations for GATT (General Agreement on Tariffs and Trade), that too became off limits for me because of the potential of a conflict of interest.

Conflicts of interest and potential conflicts arise when a reporter has a personal interest or stake in what he or she may be covering. If a reporter's husband, wife, son, daughter, mother, father or significant other is a candidate or campaign official, the potential of a conflict of interest arises. James Carville, an advisor to then-candidate Bill Clinton, and Mary Matalin, a campaign advisor to the first President George Bush, were dating during the 1992 presidential race. In order to avoid an obvious conflict of interest, they put their relationship on hold until after the election. They subsequently got married.

The SPJ (Society of Professional Journalists) Code of Ethics says journalists should "be free of obligation to any interest other than the public's right to know." It advises reporters to "avoid conflicts of interest, real or perceived," and recommends that reporters "disclose unavoidable conflicts." (Access the code at www.spj.org .)

A subset within the realm of conflicts of interest and potential conflicts is whether journalists ought to make speeches or other presentations to outside groups and get paid for them. Some news organizations have written standards and practices which prohibit reporters from making speeches and/or receiving speaking fees. The premise is that if a reporter is paid for making a speech or presentation, that reporter may be, or appear to be, beholden to those who paid him or her either directly or indirectly. For example, if a reporter were paid for making a speech to the Rocky Mountain Ford Dealers Association and subsequently was given the assignment to cover a safety problem involving Ford vehicles, would there be an actual or potential conflict? Is there the potential that the reporter will in some way go easy on those people who have paid him or her to perform?

A significant number of high-profile journalists make speeches and other appearances and get paid for them. Some reporters write books and make appearances for which they are paid in connection with the books. While there is no hard-and-fast rule, reporters need to weigh carefully whether their journalistic credibility is being jeopardized.

In some cases, it goes even further, to encompass conditions of employment. Some local television and radio stations require their on-air talent to make personal appearances on behalf of the stations. While these appearances are generally not paid for by the groups before which the on-air people appear, it sets up the potential of a conflict of interest. If the local anchor, as an example, is the emcee at an event sponsored by a church, service club, business group or civic organization, does that imply that the personality or the station endorses the positions of that group? If the anchor speaks to the annual meeting of local public school teachers, is that an endorsement of the positions of the teachers' unions? Most stations and local TV news people look at it as station promotion. But the potential dangers and threats to journalistic credibility need to be considered.

Credibility is a measure, some argue the sole measure, of a journalist's value. When credibility is diminished, the reporter's worth is diminished and his or her news organization is negatively impacted.

12.3 Socializing

There are two types of political reporters: those who socialize with the people they cover and those who do not. When I was reporting in Washington, I opted not to socialize with those I covered, although there were times when it simply couldn't be avoided. If I attended the annual congressional or White House Correspondents Association dinners, socializing was part of being there. Occasionally I would play in a charity golf tournament and end up playing with a politician or political appointee.

There is no consensus among the pros, so herewith I offer the views of some of the best in the business. Each individual reporter must make up his or her own mind.

David Broder of *The Washington Post* said he understands both sides but has made a decision for himself: "My wife and I have not built our social life around the people that I cover. I like many of them but I don't socialize with them. I find that makes it much easier to do my job. You give up what I'm sure would be some pleasant evenings and conversations. I listen sympathetically to people who say you really get to know these people if you have them over for dinner or they have you over for dinner. I'm prepared to believe that's the case, but it's not a relationship that I've ever wanted. I'm very comfortable being with them on my job."

Bob Schieffer of CBS News said, "It's possible to be a reporter and know the people you're covering. It's easier to cover people that you don't like than people that you do like. It's not that you're going to take sides with either one of them. You have to keep a certain distance, but I'm not one of these people that thinks you have to keep yourself completely separated."

He added, "When you've been around as long as I have you know people. The 2000 presidential race was the first presidential campaign where I had a personal relationship with the major candidates on both sides. Al Gore's kids had gone to school with my kids. I had seen the Gores over the years at various kinds of parent-student events. I thought they were a wonderful family. I came to know Bill Bradley when I was doing the [CBS] *Weekend News*. I was flying back and forth to New York on the shuttle. He was representing New Jersey [in the U.S. Senate] and I'd often sit with him on the shuttle and we'd have these great conversations. He's a true intellectual. John McCain [R-Ariz.] and I are about the same age and we've had a lot of fun over the years jousting with each other as I covered the Senate. And George [W.] Bush I knew because my brother was his partner in the [Texas Rangers] baseball team."

"You have to be careful about developing genuine friendships because it's inescapably going to faze the way that you cover things," said Brit Hume of Fox News. "A minimum amount of socializing is acceptable. But you have to be careful about it. You don't have to live like a monk, but you have to be careful. It ultimately gets you into the back-field and you don't want to be there. You want to be on the sidelines."

Newsday's James Toedtman said, "I have chosen to keep a very, very fixed line between work and play, or work and non-work."

CBS Radio's Bob Fuss said sometimes just doing the job creates a semi-social environment. "On the campaign, you're together all the time. You can't help but develop relationships with people, but I certainly try never to become their buddies. There's a long Washington tradition of a lot of socializing between politicians and reporters. It's always made me a little bit uncomfortable."

Candy Crowley of CNN said it's a mistake. "I figured out a long time ago that if you cover somebody you know in some other part of your life, if you cover someone who comes to your house or who you play golf with, one of two things is inevitably going to happen. Either you will at some point become a compromised journalist or you'll be a lousy friend. And I don't want to be either one of those. Actually I don't think they've got any more interest in socializing with me than I have with them."

Cox Radio's Jamie Dupree said there is nothing wrong with it. "I would say I am pals with a number of them that I have covered for a long time. I run into them and they're always very friendly. Do I go out to dinner with them or play golf with them? Very little. I don't worry about getting sucked in."

"Occasionally I'll go to a reception or a cocktail party where I'll see a member of Congress and talk to them a little," said Elaine Povich of *Newsday*. "These people aren't your friends and they're not meant to be. That's one thing that you always have to keep in mind. Reporters tend to be friends with other reporters and the people they cover tend to be friends with each other. It's a small-town atmosphere. Everybody knows everybody and everybody works with everybody."

12.4 New Ethical Dilemmas

Some news organizations, as a matter of policy, have adopted an activist position with regard to journalistic ethics. CBS News, for example, holds regular staff discussions as much as two years before an election cycle. "I just sent one of our political producers to an ethics program at Washington & Lee University," said Tom Mattesky, deputy Washington bureau chief for CBS News in May 2003. "We want our reporters and our producers to, at times, step back and think about the ethics, so when they're faced with these decisions and these dilemmas in the heat of battle they'll have some perspective or some foundation on which to draw."

There is a clear strategic purpose in considering ethical questions well in advance. "We know that there are some questions concerning ethical dilemmas that will surface that we can at least begin pondering in advance and that's what we're trying to do in this case," said Mattesky. "Clearly when you have deadlines, ethics questions cannot be discussed forever and they can't be put to bed for the night and talked about the next day. These are real-time decisions that we have to make. So we try very hard to prepare the people that we're sending into the field that will have to deal with these questions when they don't have a great deal of time to discuss them. By bringing these discussions up in advance, we can at least get them to begin to focus on what is their responsibility ethically and what decisions can they make in consultation with their editors and their producers."

He added, "Most ethical decisions that we face are one of a kind. They jump up and face us almost immediately. But talking about ethics, putting ethics in the forefront underscores that ethical considerations are an important part of what we do and a very important consideration in how we do our jobs."

Obviously, not every ethical question can be anticipated. For example, when there were regular disclosures being made public about President Bill Clinton's relationship with Monica Lewinsky, the ethical issues arose about how much information should be released and how carefully it was checked out and sourced. Deadline and competitive pressure meant that some of those ethics discussions did not take place until after the fact. Marvin Kalb, senior fellow at Harvard's Shorenstein Center, lamented such common occurrences as failure to second source material and failure to attribute information in his book, *One Scandalous Story*. He suggested that individual reporters very often know when they are not making the correct ethical decision for whatever reason. "Most people know when they're doing the right thing and when they're cutting corners, when they're going over the edge, when they're being naughty."

"I think the biggest dilemma we face is attempting to weigh the ethical concerns with the desire to have things on the air as they happen," said CBS's Mattesky. "The traditional network perspective is still pretty much to have an edited product on a regularly scheduled newscast, like the [CBS] *Evening News*, or an hourly radio broadcast or, for that matter, a magazine show that is edited before it hits air. But I do think that with the increasing competition from the cable partners, we are seeing, in the breaking news area, a desire for the audience to see things live. As a result the editing process often times is eliminated."

That raises ethical questions about how something was received, how something was transmitted and the content of what was put on the air. Newspapers have the luxury of not presenting material in real time, but many of their web sites do try to present news as close to when it happens as possible, so the same considerations apply. In addition to ethics, Mattesky said it goes to the equally important issue of fairness. "Are we doing our jobs as journalists by filtering through what has been said and highlighting the important issues, important statements, or are we simply letting the technology take over. That's a continuing dilemma whether it's political coverage or whether it's in news coverage of any variety. How important is an edited product compared to a live product? And which, to the audience, is more valuable and more important?"

12.5 Anonymous Sources

A student of mine called me one night panicked about the looming deadline on a story she'd been reporting for a class exercise. It was the major project for the semester. Her story involved the relationship between TV ads for prescription drugs and whether doctors were giving in to patients' pressure to prescribe those particular drugs. She had been trying, without success, to find a pharmacist who would discuss the issue, on the record, from the perspective of the person filling the prescriptions.

Her call was to say she found a pharmacist who would talk, but only on the condition that his name not be used. Even with a student's classroom exercise, local pharmacists in a small town like St. Augustine, Florida, were concerned about professional backlash.

I asked her to explain the reasons for the request and whether there was any possible way to obtain the same information from a source who would let his or her name be used. She said there were no other ways to get the information, that she'd hit a brick wall in getting someone to talk on the record with full attribution. She said the source agreed to let her say he was a "local pharmacist," but not where he worked or anything more. I agreed to let her use the anonymous source in this case, but I suggested that she find another pharmacist who would confirm and verify what her anonymous source said, lest he have some kind of axe to grind. She did and turned in a fine bit of reporting.

Reporters run into circumstances where people do not want to be identified in print or on the air. It is simply not satisfactory to grant anonymity to somebody because they're embarrassed or shy about having their name used. Find somebody else to quote or persuade them of the importance of identifying the sources of information in your story. Tell them that naming them and identifying them lends credence to what they are saying and allows readers, viewers and listeners to assign value to the information.

There are rare circumstances that require granting anonymity. If identifying them could cause them or their families physical harm, if it could cost them their job, if it could do some kind of measurable social or economic damage to them, there may be legitimate reasons for granting anonymity. When I covered Congress, it was sometimes the only way to obtain important information. A staff member with access to certain information could be fired or have a career ruined if identified as the source in one of my stories. Nonetheless, it was always useful to give my viewers and listeners as much information as I could about the source by naming his or her political affiliation, the representative, senator or committee involved, or some other way of adding credibility to the information.

There has been a significant swing in the news business away from the use of anonymous sources. It is always preferable to identify sources in a story. It tells the readers, viewers and listeners who's talking, and allows them to evaluate the information. Anonymous sources generally weaken a story and, frankly, overuse of anonymous sources by news organizations has made the public skeptical about the accuracy of information so attributed.

In cases where use of an anonymous source is absolutely necessary, any kind of partial identification is better than simply saying "a source said." Tell your readers, viewers and listeners something about the source, if possible, to underscore the credibility of the information. Even without a name, some kind of identifier will help your audience put a value on the information—"a source close to the investigation," "a committee staff member," "a Republican campaign official," "a Democratic pollster."

Political reporters encounter people who demand anonymity with great regularity. Examples include people who want to leak information to you from within a campaign, people in an opponent's campaign who want to leak information to you, pollsters showing you proprietary polling data and ad agency people who'll let you see a campaign commercial before it airs. Sometimes campaign officials who are explaining a candidate's position on a certain issue demand anonymity because they feel having a name other than the candidate's associated with the position weakens the candidate's position.

Individual reporters make the preliminary decision regarding whether or not to grant a source anonymity. Reporters need to make it clear to their sources that their anonymity will not be absolute because most news organizations require reporters to reveal the names of their confidential sources to their supervising producers, editors or executives. In addition, most news organizations now have written standards for granting anonymity to a source, virtually all of which place severe restrictions on the practice and favor full attribution within news stories.

13

Roadmap for Reporters: Advanced Techniques

Some of the best political stories are not necessarily those that the candidates and/or politicians want covered. The best political stories look below the surface and probe the "how" and "why" of issues and actions, the same as good journalism in any other area of inquiry. In the political arena, the dimension of a reporter's knowledge and understanding will have a direct impact on the type of stories he or she writes. It is the same as covering any specialized beat.

"For reporters it means that they need to become [campaign] experts themselves. They need to be able to contact other experts. And they need to know what questions to ask those experts," said Stephen Hess, senior fellow at The Brookings Institution.

Events, speeches, news conferences, news releases and the superficial trappings of a campaign can provide a backdrop for news stories, but the texture and fabric that makes those news stories interesting and relevant to readers, viewers and listeners comes from the training and instincts of the journalists covering them. Knowing what to look for and where to look is absolutely critical.

13.1 Tracking the Money

Computers have made the job of covering politics easier. In particular, the evolution of database managers and relational databases has allowed journalists to plumb areas that were all but inaccessible 20 years ago or less. In no area is this more true than in tracking political money. Reporters can now find out who's giving it, who's getting it and how much is involved. What now can be done with the click of a mouse used to take days or weeks of searching through spreadsheets and financial documents.

"Money will lead you to a lot of stories about candidates," said Hess. "You've got more tools today, partly because there's a lot more transparency in this field. But you have to go into the records. And when you pull the information together you often say, hmmm, isn't that interesting? Most of [Sen.] John Edwards's [D-N.C.] money is coming from tort lawyers. I wonder what that means. Or how come so much of [1988 Democratic presidential candidate Michael] Dukakis's money is coming from Massachusetts or from the Greek community? You take the information you've pulled together and use it. Today political reporters have access to much more information than they ever had before."

The key for reporters is finding, managing and using the information.

Most news organizations, even many smaller television stations and newspapers, have their own electronic libraries, complete with a database manager and the ability to access relational databases. Relational databases permit the user to call up information about a single subject in many different forms. For example, if a reporter wanted to access the campaign contributions to a particular U.S. House candidate and had only a flat database, the information would appear as a spreadsheet with every single contribution and contributor listed. (In the old days of hand-printed spreadsheets the information was not necessarily even in alphabetical order.)

A relational database allows the reporter to look for specific information within the data. It allows a search of contributors by any of a series of criteria, including occupation, amount given and whether the contributor is an individual, corporation, union, interest group or political action committee. The search can be narrowed to specific names, geographic locations, gender or other demographic criteria. (So if you want to find out how much the tobacco industry gave to a candidate, this technology will allow you to do it with relative ease.)

In addition to the news organization's own database manager, many web sites that reporters can access have relational databases of varying degrees of sophistication. "There are good public interest groups, such as the Center for Responsive Politics—www. opensecrets.org—and Political Moneyline—www.tray.com. I can't say enough about them. They track money," said Elaine Povich, *Newsday* political reporter. "They tell you who's giving, who's getting, where the money comes from, where it goes. It's great."

Several other useful web sites for reporters on the money trail include the newly redesigned site of the Federal Election Commission—

www.fec.gov—that provides a treasure trove of information on all federal races including president, U.S. senator and U.S. representative. Another wonderful web site for reporters—www.campaignfinance.org—provides access to campaign finance information for races in all 50 states. (See Appendix B for other useful websites.)

Bear in mind that the final tally of campaign contributions is often not posted online or otherwise available until after the election. Just because the election is over does not mean that a money-trail story has ceased to be relevant. In addition, what happened in the last election cycle can provide interesting fodder for a news story early in the next cycle. This applies both to incumbents and to challengers who lost and may want to try again.

Some of the questions to look for in a post-election analysis or in an early-cycle story based on money-related data from the previous election include whether the same contributors will contribute to the same candidate or candidates again. What interest groups, unions, corporations and/or PACs gave money to the incumbent and to the challenger? Did an incumbent fail to keep promises or take positions that will alienate prior campaign contributors? Did an incumbent make promises or deliver actions that will help generate contributions from new sources? Can a candidate who lost once get enough money to run successfully another time?

Developing these kinds of stories takes time and effort on the part of political journalists, but they can provide interesting insight for voters.

Finally, when tracking the money, reporters need to look for the unusual, for anomalies, such as illegal or questionable contributions. Were contribution limits evaded or ignored? (For example, if you see the maximum contribution from four or five people with the same surname at the same address and in checking you find out that two of them are under the age of 6, you might just have the makings of a story.) Look for famous or well-known names on the lists. Use your relational database to check the contribution list for both the winner and the loser and see if any names appear on both lists. If they do, find out why.

13.2 Behind the Props and Stage Sets

Many political campaigns expend significant effort and money on packaging and presenting the candidate to the public. It has become a subset of the media-relations function within a campaign's organizational structure. "That's why advance people are hired. That's why communications specialists are hired. That's why press secretaries, frankly, are hired," said Tom Mattesky, deputy Washington bureau chief for CBS News. The key for reporters is to know it's happening and why. "I wonder sometimes if we, as journalists, think carefully enough about what we're airing," added Mattesky. Too many reporters accept the packaging as a true representation of the candidate.

The best political journalists manage to get behind all the Hollywood veneer and find out something about the candidate as a person. What is this man or woman really like? What are his or her core values and beliefs? Finding that kind of information harkens back to the advance preparation a journalist does in the early days of a campaign or even before a candidate has declared his or her intentions to run.

One of the best tools is a candidate profile, often done very early in the cycle. In preparing one, it is useful to talk to people who know the candidate personally, not just people in the political arena. Wally Dean, senior fellow at the Project of Excellence in Journalism, suggested that reporters "might interview neighbors of a candidate, on the theory that you can learn a lot about a person from their neighbors. They might interview coworkers, not just in the job they have now, but maybe in their previous job. They might spend some time with the candidate's family or friends. People have the kind of information and anecdotes that not only provide interesting stories, but help give people the kind of information about issues and candidates' character and style that has real meaning to [the voters]."

By archiving the quotes and/or sound bites (see chapter 5.1) from those early days in the political race, you have material on hand that can give readers, viewers and listeners some depth and perspective about the person even though the campaign's advance teams and event stage managers may be packaging and presenting the candidate differently.

As a campaign enters its final weeks, reporters can get beyond the horse-race aspects of it by talking to voters. The key here is to differentiate between those people who are likely to vote and those who aren't. *Newsday's* Elaine Povich says a very good barometer of how well a candidate's message is resonating with likely voters is to talk to people who are in the audience where a candidate appears. "The people who attend a political event, attend a rally in a park, are a different sub-species of a community than just knocking randomly on doors. These people actually care about events and care about politics." An important line of questioning for reporters at this stage of the campaign is: do these active and interested voters care about the same things that the candidate is talking about in his or her stump speech?

The waning days of a campaign may also be a good time for reporters to revisit swing neighborhoods or communities. (See A *Conversation with David Broder,* following chapter 4.) While polling can provide some information about whether the candidate has been effective in reaching swing voters, there is no journalistic substitute for talking to these citizens yourself. Wade through the advertising, the campaign appearances, the free media, the debates and the careful packaging of the candidate and talk to the people who will have a direct impact on the outcome of the election. If the candidate's message has resonated and been effective, examine why. If not, why not? What is it that has persuaded the swing voters? Are they still undecided? Why? Will they vote at all?

13.3 Core Constituencies and Demographic Groups

For much of the last half century, the political parties have been able to count on the support of groups that politicians call core constituencies. Democrats traditionally could bank on the support of blacks, Jews and union households. Republicans traditionally relied on the support of business, white suburban voters and conservative Christians.

People associated with various interest groups are also often identified with certain parties. Pro-life voters and members of the National Rifle Association tend to vote Republican; pro-choice voters and environmentalists tend to vote Democratic. Similar lines are drawn among other groups in various communities and should be monitored by reporters. They include real estate interests, physicians and the medical community, the insurance industry, the energy industry, the tobacco industry, trial lawyers, farmers and teachers.

While the political pros will tell you that party registration is a bellwether of how people will vote, it is not always an accurate predictor. Republican Ronald Reagan's campaign for president, for example, managed to make inroads into some bedrock Democratic strongholds.

The campaign labeled these people Reagan Democrats and relished being able to identify groups of them to reporters. Reagan's pollsters isolated pockets of "soft" Democratic support and co-opted them.

Reporters covering politics should be aware of trends among groups and core constituencies. One of the most important groups in the country to watch is Hispanics. Reporters should know that while Hispanics are the fastest growing minority in the United States, the Hispanic vote is not homogeneous. Cubans in Florida tend to vote Republican; Puerto Ricans in New York tend to vote Democratic. Panamanians vote differently than Nicaraguans who vote differently from Mexicans. Hispanic voters (mostly Mexicans) in California tend to vote Democratic, but it is not hard-core support. When actor Arnold Schwartzenegger was elected California governor in 2003 as a Republican, he generated significant support among Hispanics, even though one of his opponents was Democratic Lt. Gov. Cruz Bustamante, a Mexican American himself.

Asians are another significant minority to monitor. Reporters must be mindful of the cultural and social differences between such groups as Indians, Pakistanis, Japanese, Chinese, Vietnamese, Taiwanese and Koreans. Young reporters often fall into the trap of interviewing one or two Asians and presuming that they are representative of all Asians. This is journalistically naive. To Asians, it is downright insulting.

Voter turnout is always a significant issue when monitoring core constituencies and other demographic groups. Young voters (college-age people) have a long history of not voting. Native Americans have an extremely poor voting history. African Americans tend to vote in greater numbers when they are energized by a particular issue or candidate. This is true, in general, of all other groups, although some groups tend to vote no matter what. Jewish voters and senior citizens traditionally turn out at the polls in high numbers, regardless of the candidate(s) or issues. Knowing who voted and why can reveal a great deal about why a candidate succeeded or failed.

In analyzing issues, campaign strategies, advertising targets and the focus of personal appearances, reporters should not discount or underplay the significance of these voting groups. In addition, in certain local communities and areas, other important demographic groups require the attention of political reporters because of their numbers. A large pocket of people from a specific demographic group can affect the outcome of an election or skew the way certain issues are addressed by the candidates. Immigrants from Arab countries have major electoral influence in parts of Michigan, for example.

Understanding the role and function of core constituencies and other demographic voting blocs within a state or district can add a highly sophisticated element to political reporting, and provide readers, viewers and listeners with an interesting and important perspective on the campaign and the election.

13.4 Using Polls

Every journalism school in the country teaches students about polls and surveys, and how to use them. Some even require journalism students to take a course in research methods so they can understand how polls and surveys are conducted and what they do and do not do. Unfortunately, too many working journalists either forgot what they were taught, or never learned the lessons in the first place, about the appropriate use of polling and survey data. (See chapter 11.3.) Some reporters simply don't understand polls; others have developed a deathbed grip on them and use them as crutches in reporting political stories.

Dotty Lynch, senior political editor for CBS News, was a pollster in the 1970s and '80s. "Polling has stayed pretty much the same. I think journalists have gotten worse at understanding and reporting what it is and how seriously it should be taken."

She said many reporters simply don't look for the right things when analyzing the value or newsworthiness of a poll. Reporters must look at "sample size, the dates of the interviews, the margin of error and the way the interview was conducted—was it by random sample? Random digit dialing? Was it a mail-in poll? Who was the polling organization that conducted it? You need to ask if it was a candidate-associated or partisan poll." Lynch noted that "interest groups do polls all the time that, lo and behold, show that their particular cause or issue is popular with 90 percent of the people. So who sponsored the poll is another key question to ask."

Reporters must examine methodology and interpretation in using polling data, although there is always a temptation to use poll numbers that show something that appears to be significant. "We always have been suckers for numbers, because as journalists we don't understand numbers. And so when somebody provides us with something that looks like hard numbers we think: look, a fact! We can report that," said Deborah Potter, executive director of the TV news research and training center NewsLab. "It's true in science coverage; it's true in economics. Anything that has some numbers in it, we love those because they look indisputable. The trouble with polling is that none of those numbers is indisputable."

One technique for reporters is to compare similar polls. If they were conducted roughly at the same time and ask roughly the same questions within the same approximate universe of potential interviewees, did they produce roughly the same results? If the results are not similar, it should raise a red flag that one of them may be suspect. Maybe both are.

"There's a lot more polling available, which we always thought would be better because there would be a check, one on the other," said CBS's Lynch. "But often these polls aren't conducted [scientifically]. You have these Internet polls which aren't really valid. You have the sample that was conducted four to five weeks ago and it's just processed right now. You need to look and see what the sample size is, the dates of the polls. These are snapshots now and things will change, or can change . . . Reporters have made a lot of mistakes in presidential campaigns—writing candidates off who are low in the polls early, and giving too much credence to somebody who's ahead just because of name recognition. It can become a self-fulfilling prophecy."

Lynch said that not only is misuse of polls by reporters bad journalism, it can have an impact on the political process. "Those candidates who are doing well can raise more money and do better if those polls show them ahead. On the other hand, it can be really damaging and misleading to assume that somebody who starts a race with only 4 percent in the polls is not going to go anywhere."

In checking the elements of campaign-related polls—date, sample size, margin of error and questions—one very important distinction to draw involves one particular issue. Is the poll measuring the responses of registered voters or those people likely to vote? The closer the poll to Election Day, the more impact that distinction will have on the polling data. As many as half of registered voters do not necessarily vote. Thus, a poll that samples the opinion of likely voters will be more valuable in the last weeks of a race than will a sample of registered voters.

Political analyst Stuart Rothenberg, editor of the Rothenberg

Political Report, said, "One thing that drives me crazy is how polls are reported. TV people are particularly inept on this. You'll see a movement of a couple of percentage points. It'll be within the margin of error, and reporters—sometimes print, always electronic—will report it as some kind of dramatic movement."

He suggested that in the quest for a dramatic story, reporters often ignore polling fundamentals. If the margin of error is +/- 3 percentage points, anything within a 6 point range is a statistical dead heat. "If the president's approval [rating] is 61 percent one day and 59 percent the next," added Rothenberg, "that's well within the margin of error in a survey, so from a statistical point of view, the numbers are the same. But you know you're going to hear some anchor or reporter go on the air and say, 'Well, the president's job approval is down two points.' It's crazy."

While reporters often draw their own conclusions from the raw data provided by polls, it is useful to seek interpretations from outsiders. "The problem for reporters, as you watch the pollsters, is the degree to which this is still an art form," cautioned Stephen Hess, senior fellow at The Brookings Institution. "You go to [name of a Democratic pollster] and you read his analysis. I wouldn't call it fiction but here's a man who sees the data and carries it forth saying this is what it means to me. And then if you turn that same data over to [name of a Republican pollster], it doesn't mean that at all to him."

Hess has used and applied polling and survey data for decades, as a political insider in the Eisenhower and Nixon Administrations, as U.S. delegate to the United Nations General Assembly, and as a scholar specializing in government and the press. During a lengthy discussion on a dreary Friday in May 2003, he offered the following advice and analysis with regard to the use of polls and polling data:

> You've got to be awfully careful about reporting what this material means. I'm skeptical about polls, because very often I think it means nothing. There are certain things about which people care very deeply. They have very fixed opinions. Abortion. If you get a poll on abortion, whatever it tells you, put it in the bank. People have been thinking about that for a very long time. But a lot of these polls are about things that people haven't given any thought to.
>
> Americans don't spend a great deal of their time thinking about most public issues. Ask us about our families, ask us

about out health, ask us about our leisure and we can tell you. Ask us about H.R. 193 and we don't know anything about it. But we may give an answer. We don't want to seem stupid. We're polite and we'll try to answer. So I always look at whether it's a question on which people are likely to have an opinion.

A Conversation with Candy Crowley

Senior political correspondent: CNN

Candy Crowley is one of the best reporters and by far one of the best writers in television news. In the world of 24-hour news, where speed is often more important than the craft of storytelling, Crowley hones her stories with verbal artistry. She picks her words like a poet, conjuring up just the right image, finding just the right nuance, turning phrases that resonate with viewers. Some of that is certainly the result of her years in local radio and with the wire service Associated Press. But some of it is also the result of dogged hard work.

The amazing thing is how easy she makes it look. The CNN booth was two doors down from where I worked on Capitol Hill and we often covered the same stories. I'd emerge from filing looking and feeling like I'd been hit by a bus; she'd come back from a live-shot or several live-shots cracking jokes and looking like she was ready to party. She has a robust sense of humor and an uncanny knack for getting people, especially politicians, to open up to her on camera.

She's collected a closet full of awards, including the DuPont-Columbia University Silver Baton in 1999 for her Clinton impeachment coverage. So what should aspiring reporters do while they're still in school?

C.C.: "Attend any history class you can find, because what goes around comes around. In history there is some reason for the present. That is true in politics too.

"History, history, history and English, English, English. You can know everything in the world and if you can't communicate it doesn't matter. In English I mean, yes, knowing that your subject and verb ought to match, but also knowing the power of words, that words have resonance.

"Radio is the best thing in the world for learning how to write and tell a story. . . . Read authors who know how to tell a story. Read really good writers and try to figure out why they are really good writers. Do the same things with journalists. If you really like a journalist try to figure out why. John Burns of *The New York Times* may be one of the finest writers of our time. He wrote some brilliant stuff. But don't dismiss the greats. The way to become a good writer is to read good writers. And then write, write, write yourself.

"So history and writing. History gives you backdrop and context. Writing gives you the tools with which to communicate. The present's just going to come at you, and if you're prepared, that'll take care of itself."

R.A.: *I've known you a long time, but I never asked you about your background. I know you were with AP?*

C.C.: "That was a little later. I always wanted to write. So I started out working for a trade association. And I met somebody, who I started to date, who knew of an opening at a local radio station for a newsroom assistant-type of job. I called up and got it. That was at WASH, a Metromedia station. And you know here [in Washington, D.C.] there are so many police jurisdictions that I was the cop person. I'd call up and say, 'Hi P.G. [Prince Georges County, Maryland] county police. What do you have?'

"And they'd say, 'A double homicide at such and such location.' And I'd write it up for the person who was doing the news at the station. I did the traffic reports. Erased the carts [audiotape cartridges]. I worked a split shift—morning drive and afternoon drive and went home and slept in between.

"I went from there to the AP [Associated Press radio] network and I did editing and reporting. From there I went to Mutual Broadcasting and was the first woman among all these men who were at the end of their careers, all these famous old radio voices. And I got pregnant and they treated me like the queen of Sheba. Not only was I the first woman they'd ever worked with, I was pregnant. Went off. Had babies. And came back to work for AP. I anchored for a while and then went to the White House.

"I got a call from NBC asking if I'd ever thought about TV. I said no. They said well come over and let's talk about it and NBC hired me. And then I talked to CNN and here I am."

R.A.: *When was your first political campaign? Do you remember?*

C.C.: "The first one that I covered was Teddy Kennedy, who was challenging Jimmy Carter. That was 1980. That was the first time I ever traveled with a candidate. It was the first time I was ever really touched by a political speech—Kennedy's concession speech at the [Democratic national] convention, the dream-never-dies speech. I was on the floor and I remember listening to that and getting reaction to it. That was my first time."

R.A: *Does anybody jump out as a favorite?*

C.C.: "George [W.] Bush was a lot of fun to cover. I like covering the non-incumbents because they haven't yet collected all the paraphernalia and Secret Service and all the people around them. I liked covering Bob Dole. I thought he was an interesting guy with a great story, the last of a generation. You were aware that this was the last World War II generation guy who was going to run for president. I found that interesting.

"I loved covering Bill Clinton. You just never knew what you were going to wake up to. And you'd go to these events and the crowds were [gestures with both hands] . . . I've just never seen such juice in my life from a candidate. George W. was close in a lot of ways. He can light up a room in the way Clinton can. But George W. can't light up a crowd the way Clinton could.

"I remember coming into these giant arenas and there were people everywhere. I always wondered if there was something Bobby Kennedy-esque about the crowds, because reporters always talked about the crowds around Bobby Kennedy. He was the first politician [as an outside observer] I paid much attention to. He could just wow them. You could see how a really good politician in the olden days could just start a buzz. He had so much electricity.

"I sort of feel like they're all my children. They all had interesting things about them. Even the losers. I found the Dole thing poignant and touching. I haven't really disliked any of them. I liked some better than others. And I've learned about people and politics. And politics, at its base, is all about the person."

R.A.: *This is more true in local than in national news, but the news directors are hearing from their consultants, and the managing editors are hearing from their consultants, that the public doesn't want political news. The public isn't interested in political news. And so they don't put it on TV or in the paper.*

C.C.: "I think that's really true. I can tell you that in the midterms I went to Minnesota, Missouri, South Dakota, all the hot Senate races. And 95 percent of the time we were the only camera at an event. These were the hottest, most important Senate races in the country and there wasn't a local camera anyplace. I was astonished. It used to be California was the only place where they didn't cover politics.

"It was only in the Coleman-Wellstone race after the plane crash [that killed incumbent Democrat Paul Wellstone] that it got to be a very media-intense race. But all the way down the Mississippi River— Arkansas, Louisiana—those were hot, hot races. And we'd show up and have the candidate to ourselves. Not a local reporter anywhere. There may have been a few print people scattered around. I'm not saying they didn't do it at all, but we showed up toward the end of the campaign and did not see much local coverage.

"Even at CNN, if you say politics, sometimes about 70 percent of the people will roll they're eyes and groan and think, 'Yeewwww, white men talking!' It's more than that. Sometimes you have to convince them. What I hope is that I am at the point in my career that I have done enough and have a body of work large enough that they'll look at it and say, 'Okay. If you think it's interesting, go do it.'

"It's a tough sell at any level, but one of the reasons that I have less trouble than, maybe, a younger reporter is that I'm a known factor. And they count on my making it relevant, interesting, watchable, all those things.

"I always consider it my own failure if somebody doesn't want a story I've done. If you can't reach your editor with the importance of a story and why it needs to go on, chances are you're not going to convince the viewers either. You don't just do these for your own intellectual curiosity. You've got to relate it to why anybody would give a darn about, say, campaign finance reform. How's it going to change your life in Skokie, Illinois?"

R.A.: *How do you know you've got a really good story?*

C.C.: "It's an adrenalin rush. You just look at it and you know. Oh, my God! What a great story. I've been doing this a long time. And sometimes you've got to be careful that you don't miss a good story because you've been doing it a long time. You know, if I've got to do another budget cycle I'll just scream! Been there; done that. But I just know it. I feel it. It's like that pornography thing—I know it when I see it.

"I've rarely missed a story. Sometimes I've misjudged the size of the legs on a story. I may not even want you to use this, but I didn't immediately recognize the enormity or the impact of the Trent Lott statements. [In 2002, Senate Republican leader Trent Lott of Mississippi said the country would have been better off if then-segregationist presidential candidate Strom Thurmond had won election to the White House in 1948.]

"I knew that it was a story, but I would not have said to you, 'Holy cow, this is going to blow this town wide apart.' I didn't recognize that. I wasn't there, but when I read about it I said to myself, oh, boy, he's really stepped in it. But if you'd have said to me that he'd step down as majority leader, I wouldn't have believed it. I missed that part of it. It became clear over time."

R.A.: *You always seem to be able to get a lot out of your interviews. What's the technique?*

C.C.: "I don't write out questions. I'll put topics down. I find that writing out the questions gets in the way of listening. The best interviewer is the best listener. The people you're interviewing will lead you places. I've heard way too many interviews where it's question one, question two, question three, thank you very much. I don't like to just go after the sound bite. I like to learn stuff and that makes it more of a conversation. The more of a conversation it is on your part, the more they're likely to tell you something. If they can sense that you really want to know something, they'll usually tell you. One of my techniques is that before the interview I'll talk about almost anything other than what I want to talk about when the camera's on. I want them to know that I'm a human being.

"One of the things that helped me most with my interviewing was sitting down with Lee Hamilton [former Democratic congressman from Indiana]. This was fairly late in my career because he was retired. It had just come to light that Henry Hyde [R–Ill.] who was managing the [Clinton] impeachment [in the House] had had an affair of his own.

"We were going to do a story about political hypocrisy and I thought I'd go talk to Lee Hamilton. He's a straight-up guy. He'd been around for a long time. So I asked him his definition of political hypocrisy. And then I asked him about the notion that one side comes at it one way when it's their party under fire, and they come at it from another when the opposition is under fire.

"And this look came over him. I'll never forget it. It said he thought I was going to play gotcha. He finally said, 'I have no doubt that you can go back and find a sound bite that makes me look like a hypocrite.' I didn't have one and I wasn't going to do that, but he thought that's what I was doing. He had become closed and guarded and I had to try to persuade him that I wasn't playing that game.

"That moment with Lee Hamilton became instrumental in my approach to interviews.

"I try to make people feel—and it's the truth—that I'm not there to get them. I'm there to find out what they know and, if they're under fire for something, I really am there to hear their side. I'm not there to make them look bad or make them sound stupid. I'm there to find out where they're coming from and to walk a mile in their shoes.

"You're going to get more from an interview if they're comfortable. They close up when they're on guard."

R.A.: *But aren't they always on guard? Aren't they always spinning?*

C.C.: "Sure. You've got to know that the first thing out of their mouth is going to be what they're supposed to be saying. You've got to let them do that. I generally sit back and let them say whatever the message of the day is. Then I move it from there to where I want to go with the interview. I say something like, 'That's really interesting and it makes me curious about this.'

"It's also easier with somebody you've interviewed before and done a story on before, because then they know that you're not trying to screw them. Maybe the net effect may be that. It's never my intent going into an interview to say I'm going to get this guy, I'm going to nail him to the wall. But that's what they think. Sometimes it works out that you do get this guy. Really they get themselves. It's not my questions; it's their answers. The more they see that my questions are not a trap, the more they tend to show you what there is. And if what's there is objectionable, it's going to come out."

R.A.: *Is it easier for a woman to interview a man?*

C.C.: "Sometimes I think it's helpful to be a female interviewer. Sometimes it's not. Sometimes men think you're just a girl and therefore they can get away with not answering your question, or they can charm you out of it. Other times they're more willing to see you as a non-hostile force than a guy, because there's a territorial guy-to-guy thing that goes on. It's a sort of power struggle."

R.A.: *What about interviewing women? Does the reverse hold true?*

C.C.: "I tend to think that girls bond pretty well. For a long while there weren't that many women politicians and there weren't that many women journalists. Now, gender is probably the least of most people's concerns. They're a lot more concerned with which organization you work for or can they trust you. It plays in some way, but I'm not sure how much. I do think that early on it was a relief for women to see another woman in that world."

R.A.: *What am I missing? Anything else I should have touched on?*

C.C.: "I'm always amazed at how many people don't understand what it is that we're trying to do. Journalism is about telling the story of something that happened. But a lot of people think we all have agendas—to be hostile, to be anti-government, to be iconoclasts. Sure, I think it's the nature of journalists to be pretty iconoclastic. But it's troubling because I think that in the same way we doubt politicians' motivations, a good many people doubt our motivation. What makes us tick? Why do we want to be there? Is it for the great glory of it? No. The great glamour of it? No. Is it to get these guys? No. It's to tell people what's going on. There's a huge gap between what we think we're there for and what viewers and readers think we're there to do.

"I think that's why they don't like us. I think we're pretty likable people. [Laughs.] Somebody gave me a luggage tag that says, 'Trust me, I'm a reporter!' People laugh at that when they see it on my suitcase. I thought it was a serious thing. And they laugh at it. That's not good."

Section IV
Where Do We Go from Here?

14

Learning from Our Mistakes

Political journalism is a work in progress. It has traveled the rocky byways of the political wilderness since the post-colonial days when newspapers all had political agendas and facts were not a necessary part of a political article. That wilderness is still there, but the way in which reporters explore it is substantially different. It is still not perfect. It's doubtful it will ever be perfect as long as you have the human element involved in news-gathering.

The key is not to keep making the same old mistakes over and over again, like the Peanuts cartoon with the recurring theme of Lucy pulling the football away from Charlie Brown just as he tries to kick it, sending him sprawling. Journalists need a steeper learning curve than that.

14.1 Duh, What Story?

The late Bob Martin, one of the greatest sports reporters I've ever known and my mentor as I was learning the ropes in Denver, once told me about a young reporter being sent out to cover a wedding. "A few hours later his boss found him with his feet up on his desk doing a crossword puzzle," said Martin. "He asked, 'Where's the wedding story?'

"'There's no story,' said the kid. 'The wedding was canceled. The church burned down and everybody inside was killed.'"

Well, duh!

The wedding anecdote is obviously an exaggeration. But stories are missed all the time. Sometimes they are missed because they may be too obvious or because reporters and news executives are too busy looking for the big picture to grip what's right in front of them. Sometimes it is the result of an individual failure—inexperience, reportorial myopia, even stupidity.

"In late 1999, 60 percent of the people in Denver said sprawl, development and traffic was the city's number one problem," said Wally Dean, senior fellow at the Project for Excellence in Journalism. He had been involved in a study of broadcast news there at the time. "Less than 3 percent—2.6 percent—of the stories on Denver television six months later during sweeps period, for two weeks of monitoring, had anything to do with sprawl, development or traffic. That's a case where obviously a huge segment of the community was talking every day about it, but it wasn't even on the radar screens of the broadcast journalists. And that's how these disconnects happen, where the public says the media isn't talking about things we're concerned about."

Management attitudes can, and do, contribute to missed stories. When management says to reporters that politics is boring or government is dull, it is no surprise that stories involving politics and government get missed. There is little incentive for reporters to find and report those stories. Media consultants are telling radio and television news directors that politics is, in the words of Deborah Potter, former network correspondent and executive director of NewsLab, "ratings poison."

"What they're saying is we don't want politics at all," said Potter. "So when they do send somebody out, it's because they feel obliged or it's a slow day or the candidate came to town; they have to do it in the quick and dirty way." Quick and dirty usually does not produce great or even good journalism and often results in stories that are about as interesting as watching a fly crawl up a drape.

To a degree, newspaper editors also are hearing that there is a lack of interest in political stories on the part of readers. Most of the experts interviewed for this book, however, feel that newspapers, in general, make a greater effort to cover politics than local radio or television.

The management attitude, especially in the broadcast realm, has the effect of telling reporters that political stories are not important and if they get missed, well, that's okay. Reporters know that missing a political story is not going to have the kind of negative impact on their careers as missing a big crime story or a scandal involving the local college president.

"There's a lot of data on this," said Stephen Hess, senior fellow at the Brookings Institution. "You look at local television stations—and this was done in California, particularly in Los Angeles—before an important gubernatorial contest and there's nothing there. No coverage.

There is an obligation that this is important stuff. Unless it's treated importantly, you're not going to have journalists who want to go into that."

Hess noted that the trend is not just away from electoral politics but from the politics of governance as well. "In California, you look at coverage of the state legislature. I don't think, at this time, that there is a Los Angeles [TV] station that has a full-time person in Sacramento," he said.

Yet Potter and Dean both cited a recent survey that indicated that well-done political stories will not result in the flight of viewers and in fact will serve to attract them. Potter noted that it is just one study against the advice of a battalion of highly paid consultants. "The word politics seems to have a negative connotation," she said. Viewers "think of it as mudslinging, dirty and, frankly, not relevant to them. So some of what has to happen here is the redefinition of what is politics, in terms of its coverage, and a new way of doing stories."

The anti-political culture in many newsrooms is causing reporters to downplay and even ignore political stories. "Reporters who can turn a perfectly good story around in a day, a feature for example, lose their vision of what makes a good story as soon as the topic switches to politics," said Potter. "They forget that stories are about people. People are interested in other people. People are interested in what affects them. All of a sudden the basic rules of storytelling just go whsshhht! out the window as soon as the topic turns to covering a campaign."

One ongoing mistake involving political news coverage is falling victim to a self-fulfilling cycle: the audience tells consultants and pollsters that they don't like politics; therefore news organizations don't cover politics (unless there's scandal or corruption); therefore the audience doesn't know anything about politics; therefore when consultants and pollsters ask if viewers and readers like politics they say no because they don't know anything about it (except it's sleazy); and on and on. The self-fulfilling cycle produces poor journalism that does little to encourage editors and news directors to expand political coverage.

Veteran *Washington Post* reporter Helen Dewar said that occasionally it gets pretty bad at some smaller papers. "They're writing stories from news releases or what it was like at Senator So-and-So's picnic." Nonetheless, she adds that many smaller papers "do a very good job of truth-squadding the claims by the politicians."

Reporters are not in the military, going where they are told, when they are told, even though most campaigns and politicians try to regiment the press. Journalists must be actively engaged in their coverage. If reporters miss the story or don't recognize its value, it's very hard for them to take a proactive position with regard to selling it. "There seems to be less interest at the top," Dewar said, noting that it is often up to reporters to persuade reluctant editors of the importance of a story. "You're hard pressed to make the case that the public is demanding it. But it's part of the essence of newspapering. Some of it's an appeal to their better instincts, that it's necessary for people to participate in a democracy. That, coupled with the fact that you can write very readable, interesting stories about politics. But then you have to show them you can."

"When it comes to political reporting, too many local reporters have too little in the way of political background," said Stuart Rothenberg, political analyst and editor of the Rothenberg Political Report. "They don't ask the probing questions. They haven't spent enough time around politics. They're young and green. They do tend to do more of the straight reporting, but they do it without very much depth. They don't get into where the candidates stand on key issues, how they're raising and spending money, who's contributing to their campaign. Too many small newspapers have a reporter who one minute is covering politics and the next minute is covering a sheep-shearing contest."

14.2 News Policy versus News Judgment

When William Paley owned CBS, he was in the business of making money. He made a lot of it. But Paley believed that news was an important public service and as a result, the news division at CBS was isolated and insulated from the rest of the company. The business decisions that governed programs like *The Ed Sullivan Show* and *I Love Lucy* did not govern news programming like *See It Now* and *CBS Reports*. News policy (the decisions made by the management side of the news business) and news judgment (the news-gathering and reporting decisions made by the editorial side of the news business) were walled off from entertainment programming, sales, marketing and corporate promotion.

Today, at CBS and elsewhere, corporate decision making and news policy are much more closely intertwined. Former CBS News correspondent Marvin Kalb, now senior fellow at Harvard's Shorenstein Center, said, "Contemporary news is defined in large part by the new economics and the new technology. The new economics would provide an answer, discomforting to me but probably realistic, and that is there is no realistic way to persuade the current owners that it is in the interest of the people that they have more serious news programming. . . . In essence there is an economic culture in the news business today that obliges news directors to think about ratings, to think about profitability, and that very central factor determines how you select the news that goes on the air."

Kalb added, "Journalism is a business that lives in the real world, composed of bottom lines, competitive values, a sense of fragility in the economy, the need to make money now, even if you have to cut a corner. And in the mind of the general manager and in the mind of the owner it isn't that they're doing something bad. They're not bad people. They're probably good people. They are living in a world that requires them to make certain decisions."

Helen Dewar of *The Washington Post* said that economic realities have a profound impact on news coverage, in general, and political coverage in particular. "Editors have less interest in covering politics and political campaigns, investing the time and money, particularly when ad revenues go down in a recession. When ad revenues go down they clamp down on the travel budget. I think a lot of papers that are not in particularly strong financial situations have cut back on political coverage."

The media environment, as it relates to journalism in America, has been transformed over the last two decades. It used to be that there were three commercial television networks and a handful of radio networks. Almost every large and medium-sized city had a morning and an afternoon newspaper. The thumbnail version of what happened is that the number of delivery platforms in the electronic realm expanded, the number of newspapers declined, the Internet emerged as a news delivery vehicle, and they all became owned by fewer and fewer enormous media conglomerates.

News organizations used to have a twice-a-day news cycle: morning and late afternoon. Only the wire services and radio had a 24-hour news cycle. What has developed—as a result of the 24-hour cable news channels and the Internet—is that the news business now is on the 24-hour news cycle. "Every 20 minutes there's got to be a new headline, because the cycle spins," said James Toedtman, associate editor of *Newsday*. "Good old 1010 WINS set the standard for that." WINS is an all-news radio station in New York City which has long used the slogan, "You give us 20 minutes and we'll give you the world." It's become part of the modern media culture.

While the 24-hour news cycle was evolving, the level of business competition among those organizations delivering news became cut-throat. An increasing number of organizations were competing for a relatively finite number of readers, viewers and listeners. Those who succeeded saw their market share flourish along with their ad revenues. Those who did not found themselves in difficult financial straits, sometimes sold and/or merged with other organizations, and some simply closed. The convergence of these factors—competition, business economics, corporate policy, news policy and news judgment—has created the new reality of journalism.

For political reporters, it has created a series of challenges that didn't exist at this level of intensity before the 1980s. Politicians and their handlers are all keenly aware of the changed media landscape and the heightened importance of television and, more recently, the Internet within that new environment.

Toedtman said that as a newspaperman he worries that a lot of politics is being driven by this new highly competitive TV-centric 24-hour environment, and everybody's playing to the cameras. He pointed to the events surrounding the impeachment of President Clinton. Special prosecutor "Kenneth Starr delivered his report to Congress in a convoy of jeeps at 6 o'clock, just before the evening news shows began. Clinton held a pep rally on the [White House south] lawn." He noted that "it was all staged and driven by this constant need to get on top of the news of the day," that is the direct result of the 24-hour news cycle on television. "It presents us with an enormous challenge to keep our balance and maintain some sense of perspective. Especially when it comes to recognizing that events are being artificially driven by this demand for the new headline," said Toedtman.

The new environment, in some organizations, has changed news judgment itself. In order to garner ratings and readership, editors, producers and news directors are requiring different journalistic values. Such traditional news values as impact and importance have given way to sex and sleaze. This has created a difficult hurdle for serious political reporters.

CBS News's senior political editor Dotty Lynch said, "The constant 24/7 appetite for news is resulting in the hyping of stories. If it's scandal, it's the lead of the show, and if it's a nice story, it's toward the back. . . . You get into the problems of ratings and competitive pressures that's caused some problems and some skewing of stories toward the negative and toward the sensational."

Many news organizations have deliberately adopted a news policy of appealing to the greatest number of people while offending the fewest number of people in order to maximize audience. To Harvard's Marvin Kalb, the central journalistic issue is the dichotomy between giving news consumers what they want to know as opposed to what they need to or ought to know.

"If you had a very high rendering of the intellectual, moral quality of the American people, you would be reaching to that standard in the presentation of news," he said. "But the fact is that you do not have that high level judgment of the American people. You have the middling level. Some times it goes up. Most of the time it stays there in that sloppy, gucky, happy middle ground where people receive information that doesn't jar them or upset them in any way at the dinner table or at breakfast. It makes them happy. It doesn't hurt them, doesn't jar them, doesn't negatively affect them."

For the reporter in the field, the demand is frequently for nonstop coverage and as a result the amount of actual reporting is outweighed by the demand to be on the air or to file. Fox News's Brit Hume said, "What happens in 24-hour news is you send somebody out to cover a story and he or she has to go out and lash himself to a live shot and sort of figure out what's going on between live shots. Whereas in an earlier time, you might be able to go live at the end of the day, and you could spend all your day, up to a point, covering the story. Now you sometimes have to cover it by osmosis, from your vantage point at a live location somewhere in a forest of satellite trucks. That sometimes cuts into reporting time and that's something you have to worry about. On the other hand, there's a limit to how many times every hour you're going to keep coming back to a correspondent who has nothing new to say because he or she can't get away from the truck long enough to find anything new to talk about."

While there is a demand for more coverage of some stories there is a collateral trend to restrict the length of stories. "In broadcasting, there has always been a problem of superficiality because the time frames are so short," said CBS Radio's Bob Fuss. "They've gotten shorter. When I started out, a spot was generally 45 seconds. I could sometimes push them to 50. It's gotten to the point now that I'll go on and very often the time I'll have is 20 or 25 seconds. It's always been a problem. It's just gotten worse."

Fuss added, "The competitive drive to get news on faster has had a negative side-effect, giving us less time to think about the news and time to report it carefully. It's led to more mistakes. There's no question about that. You make more mistakes when you go on so fast that you don't have time to think about what you're saying."

News managers making policy decisions that impact both how the news is reported and how it is received by the audience are getting input from various sources, primarily consultants and their affiliated stations that are, in turn, listening to their own consultants. The news managers are hearing about a desire for a high story count, fast pace, cleverer writing, snappier presentation and up-tempo delivery. Some of the presumption is that the audience is highly influenced by what might be called the MTV factor, the way music videos are cut providing a frenetic amalgam of images and sound.

My own research is anecdotal, not scientific. For the last five years I have exposed my intermediate reporting students, a majority of whom are college juniors, to a variety of radio and television news presentations. The results have been consistent in 10 separate classes. The students, by a wide margin, prefer a slower, more traditional news delivery than a fast-paced presentation. At the same time, they find the National Public Radio (NPR) delivery style a bit too deliberate.

In the newspaper world, a significant influence over the years has been *USA Today*, which tends to write much shorter, tighter stories than most traditional dailies. In the early years of *USA Today*, reporters for other papers would dismiss it as McPaper and call it fast food for the eye. Today, *USA Today's* influence is evident in the design, layout and story length of other publications. *Newsday's* Toedtman said a number of factors have contributed, including a shortened public attention span. "Over the years we've been writing shorter and shorter stories than we used to. We have certainly been influenced by the fact that our editors are watching TV, watching CNN and CNBC every minute of every day. And they'll frequently be obsessed with what they'll see on television as a story and what they think we ought to be doing as a result of it."

He added, "[The] media economy is tough, but when you've got a good story people buy the paper. We've certainly seen that in New York between September 11th, plane crashes and the Iraq war. Nothing sells papers quite as well as good journalism."

14.3 The New Landscape

The evolution of the 24-hour news cycle and the development of myriad new platforms from which news and information are delivered have joined together to create a dizzying new landscape. Add to the mix celebrity journalists, vastly increased demands for reporters to file quickly, the corporate drive for ratings and profit and the picture approaches the surreal.

When CNN (Cable News Network) went on the air, it was envisioned to be a 24-hour purveyor of news. But filling a day with what had come to be viewed as TV news—the model of highly polished, edited and produced news packages established by the three major networks and their evening newscasts—proved to be daunting at best and impossible at worst. It was costly, repetitive and did not generate the kind of audience that was expected. All-news radio was discovering much the same thing and a hybrid format "news-talk" was developing at the same time. Both media found that talk shows with interesting, sometimes outrageous, personalities were the ticket for cheap programming that delivered an audience.

Of course, the three major networks had long been in the Sunday talk show business: CBS's *Face the Nation,* NBC's *Meet the Press* and ABC's *This Week* were a staple of hard news, usually with guests who could discuss public policy issues. They drew a relatively small audience, but held an enormous level of prestige for the networks that aired them. They generally made news; they were quoted in all the Monday newspapers; they were featured on the Sunday night and Monday morning newscasts nationally and locally.

But the new breed of talk shows was less interested in a public policy discussion than an ideological conflagration. The cable channels and radio stations that aired them wanted something flashy that would draw viewers and listeners. Demographic studies revealed the nature of the radio talk show audience was predominantly white, male and conservative. Radio talk shows sought to appeal to that audience and started delivering a steady diet of mostly conservative talkers, such as the hugely successful Rush Limbaugh, G. Gordon Liddy, and Laura Ingraham. CNN's Larry King was one of the most successful early cable talk-show hosts, following a huge success on the now-defunct Mutual Radio Network. The field of cable TV talk shows quickly grew to include Fox's Bill O'Reilly and CNN's *Crossfire*.

The genre draws low marks from top political pros, such as analyst Stuart Rothenberg, who said it's become a standard formula with little real substance: "You put a loudmouth right-winger on one side of the set and a loudmouth left-winger on the other side of the set—a Republican and a Democrat—and you let them argue. And at the end of the half hour the voters are supposed to have an answer? They're supposed to have a clue? They're supposed to have an insight? I think that just confuses people. There are so many half-truths, so many phony arguments, and so much posturing. I would much prefer to have two serious people having a discussion of an issue, acknowledging weaknesses and strengths on both sides of the same question. But you don't get that. You get yelling back and forth."

CBS News's senior political editor Dotty Lynch agreed, "The more sensational you are, the louder mouth you are, the more extreme you can make your argument, the more likely you are to get air time and to grab people's attention. What they show as evidence is that the Jim Lehrer public television, public radio shows everybody might think are very solid and very complete and nobody turns them on. And you get these hot cable shows or talk radio and they get audiences. The competitors put one on to counteract that. And you've suddenly got five screaming crazies."

For the public, the rise of talk shows on radio and television has not been to the benefit of journalism in general and political journalism in particular. The public tends to blur the lines between news and entertainment. The fact is that most of these talk shows are entertainment, even though they discuss public-policy issues. Most have a distinct point of view.

Journalists, themselves, have not been as careful as they should be in articulating and illustrating the differences between news and entertainment. "Some of these debates that we now see on television become almost cartoon-like," said CBS News's chief Washington correspondent Bob Schieffer. "They say we're going to have a—quote—conservative and we need to go find a—quote—liberal. And in order to make a better show we need to find somebody as far to the right to debate somebody as far to the left as possible. We tend to focus too much attention on the people who come up with the most extreme answer either on the left or on the right because it's so different from what the rest of the information is. We have to be very careful as journalists that we don't let that become the driving force."

"The problem goes even deeper," said CNN's senior political correspondent Candy Crowley. "Sometimes the people who deliver the news one hour pop up the next on one of the talk shows and talk about it. But part of it is that we have blurred the lines. . . . You see someone standing in front of the White House or some other location and the next minute they're sitting around a table with six other people telling the public what they should think. I'm not saying for a minute that those people who do that dual sort of thing can't be good reporters. But what do we beat politicians up about? We beat them up about perceptions. And if all day long you're reporting on George Bush, and then you go in and sit around a table and say, 'The president has the whole wrong idea. He should have done this or shouldn't have done that.' Well the next time viewers see your hard news report people are going to find stuff that may not even be there because you've laid yourself open to that." In fact some radio and television journalists are required, as a part of their job description, to appear on their station's or network's talk programming. Some newspapers encourage their reporters to appear on talk shows because of the free publicity it generates for the publication.

Some well-respected journalists, such as Jamie Dupree, news director for Cox Radio's Washington bureau, see a beneficial side to talk shows. He argued that talk shows are often focused on the issues of the day, which provides him with a greater ability to sell political stories to his news directors. He reckoned that the talk shows give him the ability to inject some serious hard news about the issues to that same audience duriig the stations' newscasts.

Journalists, especially those with an institutional memory of earlier times, bemoan the blurring of the lines. But there is ample evidence that many station managers, and even network executives, not only fail to recognize the problem, they actively seek to make the distinctions less clear because of the way they use their reportorial employees. Often reporters have little recourse.

In some cases, the reporters themselves contribute to the problem. "Some hard news reporters have tended to drift more and more toward analysis and once you talk about analysis you are talking about opinion," said Stephen Hess, senior fellow at The Brookings Institution. In some cases the requirement of appearing on talk shows automatically translates into the necessity to deliver opinion. But Hess said part of it is that journalists, themselves, are different today. "These reporters are better and better trained. They went to college. They went to graduate school. Seventy-five years ago they started as apprentices filling the paste pot for the city editor."

Harvard's Marvin Kalb said, "The blurring of the line between hard news and soft news is well documented. The blurring of the line between journalists and politicians. The blurring of the line between a communicator—like Rush Limbaugh or Larry King—and a journalist such as [Ted] Koppel or [Dan] Rather. That blurring of the line . . . is a very strong force for the erosion of clear judgment as to what a journalist does."

Crowley added, "Journalism is a very misunderstood business. I've had people come to me and think that I worked for the campaign I was covering. This is the United States of America. I don't work for Tass or Pravda, for heaven's sake. Part of it is that the public doesn't know what we do."

While the experts interviewed here generally concede that there is a problem with the blurring of the lines, Hess said news organizations, reporters and the public all bear some responsibility. "Journalists have to be more cautious—and the consumer has to be more cautious—about what is opinion and what is not in the so-called hard news area."

The twin peaks of this new journalistic landscape—greater demands for speed and output from reporters and blurred lines between news and entertainment—pose some serious dangers for the institution by undermining public trust.

"Dilute the purity of the journalism and the public then begins to question the reliability of the information," said Michael Freedman of The George Washington University. "We have moved away from the basic journalistic principle of gather, sort and report. We now are reporting, in some instances, while we are gathering and before we sort."

14.4 Celebrity Journalists

This is the age of the celebrity reporter. Their names and faces are nationally known. They command enormous salaries. Print reporters, who once labored anonymously, even at the biggest newspapers, are in the ranks of the stars as well because many of the big-name print reporters find themselves on television.

The issue is not fame. Fame is not a bad thing, even for a reporter. But when Dan Rather, Peter Jennings or Tom Brokaw shows up at an event, they automatically become part of the event because of their celebrity status. These superstars can no longer simply report a story. They travel with an entourage—producers, camerapeople, technicians, sometimes even a makeup artist. And it's not limited to the network heavyweights. Local anchormen and women in many cities enjoy the same celebrity aura. In fact, many of them cultivate it and are encouraged to cultivate it by their bosses.

The peril in having a journalist become part of the story is that the whole notion of journalism is to gather the news, seek the truth, find the facts and then report them. The presence of a celebrity journalist changes the nature of many stories and as a result the public gets something that is different than if it were covered by rank-and-file reporters. One network veteran, who spoke about this subject only on condition of anonymity for fear of reprisal from within the news organization, said, "When the anchorman shows up you're naturally going to have more coverage of the event where he is. You're going to have it whether there's any news or not just because the anchorman's there. It skews the coverage. The anchor should stay in the damned studio."

Many network correspondents and executives disagreed and noted that the top network anchors are also exceptional journalists. "Tom Brokaw, Peter Jennings and Dan Rather—whether you like them or hate them—all share the fact that they paid their dues. They were all reporters before they came to these jobs and that's reflected in their performance," said Bob Schieffer, CBS News chief Washington correspondent.

Schieffer said there's a difference between network anchors and local anchors. Many local anchors have done nothing else and he compared them to hothouse plants that have grown up under the hot lights. "Finally, you've got 10 years experience anchoring . . . and you have not learned how to report a story, how to write a story from scratch. That's the basis of all journalism. I believe that the basis of all art is drawing. I like abstract art, but it makes me feel a little better if I know that the guy can also draw. The plant, in real life, that grows up in the sunshine is a little stronger in the long run than that plant that has grown up in the hothouse. We have got to insist on the people getting out and learning how to be reporters. You can always learn how to read a Teleprompter. That's a skill that doesn't require much brains. It just requires practice."

The impact on the news of celebrity journalists has fostered an ongoing debate, and while it is doubtful that networks and local stations are going to stop sending their stars out into the field, it is an issue that should be addressed and considered by reporters and news executives alike.

In addition there is the question of how megabuck superstars can relate to the general public, to the voters, and to the citizens in a community. University of Virginia political science professor Larry Sabato minced no words, "They are totally out of touch with middle-class America, much less the poor. Anchors being paid 8, 10, 12 million dollars a year? It's insane. They are part of the elite and they are really out of touch because of their economic circumstances. . . . Those ink-stained wretches of bygone days who made 25 or 30 thousand dollars, who went to the races and had a beer with their buddies, were a lot more in touch with what people were thinking than they are today."

Sabato went on to say that local reporters are closer to their communities and thus closer to what concerns the citizens: "Local reporters are really there at the grass roots. They go to the city council meetings, to the local school board meetings, the local demonstrations on the right and on the left, and they have a real sense of what people are thinking and they relate to people at the grassroots level. I've found a big difference between local reporters and national reporters. National reporters focus a lot on esoterica. They're covering events that the average person just can't relate to. You know, like a G-8 summit? The average person can't relate to a G-8 summit. . . . But that local reporter is covering a discussion of zoning laws and whether or not we're going to be able to build something in our back yards or not. We can relate to that."

Tom Mattesky, deputy Washington bureau chief for CBS News, noted that few local TV stations have the luxury of having full-time political reporters and that, in itself, changes the dynamics of political coverage. "In terms of network correspondents or anchors, what you're getting is simply the best. These are people who cover politics every day. They know the issues and I think that gives them a much different perspective and a much better view of what's being said."

A Conversation with Marvin Kalb

Senior fellow and founding director: Shorenstein Center for the Press, Politics and Public Policy, John F. Kennedy School of Government, Harvard University

Former correspondent: CBS News and NBC News

Author: eight non-fiction books and two novels, including *One Scandalous Story: Clinton, Lewinsky and 13 Days that Tarnished American Journalism* (Free Press, 2001)

If I ever doubted that I had entered the big leagues when I joined CBS News in 1974, it took only weeks to set me straight. I was working on the Washington bureau's news desk less than a month after I started and I answered the telephone, which was a part of my job. "May I speak with Marvin Kalb," rumbled the voice at the other end. I knew the voice instantly. It was deep and resonant with a slight German accent. It was the secretary of state, Henry Kissinger. Dorothy clearly was not in Kansas any more.

I had the pleasure of working with Marvin Kalb until he left CBS for NBC. I subsequently spoke to him periodically after he founded Harvard's Shorenstein Center. From the first moment I met him my impression was that he may be the smartest, most intellectual reporter I've ever known. Nothing since 1974 has happened to diminish my opinion of Kalb's keen mind. Over the years my respect for the man has done nothing but grow.

While he has been in the academic world since 1987, his journalistic

prowess remains as solid as ever. His 2001 book, One Scandalous Story, *is a case study in what's wrong with American journalism at the dawn of the 21st century.*

R.A.: One Scandalous Story . . . *what made that period so bad, what made the reporting so bad?*

M.K.: "Piggybacking. Very few reporters knew the story but all reporters felt the obligation to report the story because it was so hot, salacious, interesting. *The Washington Post* had that story. *Newsweek* had that story. *Newsweek* had it first. The *LA Times* had a good chunk of it. And ABC had part of it. But when the story broke in *The Washington Post* on that Wednesday morning, January 21, 1998, everyone went with it as if everyone had the story.

"At the very beginning they did ascribe information to *The Washington Post.* But then within one news cycle it was all simply out there. Once it was out there, it was everybody's. And once it was everybody's, most journalists did not feel the need to do the reporting themselves. They depended on others to do the reporting. That, to me was the worst of it. . . .

"A lot of journalists say that they were simply taking the story to the next level. That's fine, if you know that the first level is accurate. Everybody assumed that it was accurate. It was too good for it not to be accurate. They'd always assumed that the president was a philanderer. So if you have a story that comes in saying he was a philanderer, you simply accept it. You don't check it. And that had to do with Clinton, that had to do with sex as an ingredient in a news story. Now that was not always the case, but it certainly is the case now."

R.A.: *You start with the anecdote about John Kennedy. Journalism was much different then.*

M.K.: "It was very different. The anecdote was about something that happened in the early '60s. That was 40 years ago. And 40 years ago journalism in Washington did not believe that the private life of a public official should be exposed to everyone's perusal for everyone's titillation. It was regarded as private information.

"I can hear students go after me immediately on this point. Was that better? Was that worse? I don't know if it was better or worse. I know that it was different. I know that, as a journalist, I did not feel that I had the right, and it was certainly not in my judgment at the time that I had the responsibility, to report on the private life of any public official, including the president.

"And in my particular case, as I post facto rationalized it, what is it that I actually knew? What did I see? The fact is I saw a beautiful woman being escorted into an elevator by the Secret Service presidential detail. It was obvious what was happening but was it obvious enough for it to be a news story? In my judgment at the time it was not a news story. I even rationalized that if I had brought the news to Cronkite and said, 'Walter, what a great story!' he'd have looked at me as if I was nuts. Because it was so far off the radar screen.

"In 1962–63 we were focusing on the Cold War, the Cuban missile crisis, the beginning of Vietnam. We were in the middle of the Civil Rights movement in this country. It simply seemed inadequate, it didn't measure up to the standards of the news that we were reporting. Were we right? I have no idea."

R.A.: *Would you, could you, make the same decision today?*

M.K.: "No. Today it would not have worked in news, it would not have worked in politics. The news business is radically different today than it was 40 years ago. Forty years ago there were the three networks. Today you have so many other networks around and so many other organizations that call themselves news organizations. The standards of the country are very different today, too. We, as a people, seem to derive pleasure out of talking about the most personal facets of our lives.

"There are programs that are devoted to people exposing the secrets of their lives and they seem to get great pleasure out of it. It's a very sad phenomenon, actually. I don't watch or listen to these programs, but I'm told about them. What I'm told makes me feel as if people ought to keep private things private and not make them public, unless the democracy itself requires the information.

"In other words, if I knew during Kennedy's time that he was having an affair with an East German woman, I sure as hell would have followed that story. That would have been within the Cold War context. That would have suggested to me that a president could be having an affair with a woman from East Germany who was in the employ of the Communist government of East Germany or in the employ of the Kremlin. That's big-time. That would have been a news story without any doubt. That he was fooling around with a beautiful lady from Hollywood? Didn't seem like news."

R.A.: *Isn't some of this driven by the technology? In those days news was shot on film. Newspapers were printed in hot type. The timeline was much longer between covering a story and putting it on the air or getting it in the paper. Today, almost everything is live. Everything moves faster than the speed of thought.*

M.K.: "That's part of the problem, but that's not the heart of the problem. The heart of the problem is that we, as a society, have changed. What we didn't consider central to our knowledge, we now consider central. We are more prone to expose personalities and personal aspects of our lives.

"I think our definition of news has changed. And that, in part, is a reflection of the new technology. The new technology has certainly changed the way in which we report information and the way in which the public absorbs information and marginally affects our definition of news. But I don't think it is the reason why our attitude toward news and our understanding of news have changed. I think the reason is societal, and under that I would put technology and I would put economics as two major factors.

"But you have to think about huge events in this country, such as the Civil Rights movement. [They] transformed the country and the way we think about one another. It isn't a finished revolution. But when it happened in the late '50s and early '60s it did change our vision of ourselves. Put Vietnam into that mix and you had explosive components of change. That our attitude toward sex changed is not surprising, but it is a reflection of all of these other changes sweeping through the country in the '60s and into the '70s.

"When you are living through a societal revolution, many, many times you are not aware of it because you are living it on a day-to-day basis. It takes 10, 15 years—or even 20, sometimes—to look back at yourself and say, 'Hey Marvin, when you arrived in this city in 1953, blacks did not feel comfortable even walking down the same sidewalk with you.' You would feel odd and they would feel odd if they were sitting in the same restaurant. It was a totally segregated environment.

"And look at it now. We have experienced a revolution. It's incomplete. But huge changes have taken place. . . . In a sense we're much more profligate with news today, as we are in the acting out of our private lives. There is a greater ease toward standards, towards morality, towards any number of issues that determine and define a society."

R.A.: *Has the news business, itself, changed from the '60s to the present in such a way that the business no longer sets its standard on what people ought to know but more on what they want to know?*

M.K.: [He explained that a Japanese student had asked virtually the same question from the same chair in which I was seated about 24 hours earlier.]

"I said, 'Oh Kioshi, you are now touching on the great philosophical divide in American journalism in the 21st century. Should news be what people want to hear? Or should news be what they ought to hear?'

"There is absolutely no question, as someone who was hired by the great man himself [Edward R. Murrow] in 1957, news was something the American people should know about. Now it appears that news is what the American people want to know about. I still think that Murrow was right. This is a very elitist view, but I think news is what people should know.

"Maybe there is a point at which the two converge. But if people were told what they should have known through the '90s, when 9-11 took place most people would have known that there was a terrorist threat. Most people would have known that there was an Osama Bin-Laden. Most people would have known, because they would have been told, that there was an Al-Qaida. They were stunned. We were all stunned, no one more than the man who lives at 1600 Pennsylvania Avenue. No one more.

"To me that is the reason why people, in a free society, ought to be told what it is that they should know. [Thumps desk.] Ah, a question then: Who the hell are you to tell people what they should know? And the answer is, 'I'm a pro. I'm a professional journalist. I'm a good, serious professional journalist. And in my gut I know what is important. I want to tell you what is important. And as long as I have the freedom to do so, I'm going to do it.' That, to me, spells out a philosophy of news. Granted, it's almost totally out of synch with today's judgments. But I truly feel that way."

R.A.: *If you are giving the people what they do not particularly want, they're going to change the channel. I've got my TV clicker, my car radio has 18 stations programmed into it, and if there's something on that's boring me or I'm not interested in, I'm gone.*

M.K.: "There's a highly competitive environment. Lots of people want to make money. People believe that the transmission of information is a way of making money. And if they feel that the American people want something and that they won't leave if you present them with a high level, high fiber [news] diet—you're going to go after them with very solid news—then you'd probably give them high quality news. But your feeling is they will leave you and there is evidence that they will leave you, so you give people what they think they want, what they appreciate—and that is that sloppy middle level."

R.A.: *How, then, do young reporters close the gap? How do they cover stories that people need to know about and do it in such a way that people want to know about them too, to make them interesting?*

M.K.: "I'll be damned if I know. I've thought about that question since I've been teaching, 16 years, and I do not know the answer. I don't know how you persuade a young reporter that it is the right thing to do.

"Oh, I've seen them in the classroom. Some of them are so smart. They are so eager to do the right thing. And they want to follow the Murrow tradition. But then one wise-[guy] kid will stand up and say, "Well now, didn't Murrow do *Person To Person*? Didn't he reach out to the public in that way. Didn't he go for the lowest common denominator?'

"I say, 'No. He was doing interviews with [former Israeli Prime Minister] David Ben Gurion.'

"And the kid says, 'No, no, no. He was doing interviews with Marilyn Monroe.'

"We're both right. News cannot always live at a stratospheric level. It has to live where the people are. If the people want Marilyn Monroe, you've got to provide information about her. That too is news. No question about that. But in the back of the reporter's mind there should also be a fierce, relentless determination to provide other news also, not to be stuck at the middle or bottom levels of definition.

"They need to reach out and push the boundaries of news that tells you about where you live in society, and where your society lives in the country, and where your country lives in the world. To me that should be a never-ending quest for good journalists. You must always have in the back of your mind that you want to raise levels. You want to keep standards as high as possible. You want to push the barriers out, not allow them to crumble before your eyes, which is what a lot of journalists are doing today."

R.A.: *The public trusts the news media less than they did back in the '60s and '70s. If the public loses trust in the institution, doesn't that pose a danger to the democracy? And in addition, isn't the news media itself contributing to that diminishing trust?*

M.K.: "The answer is 'absolutely' on both counts. The public will suffer in the long run and the news business will suffer in the long run. I think it's suffering already in the short run. People don't want to be jarred into accepting the new realities of Osama Bin-Laden. Why should they? It's so much easier to live in the comfortable world of Disney. That's overstating the point. If they cannot be made aware of the importance of hard news—and I think they probably can't—then they're going to suffer the consequences of ignorance.

"If you live in a world of comfortable ignorance you resent the people who want to disturb that world. And to the extent that journalism disturbs that world they will resent journalism. To the extent that journalism, in its quest for profit, tries to be a street-corner vendor selling his product to as many people who pass his corner as possible—not thinking about quality, just thinking about quantity, just reaching out as far as he can—then more and more people are going to say to themselves, when their views don't mesh with what they're being told, that the messenger is carrying the wrong message. And therefore they don't like the messenger. I don't like the message and I don't like the messenger. . . .

"There are so many ways in which people can absorb information that they are overwhelmed with it. And somebody has to be there to sort it all out. And that's the job of journalism. . . .

"If a Murrow type brought you hard news, tough news to absorb, you'd listen to him because you respected him and you'd figure that it was important. Today, who is Murrow? There are some terrific journalists around. But who is Murrow? There isn't anybody."

15

Roadmap for Reporters:
Better Stories, Better Coverage

One of the first people I met when I walked in the door of CBS News in 1974 was a wonderful woman named Anne Reilly. She worked on the Washington assignment desk and was a radio editor until she, tragically, lost a long battle with cancer. Little escaped her analytical eye or her rapier wit. "You're only as good as your last story," she admonished me and everybody else with regularity. "You can always make it better." The more stories I covered, the more I realized the truth in what she said.

Sometimes you hit potholes and speed-bumps along the way, and sometimes you soar to spectacular heights. But the fact remains that reporters are always looking ahead to their next story. Political reporters are no different.

15.1 Old Wine, New Bottles

"What reporters have to remember is that what we do and what we do best is not too complicated," said CBS News's chief Washington correspondent Bob Schieffer. "We simply want to get at the truth, get to the story, get as close to the story as you can, get to the scene of the story. Talk to as many people as you can and sort out what the story is. If you do that and you give both sides their shot, you'll get along okay."

In many ways, the job of the journalist has not changed much in a century. In other ways, it is an entirely new craft using entirely new tools. With more platforms for delivering news and information, greater competition among those platforms for ratings and readership, new technologies for gathering and presenting the news, and heightened economic concerns on the part of media owners, political journalists face enormous challenges. But the fact remains that journalism and journalists are part of the fabric of American democracy.

The concept of a free press is enshrined in the First Amendment to the U.S. Constitution, and Congress is expressly prohibited from taking it away or abridging it.

Marvin Kalb, senior fellow at Harvard's Shorenstein Center for Press, Politics and Public Policy in Washington, said that political reporting is deeply rooted in fundamental American ideals. He pointed to a copy of the Declaration of Independence on his office wall. "The guys who wrote that document up there had a couple basic ideas in mind. Freedom was a good thing. . . . People do want freedom. They may not know exactly what it is and they sure as hell undervalue the difficulty in achieving it. But they want it.

"Good journalism helps them get it. Bad journalism inhibits the effort. And we're living today between good and bad journalism, with the ultimate product being shaped by economic pressures, technological forces over which one seems to have no control, by value systems that have run amok and, therefore, it is not surprising that journalism itself shows signs of running amok."

Journalism in general, and political journalism in particular, do not have to run amok, and in fact can be made better. To make it better takes the commitment of the professional community. Yet, there is often a reluctance on the part of reporters and/or news management to try new ways of approaching stories and coverage. Not every new idea will be a resounding success, but until it's tried there is no way to tell.

Sometimes reporters who want to cover politics have to sell their stories to reluctant managers. This is particularly true in local TV. "One of the unfortunate things that's happened is that local television stations have consultants and surveys that tell them you get higher ratings if you don't cover politics. And so they don't cover it as much as they used to," said Schieffer.

Some reporters circumvent the problem by not calling their stories political. They say to a reticent news director who believes political stories kill ratings, "I have a story about increased class sizes in this city next year, and by the way, the candidates for the state legislature are both red hot on that." Another technique is using an event as the backdrop for a story about a broader issue. If the candidates for chair of the county commission are going to the county fair today, that can be the frame for a story of significance to viewers in the county, such as roads or real estate development.

The trend away from political news coverage is worrisome to many journalists and scholars. "It's not a luxury. It's basic," said veteran *Washington Post* political reporter David Broder. "Most news organizations recognize that they have some obligation to cover local politics and elections." Some try to keep it to a minimum.

The best news managers (radio and TV news directors, network producers, newspaper publishers and managing editors) are willing to give their reporters a chance to test new approaches. The best reporters are receptive to new coverage ideas from their news executives. When the public perceives political coverage to be stale—been there, done that—it's because it probably is. Journalistic excellence sometimes requires the journalists to color outside the lines.

Breaking the mold of covering politics based on events, personalities and the horse-race elements of the campaign requires a commitment on the part of top management. Deborah Potter, executive director of NewsLab, a nonprofit television news training and research center, said, "The best examples of how to do it are local stations that are owned by station groups that have made a commitment to do this regularly through the course of an election cycle. So you have the Hearst-Argyle stations saying every night we're going to have five minutes of coverage between the primary and general election, or over the course of the last month before the election. And [from the top] you tell them that this is what you'll do. It's amazing how creative stations will get when they've been told 'you will do this!' by their corporate bosses."

15.2 Ask the Readers and Viewers

News consultants generally conduct a poll or survey in a particular market before they make proposals to a news organization. Some consultants perform a valuable service to their clients, pointing out weaknesses in news gathering and presentation. This serves to improve the news product. Other consultants care less about traditional journalism and journalistic values than about entertainment values and slick packaging. Few consultants, however, really talk to readers, viewers and listeners the way the news professionals do.

Some news organizations have begun to hold discussions with the people who use their product in order to find out what they want in the way of news and news coverage. This eliminates the middleman and lets the journalists hear from their audience directly.

The Project for Excellence in Journalism encourages news organizations to hold reader or viewer roundtables. "It helps the public understand how the newspeople work and it helps the newspeople understand how the public thinks. I think that at the end, the goal is to come up with some practical strategies that everyday reporters can use in writing stories that are useful, reporting stories that are more useful," said Wally Dean, senior fellow at the Project for Excellence in Journalism, who conducts some of the roundtables.

"We tend to report all political stories the same way, and we need to have readers and viewers help us identify what's important and how we can do stories that give them useful information. Consultants haven't been doing that. They've come at it from a completely different angle and that is how to appeal to readers, viewers and listeners. This isn't about appeal, this is about delivering useful information," said Dean.

Getting information from readers, viewers and listeners is not about how to write stories, report facts, edit a newspaper or produce a newscast, but it is a template for coverage based on the way that the audience makes its decisions about candidates and issues and the way that those people use the information provided by a news organization. Simply reporting what a candidate says in a speech may not provide the most useful information for a reader, viewer or listener.

"We would ask readers or viewers how they would make a decision about a candidate. What's important?" said Dean. "They might say something like, 'We look at character.' Well what exactly is character? And some will say 'honesty.' How do you determine, when you see a story about somebody on TV or read about them in the paper, if they're honest? Readers and viewers will tell you. 'Do they pay their taxes? How do they treat their family? Are they good with money? If they had a business, how did they run their business?' That gives us, as reporters, some hints about how people judge whether a candidate is honest. And we can include these things in our stories."

One of the major findings that Dean has unearthed in talking to news consumers is that event-driven news coverage and personality-driven news coverage do not address a fundamental concern of voters across the board. "All politics are based on values, so to report politics we need to report values. And we're lousy at reporting values. Values are at the heart of so much that we report and we just don't have very many reporting tools that help us explain values, especially in a 200-

word newspaper story or a minute and 15-second TV story or a 30-second radio spot."

Harvard's Marvin Kalb underscored the role of political journalists in examining values. "I think our society today reaches for immediate gratification. In that reaching for immediate gratification, we forget our long term, deep-seated values. Politicians who can convey a strong sense of values in America are those politicians who are going to win. They may be phony in the projection of those values, but they're going to persuade enough people that they're on the right side of the fence and deserving of their vote. That is because the American people believe in a strong value system. That's why the term 'values' in American politics is so important, so salient.

"Journalists have to figure out which value systems are real and which are phony, and tell the public about them, not in a judgmental way but in a factual way. What is the evidence? This is what this candidate said five years ago, 10 years ago, and this is what he's saying now. Compare that. Comparative journalism is very strong journalism."

15.3 Reach Out and Touch Someone

Journalism professors around the country sound as if they could be chanting the *Hare Krishna* in unison when they say over and over again that good journalists write compelling stories, stories that matter to the audience. I've said it several times, in several ways, within these pages. Stories that convey impact and importance are also the most interesting. In doing the research for this book, the very best political journalists in the business said virtually the same thing. It's not classroom theory. It's hard, practical reality.

It is easy to cover the speech, interview the candidate, talk to the pollsters and write a story. It takes serious work and effort to do all that and come up with a story that really matters to your audience. I always used the mom test. I'd check with my mother about what I had reported. If she said, "Oh yes, dear, I saw it or heard it," I knew it was a bust. If she remembered the substance of the story, I knew I'd done something that connected.

"Personalize your stories as much as possible," said *Newsday* reporter Elaine Povich. "When I was covering Clinton's health care plan in 1994, one of the best stories I did was about the personal health care issues of members of Congress. One lawmaker had a child who had to have a kidney transplant. That made him a big advocate for this sort of thing. One lawmaker had a daughter with mental illness. He's fighting to this day for some kind of parity between mental illness and physical illness in terms of insurance coverage. I told the story through the lives of those people who were making the law and that made it much more interesting."

Some news organizations that have in-house pollsters use them to define what's on the voters' minds. In other cases, reporters go to uncommon places to find what common people are thinking about—a café, bar, barber shop. Sometimes it will lead to issues that aren't even being discussed by candidates. That can provide the genesis of unusual and important stories based on asking the candidates why they're not talking about what matters to the voters.

In breaking away from stereotypical campaign coverage, NewsLab's Deborah Potter said reporters should look for non-traditional experts. "Not all experts have to wear ties and have titles. People are experts in their everyday lives. So, for example, if your topic is transportation in your community—traffic jams, public transit, whatever—the people who live that every day are actually experts about it. And they can help you tell great stories about the problem, without resorting to the [candidate's] debate in which one candidate says 'We really should build a new bridge.' And the other candidate says, 'We really should study it first.' The question is: what's the problem, what are the potential solutions and how are the candidates addressing it? If you frame the story that way and include what candidates are saying, you can make the stories quite interesting.

"If you recognize that your citizen/expert is not an anecdote but actually the centerpiece of your story, the backbone of your story, then you can keep your viewer or reader going all the way to the end. Instead of mentioning them in the first paragraph and you never hear from them again. We know they were just a foil and we really wanted to get into what the candidates had to say. That kind of approach leads to reorienting your storytelling and coming at it from where the voters are."

Wally Dean of the Project for Excellence in Journalism expanded on that concept. "We tend to slap Jane Doe onto the top of our stories and say, here's Jane driving to work, and then we dump her like a bad habit and let the officials and experts talk. The readers and viewers, though, are experts at living in the community. They know what the streets are like because they drive them daily. They know if public services work because they use them every day. They know what life in the community is like because they live it every day. Yet we don't give them any respect."

Nonetheless, there is a potential downside to making the anecdote the foundation of the news story. "The risk is that in order to move a person from an anecdote to an expert, they must be representative of a certain body of thought, presumably widely held," said Dean, noting that there are ways to guard against representing something as generally true when it isn't. A reporter can compare it to polls, compare it demographically and compare it using other anecdotal information from the same community or area.

"I'd like to have a Rolodex—you know, that person who everybody says is the mayor of the neighborhood, who knows everybody in the neighborhood and knows what the buzz is. I'd like to have a Rolodex full of those people. They know what's going on long before it ever hits the city council agenda," said Dean.

Reporters are trained to look for conflict, controversy and tension. Sometimes, however, finding the loudest voices or the most extreme positions in a political discussion does not make for stories that are compelling, important or interesting. Most voters are not attached to one extreme or the other, nor do most voters view issues in that way. Good political journalists are not only attuned to the controversies and the conflicts, they are aware of their causes and effects. In reporting them, journalists must be able to synthesize and separate real solutions and legitimate proposals from political hyperbole.

15.4 Covering the Beat

When the U.S. Congress was my beat, it was my job to know all 100 senators, 435 representatives, five non-voting House delegates, and all of their press secretaries, top aides and key staff members. I also needed to be familiar with major lobbyists, political analysts, think tank denizens and even members of the Capitol police. It was my job to know what was happening on my patch and who was doing what. That is the nature of covering any beat.

Some journalism students have been impacted by what they've seen in the movies and on entertainment television. They presume that covering politics is a glamorous occupation involving political megastars, celebrities, glittering events and high-powered cocktail parties. "I can't think of a single story that I've ever gotten at a cocktail party," said CBS News's chief Washington correspondent Bob Schieffer. "The way most reporters get stories is by calling up the same people every day and asking the simple question, 'What's going on? What's new?'"

Reporters who cover politics, either as a full-time beat or a part-time beat, must be experts on everything connected with the area. They must know the issues of governance as well as the campaign arena—what are the issues, what are the politicians' positions, who are the key players, who are the people pulling the strings behind the scenes, who are the consultants, who's collecting the most money, who's contributing the most money and on and on.

Covering presidential politics is, in some ways, easier than covering local politics. The field of players is smaller and the campaign issues are more tightly focused. Covering local politics can verge on being unwieldy. City politics in Chicago, for example, involves more candidates and offices than the entire political structure of some small countries.

CBS's Schieffer said part of covering the beat is knowing where to look for the news. "Young reporters need to remember that most [political] news happens because it is in the interest of somebody for it to be out. When I covered the Pentagon, I found that the best stories about the Air Force came from the Army and the best stories about the Army came from the Air Force. When I covered the Tarrant County courthouse, the best stories about the commissioners came from the sheriff and the best stories about the sheriff came from the county commissioners.

"The reason for that is that when you have two entities, two elected officials, or two people competing for the same tax dollars, they can always bring you up to date on what the other guy really has in mind. In other words, the Air Force can give you a very good explanation of how much it costs to keep planes flying off aircraft carriers. The Navy can always give you very good information about how vulnerable land-based aircraft are. They're both competing for the same tax dollar."

Newsday's associate editor James Toedtman said that good reporters and politicians know that pocketbook issues matter to voters. "Virtually all tax measures and trade legislation falls into this. If the price of clothing is going to go up or the price of gasoline is going to go up, it's going to affect the readers."

He said if something is surprising to the reporter, it will probably be surprising to his or her readers, viewers and listeners. In addition, when politicians and officials go silent, reporters should start asking why. "So one of the early clues on what's a really interesting story is how secretive are people being about it and how reluctant are they to talk about it. If people are keeping secrets, you know that there's a good story there someplace."

Appendix A

Observations from the Experts

Political journalism is as much art as it is craft. Art can't be taught. It is highly subjective, often idiosyncratic and unique. This book has included lengthy conversations with some of the best and best-known people in the business, but in collecting information for it, I found that many of the other experts I interviewed had great insight and a wealth of experience.

What follows is some of the perspective, experience and observations of those people who either are on the front lines of political journalism, who have been on the front lines, or who have a significant role in the process.

A-1 Stephen Hess

Stephen Hess is a senior fellow at The Brookings Institution. He's the author of many books including *Live from Capitol Hill* (Brookings, 1991) and *Drawn and Quartered: The History of American Political Cartoons* (coauthor Sandy Northrop, Elliott & Clark, 1996). He is coeditor (with Harvard's Marvin Kalb) of *The Media and the War on Terrorism* (Brookings Institution Press, 2003). His political savvy and knowledge is highly regarded. He is an expert on the relationship between politicians and the news media.

In the 1950s, Hess was a speechwriter for President Dwight Eisenhower. He described his routine: "We'd typically have a big full speech of the week and a couple of Rose Garden rubbishes. They can't be so casual with Rose Garden rubbish any more. With 24–hour cable, everything is on the air in nanoseconds. So now any time a president sticks his head up, he's got to assume it's going to be instantly broadcast somewhere. But a lot of the stuff we did was, 'Welcome to Washington. It's a beautiful city. Glad you were here while the cherry blossoms were out. Hope you have a good time.' We called it Rose Garden rubbish because it was.

"Now there are more speechwriters because the technology of the media devours information. Something's got to fill up those 24 hours a day, and the president is one of the things that fills it up."

Hess said that speechwriting itself is much different. "The first campaign that I did for Eisenhower was the congressional elections of 1958. You'd have a full speech, 25–minute speech. We'd worked it over carefully. We were going to the National Guard Armory of Baltimore. The place would be full. It was 8 o'clock at night. That's how it was done. It was a full-dress occasion. We looked on it as a big deal."

"It was a recession year and the Republican theme was that the Democrats were prophets of 'gloom and doom.' I got tired of writing 'gloom and doom' and so for that speech I invented the word gloomdoggler, which was a play on boondoggler. The Democrats weren't going to make work, they were going to make gloom. They were gloomdogglers.

"So we were going over the speech in my boss Malcolm Moos's office. Mostly there were lawyers checking every little thing. And they didn't really like it. And they couldn't find gloomdoggler in the dictionary, naturally, since I'd just made it up. And Moos's wife came into the room. She got very excited about it. So as a favor to her they left the word gloomdoggler in the speech. It got to the president and he loved it. So we all went off to the Baltimore Armory to hear the speech and as we came out there was the bulldog edition of the *Baltimore Sun* and across the front page was the headline: 'Ike Calls Democrats Gloomdogglers.' I've got that framed up in my office."

Television's role in our society has changed the way in which Americans experience the political process and see their politicians, observed Hess. In 1958, "people came out to watch [a speech], at night, in a city. They weren't worried about crime in the streets. They weren't lured away by *Friends* or *Emergency* or any TV series. It was still entertainment. With all the entertainment we have for free on TV, it's become increasingly hard to get people out for these sorts of things. So the nature of speeches has changed. They've become short, designed to catch a headline on the evening news or on the news that's running all day long."

A-2 Michael Freedman

Today, Michael Freedman has the title of vice president for communication and professorial lecturer at The George Washington University. In his past he was a reporter, congressional press secretary and CBS News executive.

When I first started covering Congress as my principal beat, I encountered Michael Freedman in his role as press secretary to Democratic Rep. David Bonior of Michigan, the House majority whip. It always struck me that Freedman was a little out of place in that role. "It wasn't the best job I ever had," he said. "It was a constant struggle for me as a press secretary." His journalistic training and background occasionally came into conflict with the goals and objectives of a congressional office.

On the third floor of the U.S. Capitol, just across the hall from the chamber of the House of Representatives, is a cramped newsroom called the House Radio and Television Gallery. It contains a rabbit warren of work areas for radio and TV reporters, as well as a small studio from which House members hold news conferences and conduct interviews. The backdrop, which appears frequently on television, looks like a library shelf loaded with books. Because of the extreme limitations on space, the books were all sawed in half. We used to call it the "abridged library."

Freedman noted, "There were three kinds of press secretaries who went up to the radio/TV gallery—those who went up to get information, those who came up to spin like a washing machine and then there was me. I used to go up to have lunch with friends. I was not a good spinner. I abhorred that."

Among reporters, congressional press secretaries run the gamut from pretty straight shooters (often former reporters) to those who thought nothing of playing fast and loose with the truth. Freedman said his one commitment to himself was not to lie.

He related what he called a "very pivotal" incident. "I came into work one morning. It was around 7 o'clock. I was told that Bonior was at Walter Reed Hospital because his back had stiffened up. He couldn't move, couldn't get out of bed. We were given strict instructions in the office not to say anything to anybody until we knew what's what, because it was the beginning of the campaign and it would create fodder for his opponent.

"So I was walking down one of the halls in the Capitol and one of the reporters for *Congress Daily* came up and said hello and asked, 'Anything going on?'

"I froze. This was an ethical matter to me. And so I said, 'Yes, there's something going on but I can't tell you what it is right now.' I asked him what his deadline was and he said 2 o'clock. I said 'I'll tell you before 2 o'clock.'

"I went back to the office and told one of the supervisors what I had done and she was aghast. Just aghast. She said, 'How dare you?'

"I said that I can't function any other way. I couldn't say that there was nothing going on. And if you're going to say there's something going on, you have to follow that up. So clearly I was not the kind of political animal that most people were working on that side of things up on Capitol Hill.

"Well I got chewed out royally for what I had done. But I got the information to the reporter. It turned out not to be a major story, but to me it was a huge ethical issue and I was proud that I was able to pass my own test."

National reporters know they are in competition with local news organizations and reporters. Freedman said the local newspapers in Bonior's home district were at the top of the pecking order. "They really did have top priority in terms of making sure that stories were out there that showed that the member was serving the needs and desires of the people who elected and reelected him. Yes there was a difference in the way we treated local versus Washington press and the higher priority was placed on local."

Television is always important, but Freedman said he managed to educate his colleagues about an often forgotten medium. "I'm not sure that the office understood the value of radio when I arrived. But . . . I had the opportunity to explain how radio works to the office. I told them how one interview can go a long way on an all news radio station—through the 90–minute cycle of repetition, through turning an interview into six actualities and a couple of wraps [voice reports that include sound bites]. One interview can be cycled throughout the day, sometimes through as many as three day parts."

A-3 Geoffrey Garin

I used to interview pollster Geoff Garin of Peter D. Hart Research Associates quite regularly on my radio show on CBS. He was always articulate and knowledgeable. I especially liked the way he could synthesize and explain complicated issues and ideas. When I sat down to interview him for this book, I had the opportunity to talk to him about some things we'd never discussed before, such as his own background.

"I was working for John Heinz [a Pennsylvania Republican] who was running for U.S. senator in 1976 and Peter Hart was the pollster in that campaign. And I got to know Peter. I stayed with Heinz for a year and a half after he was elected to the Senate. Peter had offered me a job right after the campaign and I took him up on it a year and a half later and have been here for a little over 25 years now."

He said that back in 1978, about half of all political polling was done in person, but that has changed dramatically to the point that virtually no political polling is done in person. "We've gone to a much greater use of the telephone and are, in some cases, starting to transition to the Internet. Although for political research, the telephone is still the best and most accurate tool."

Garin says the evolution in research technology and practice continues. "The reality is that 10 years from now the telephone won't be a telephone any more. There'll be some convergence between computers and telephones. That's already occurring to some extent. So things will change again, almost as radically as in the 25 years I've been here.

"The other big difference is the ubiquity of the research. Peter Hart worked for a senator from Iowa who was defeated for reelection. . . . When this result came in, Peter was devastated because his final poll had shown the incumbent to be ahead by 12 points or so. And he couldn't imagine how the polls could have shown somebody to be ahead by that much and the person lost. Well it turned out in those days he did the last poll in the first week in October, a month before the election. In a well-funded campaign, maybe you did two or three polls over the course of the cycle. And now we do the vast majority of the polling for any candidate in the final four weeks. But we just do a lot more polling than before."

Garin said it's often more than one campaign commissioning a greater volume of polls. "You can have lots of different pollsters doing polls in support of the same candidate's election. You could have the congressional committee doing polling, and the candidate doing polling and some issue advocacy groups doing polling all on the same race. And there are laws limiting the coordination and transfer of information. But if you live in one of those very few highly competitive congressional districts you can end up being called by pollsters every other day."

Finally, Garin said people lie to pollsters and the pattern is predictable. "They often lie when race is involved. People tend to give socially correct answers. There's a measurable impact of having an interviewer of one race and a respondent of another race; when race is the topic of the survey, people tend to give the polite answer, even if it's not the answer they mean. If a white respondent tells a black interviewer that he or she is undecided in a race involving a black candidate, very often what that white respondent is saying is that I'm voting for the other guy but I don't want to offend you.

"When you ask people if they voted in the last election, most of them say yes even though they didn't because it's the socially correct thing to say."

A-4 Larry Sabato

A Greek-style rotunda is the symbol of the University of Virginia. Looking out the third-floor windows of the rotunda at the campus feels like one is communing with the ghost of Thomas Jefferson. Down the road from the rotunda is a modern brick building that houses the Center for Politics. It's doubtful Jefferson would like the architecture; but he would certainly like the Center and its mission—to improve civic education and the political process. At the heart of the Center for Politics is Larry Sabato, political scientist, professor, author and widely cited analyst.

Sabato said that many politicians succeed by simply telling the voters what they want to hear. "You can pretty much look at any public opinion poll and tell what candidates are going to be talking about, whatever the top four or five concerns are that people mention in a public opinion poll. Most politicians that I've known personally have very pliable opinions, that is they're willing to adjust what they believe to fit whatever the public mood is at the time. Issues are walking sticks that politicians use to become king of the hill. I don't think most of them deeply believe in anything. There are exceptions on both right and left.

"I think of it as ambition. They want to be governor or senator and therefore they're willing to take on the position that the public [likes], whether or not that precisely describes what they personally believe or not."

Sabato said that the exceptions in modern politics are those politicians who stand up for what they believe regardless of public opinion, and in the process even risk being defeated. He offered two examples: "The late Sen. Paul Wellstone [D-Minn.] was a classic case. He was elected twice with 50.1 percent of the vote. Could he have gotten more if he'd adjusted his beliefs? Absolutely. [Former Sen.] Jesse Helms [R-N.C.] never got more than 55 percent; he usually got 52 percent of the vote. As a long-term incumbent you would have expected him to do much better. Why did he only get 52? Because he never changed his mind. So there you have a guy on the left, Wellstone, and a guy on the right, Helms, who were willing to sacrifice 5, 10, 15 percent of the vote to stick with what they believe in. But they're the exceptions."

A-5 James Toedtman

"When I was in third grade and some of the neighborhood kids tried to save a little rabbit on the eve of Easter, I wrote a story about the efforts to save Peter Cottontail. And my dad took the thing down to the local paper, the *Berea News*, and they published the thing when I was in the third grade. It's all been sort of uphill or downhill since then."

Newsday's associate editor, James Toedtman, grew up in northern Ohio. His father encouraged him, at a tender age, to pursue a career in journalism. He arrived in Washington as *Newsday's* bureau chief in 1995. As associate editor and chief economics correspondent, he is less involved today in news management than in covering the news. Political reporting has been part of his job for more than four decades. In fact, he wrote his college thesis about a congressional race in north-central Ohio.

"The first political candidate I covered was a fellow named John Marshall Bliley who was running for the Senate in the state of Ohio. It must have been in 1962. I was a summer intern at the Elyria *Chronicle-Telegram*. This blustery old guy was a real, genuine Republican candidate for the Senate and I traveled around the back roads of northern Ohio with him for a couple of days. . . .

"I must have liked it because I remember arguing with my editors at the *Chronicle-Telegram* that they should be paying more attention to this guy because he was actually running for the U.S. Senate and that was a big deal. That was an uphill battle even then. Politics among lots of editors has the same lack of cachet even today." As it turned out, Bliley was easily defeated by incumbent Democrat Frank Lausche.

Toedtman observed that not only has technology accelerated the delivery of news and information, the magnitude and momentum of events seems to have speeded up as well. He recalled that when he entered the College of Wooster "the dominant event had happened two years before I went to college. That was the launching of Sputnik, which galvanized schools, galvanized politics, galvanized the world. Oh my God, the Russians are really serious and the Russians are really good. It changed the way we were educated, put a whole new emphasis on science and technology, and that continued through my whole college career.

"Even with the assassination of Kennedy the dominant reality was shaped by the launching of Sputnik until Civil Rights and Vietnam in the late '60s. You go back eight or nine years today and you've had the Gingrich revolution, government shutdowns, the Oklahoma City bombing, Clinton and Whitewater, Monica Lewinsky, the Starr report, impeachment—only the second time in our history a president's been impeached—acquittal, the president's more popular than ever, the [2000] election that doesn't end, September 11th, corporate scandals, the Iraq war. . . . The pace of things happening is unbelievable."

Appendix B

Useful Websites for Political Reporters

NOTE: This is far from a comprehensive directory of political web sites. These are sites I have found useful or that were recommended by political journalists I interviewed for this book. Web addresses change and web sites move or disappear. The addresses here are accurate as we go to press.

Government

www.(agency abbreviation).gov	Most federal agencies have web sites (e.g, the Federal Election Commission is *www.fec.gov*)
www.census.gov	A cornucopia of data about us, about the states, cities and counties in which we live
www.co.(county).(state).us	To access most counties in the country (e.g., El Paso County, Texas, is *www.co.el-paso.tx.us*)
www.c-span.org	C-SPAN web page with information about congressional activities, pending business, schedules
http://thomas.loc.gov	Excellent source of federal government information, particularly about Congress (named for Thomas Jefferson)
www.state.(abreviation).us	To access the main web pages of the various states (e.g., Alabama is *www.state.al.us*)

Journalism

www.ire.org	National Institute for Computer-Assisted Reporting at the University of Missouri School of Journalism

www.journalism.org	Project for Excellence in Journalism
www.jou.ufl.edu/brechner	Brechner Center for Freedom of Information at the University of Florida, repository for First Amendment and media law
www.muckraker.org	Center for Investigative Reporting
www.newslab.org	NewsLab, television news research and educational organization
www.pccj.org	Pew Center for Civic Journalism
www.poynter.org	Poynter Institute and journalistic think tank
www.rcfp.org	Reporters Committee for Freedom of the Press, links to freedom of information laws, sunshine laws, reporter shield laws and other First Amendment issues
www.rtnda.org	Radio-Television News Directors Association and Foundation; excellent for civics issues as they apply to journalists
www.spj.org	Society of Professional Journalists

Money

www.campaignfinance.org	Links to local candidates and their financing in all 50 states
www.fec.gov	Redesigned Federal Election Commission web site with detailed campaign finance information about all federal candidates
www.opensecrets.org	Center for Responsive Politics
www.tray.com	Political Money Line, which is a good campaign finance site, but which charges a subscription fee

National News Organizations

www.absnews.com	Click "politics"
www.cbsnews.com	Click "politics"
www.cnn.com	Click "politics"
www.foxnews.com	Click "politics"
www.gallup.com	Gallup polls
www.msnbc.com	Click "news" and then "politics"

| *www.nationaljournal.com* | Includes Hotline, requires a paid subscription |
| *www.washingtonpost.com* | Click "politics" |

Political Parties

| *www.democrats.org* | Democratic National Committee |
| *www.rnc.org* | Republican National Committee |

Political Resources

www.centerforpolitics.org	University of Virginia Center for Politics
www.commoncause.org	Common Cause, citizens lobbying organization with a particular interest in campaign finance reform and political ethics
www.lwv.org	League of Women Voters
http://politicalgraveyard.com	User-friendly historical site

Search Engines

www.askjeeves.com	
http://assignmenteditor.com	
www.findlaw.com	Law search engine
www.google.com	My favorite
www.go.infoseek.com	
www.hotsheet.com	Good resource for access to news organizations
www.lawcrawler.com	Good law search engine
www.phonebook.com	Even has a limited crisscross directory
www.webcrawler.com	

Index

undecided voters, 41
voter turnout, 40–41
voting age, 39
Washington, D.C. voters, 39, 42
of women, 38–39
Voting Rights Act of 1965, 38

Warner, John (R-Vir.), 78
Warner, Mark, 72, 78
Washington, George, 11, 22
Washington Post, The, 244. *See also* Broder,
    David; Dewar, Helen
    conservative bias, 19

election news, 107
web edition, 130, 144
web site, 270
Watergate scandal, 3, 177, 179
Wellstone, Paul (D-Minn.), 161, 222, 267
Whig party, 24
Whisper campaign, 34
Wilder, Douglas (D-Vir.), 112–113
Wilson, Woodrow, 54
Wireless communication, 145–146
Women
    in political press corps, 64
    voting rights, 38–39
Wright, Jim (D-Tex.), 5, 73, 152